"A penetrating analysis of the impact of feminist ideology on the life of the churches. The author convincingly shows how this has resulted in a new 'gospel.'"

—Donald G. Bloesch, Professor of Theology,
University of Dubuque Theological Seminary

"Mary Kassian's thorough look into the development of feminist thought is a sound refutation of a movement which clearly rejects the authority of the Bible. A valuable tool for today's Christian!"

—Beverly LaHaye,
President, Concerned Women for America

"This is an important and original contribution to debates over feminist theology. One need not agree with every judgment Mary Kassian offers to see how important it is to place various strands of the movement within their cultural and ideological contexts. But Mrs. Kassian is not some mere traditionalist; she candidly exposes her own struggles and profoundly Christian commitments as she seeks to bring her life into line with God's gracious disclosure in Christ Jesus and in Scripture. I warmly recommend this book."

—D. A. Carson,
Research Professor of New Testament,
Trinity Evangelical Divinity School

"*The Feminist Gospel* is a well-researched, excellent resource tool for all seeking a better understanding of the history and philosophy of the feminist movement and how it affects and influences our thinking today. I especially appreciate that Mrs. Kassian reminds us, as Christians, to go back to our only unchanging reference point—the Bible—for answers."

—Gigi Graham Tchividjian

"This is an incisive, sympathetic, and well-balanced treatment of one of the most important theological and sociological phenomena of our age. The author understands the legitimate concern of feminists but, out of her deep commitment to the gospel and to the authority of the Bible, shows us where to draw the line between legitimate reinterpretation and illegitimate deformation of the Biblical message."

—Harold O. J. Brown,
Professor of Biblical and Systematic Theology,
Trinity Evangelical Divinity School

"Timely, fresh, succinct, and best of all, Biblical. I commend to you *The Feminist Gospel*."

—Anne Ortlund,
author of the *Disciplines* trilogy

The Feminist Gospel

*The Movement
to Unite Feminism
with the Church*

Mary A. Kassian

CROSSWAY BOOKS • WHEATON, ILLINOIS
A DIVISION OF GOOD NEWS PUBLISHERS

Cover design: Russ Peterson

First printing, 1992

Printed in the United States of America

Special thanks to Susan Olasky for her excellent editing.

Unless otherwise noted, all Bible quotations are taken from *Holy Bible: New International Version*, copyright © 1978 by the New York International Bible Society. Used by permission of Zondervan Bible Publishers.

Library of Congress Cataloging-in-Publication Data
Kassian, Mary A.
    The feminist gospel: the movement to unite feminism with the church / Mary A. Kassian.
        p.   cm.
    Includes bibliographical references and index.
      1. Feminist theology.   2. Feminism—Religious aspects.
I. Title.
BT83.55.K37 1992   230'.082—dc20   91-39139
ISBN 0-89107-652-2

00	99	98	97	96	95	94							
15	14	13	12	11	10	9	8	7	6	5	4	3	2

For the saints
and for the Lamb!

CONTENTS

INTRODUCTION

Feminism is not a neutral topic. For many, it evokes emotions of bitterness, anger, and defiance. Others regard feminism with amusement, scorn, or even disgust. Feminist philosophy addresses the deeply significant question of who we are as women and men. It provides a framework for defining the reason and purpose of our lives. Feminism is controversial, for it touches us at the practical level of our own everyday existence. It evokes strong emotions, for it confronts our personal view of ourselves, our world, and ultimately our God.

The impact of feminist philosophy is evident in North American society. We encounter and interact with the feminist perspective daily on issues such as gender roles, affirmative action, reproductive technology, abortion, rape, abuse, day care, and pay equity. Feminist ideology is also visible in the Church. Many books and articles have been published that claim Scripture supports undifferentiated roles for men and women. The ordination of women to leadership offices is commonplace. Denominational women's task forces, women's studies courses in seminaries, feminist theology, inclusive language, revised inclusive lectionaries and feminist rituals are well accepted in many denominations.

Undoubtedly, feminism is influencing Christianity. But is its influence completely negative? Or can certain aspects of feminist philosophy justifiably be integrated into Christianity? Biblical feminists believe that the Bible is properly interpreted as supporting the central tenets of feminist philosophy. They also believe that the Bible is the final authority on all matters of religious faith and practice. Contrary to *liberal* religious feminists, Biblical feminists shun the radical revision of Scripture and the alteration of core Christian doctrines such as salvation and redemption. But are these conservative Biblical feminists so different from their liberal counterparts? Do their presuppositions and methods of interpretation protect them from accommodating the teaching of the Scripture to which they hold? These are important questions for the evangelical Church to consider. For if feminism and Christianity are compatible, evangelicals should not resist the feminist movement to unite the two. But if they are not compatible — if the feminist presence compromises Christianity to any extent — then the evangelical Church must refuse to accept the gospel that feminism proffers.

This book examines the historical development of feminist philosophy. It also explores the lineage and interrelationship between secular feminism and religious feminism. I believe that an overarching pattern has emerged in the historical development of both secular and religious feminist theory. This pattern is evident when the movement is studied chronologically, from a historical perspective. In the first three parts of this book, I will present the progression of modern feminism from its beginning in the early 1960s, which gave women the right to name and define themselves, through its final stage of development, which has endowed women with the right to name God. I have included two flow charts in the appendix to graphically illustrate this development. These charts are intended to assist the reader to integrate the information into an overall picture, and to facilitate comparison of the religious to the secular. In the fourth and final section of the book, I examine the relationship of conservative, evangelical Biblical feminism to the more liberal forms of religious feminism. I seek to determine how — if at all — Biblical feminism relates to the overarching historical progression of feminist philosophy. Finally, I attempt to answer the question as to whether or not the union of feminism and Christianity is viable.

This book is by no means microscopic in scope. Rather, it presents a broad overview of the basic theories and trends evidenced within North American feminism. It is not intended only for students of women's studies or theology; rather, this narrative and critique could be read without too much trouble by the ordinary Christian who is interested and prepared to devote some time and thought to the subject. The difficulty with this type of broad history lies in selecting the writers to emphasize. I have attempted to trace the development of feminist thought over a span of roughly thirty years (from 1960 to 1990), to concentrate on a small number of writers and examples rather than to gloss over many, and to draw attention to what seems to be of major significance. The development of feminism can be traced quite clearly and comprehensively up until the mid-1970s. The explosion of literature after that point forces a review which is at best brief and partial.

There are a number of points that I would like the reader to keep in mind while reading. First, I believe that feminism has drawn attention to crucial problems that exist for women in society and in the Church. In this work I am not so much debating the validity of the *questions* that feminists have posed, but rather seeking to evaluate the validity of their *answers*. I hope to determine if the feminist answers will, in fact, solve the problems that exist.

Second, in order to understand the interaction between the development of secular feminist theory and religious feminist theology, it is important to be aware of the political climate in which the current wave of feminism originated. The early 1960s were years of social upheaval. Many rebelled against the political policies that they believed encouraged the domination of certain groups of people over others. Individuals who were involved in the civil rights, student rights, and peace movements of that era were often involved in the Church as well. Martin Luther King, for example, was an American Baptist minister. He argued that the moral basis for the civil rights movement was the Word of God. Roman Catholic priests Daniel and Philip Berrigan and the Rev. William Sloane Coffin were also well-known peace activists. As time passed, the religious ties of the various movements lessened, but it is significant to note that feminist philosophy surfaced at the point when there was close interplay between the two. Therefore, readers should understand that religious feminist theology did not develop *as a result of* secular feminist philosophy, but rather emerged and developed *concurrent* to it.

Third, the reader will note that I have traced an overarching picture of feminism and have not delineated between its specific *types* or *brands*. I do not deny that various streams of feminist philosophy exist. But I argue that in spite of their political, sociological, or theological nuances, feminists all adhere to a common presupposition. It is this common presupposition that has shaped and dictated the progression of feminism's philosophical development. Moreover, in the Church, feminism transcends denominational distinctions. The denominational ties of Roman Catholic, Baptist, United Church, Methodist, Episcopalian, Presbyterian, Anglican, and Jew are all superseded by the common bond of feminism. Feminist theologians did not care whether women's theology was furthered by a Catholic, Jew, mainline or evangelical Protestant. The major consideration was only that women's concerns were being pursued within the context of established Judeo-Christian institutions. In discussing feminism in the Church, I am therefore referring to a philosophy and theology that is not confined to denominational boundaries. The theology of religious feminism includes all those religions that use the Bible in their formulation of doctrine.

Finally, I would like to point out that the development of feminist philosophy and theology did not occur without debate or discussion. Many people offered dissenting opinions during the process. However, even though individuals contested new theories, those theories contributed significantly to feminism's overall development. Furthermore, as some radical theories were augmented by others, those early ones, with minor modifications, were integrated into mainstream thought. In tracing the development of feminism, I have therefore presented the theories that were at the most progressive, cutting edge of the movement. Even though these theories were not — at any given point in time — accepted by all feminists, together they reflect a sequence of development that is both logical and progressively imminent. In the most recent stage of feminism's development, feminists have begun to name God. They began their journey, however, by naming and defining themselves.

PART ONE

Naming Self

1

The Problem Without a Name

It has barely begun, the search of women for themselves. But the time is at hand when the voices of the feminine mystique can no longer drown out the inner voice that is driving women on to become complete.

Betty Friedan, 1963

The women's movement reemerged in North America in the early 1960s. Its aim was the pursuit of meaning, wholeness, and equality for women. Many refer to its appearance as the "second wave" of feminism, for it was not the first time such a quest was undertaken. The feminist tradition of pursuing wholeness has spanned many generations.

The "first wave" of feminism began in the late 1700s when an Englishwoman, Mary Wollstonecraft, penned *A Vindication of the Rights of Woman*. Within a year of its publication, Olympe de Gouges issued a street pamphlet in Paris entitled *Les Droits de la femme* (*The Rights of Woman*) and an American, Judith Sargent Murray, published *On the Equality of the Sexes* in Massachusetts.[1] Other powerful feminist thinkers soon emerged: Frances Wright, Sarah Grimke, Sojourner Truth, Elizabeth Cady Stanton, Susan B. Anthony, Harriet Taylor and John Stuart Mill. Together, these nineteenth-century feminists began a tide of revolutionary fervor that swept over the Western world.

In 1848 one hundred American women gathered at a convention in Seneca Falls, New York to ratify a "Declaration of Sentiments" regarding the basic natural rights of women. In the Declaration of Sentiments, drafted primarily by Elizabeth Cady Stanton, fifteen grievances were catalogued. The first two concerned the denial of suffrage and the right of the governed to consent in their laws. The next several concerned the injustice of *couverture*: the legal ordinances that eviscerated a married woman's right to property and wages, and attributed to her husband the right to her obedience.[2] The final several grievances dealt with societal prejudices rather than political rights. The authors of the Declaration of Sentiments complained that women were barred from "profitable employment" and did not receive equitable pay. They noted that women were excluded from the professions of theology, medicine, and law, and claimed that all universities were closed to females. In addition, a double standard of morality condemned women to public obloquy while exonerating men for the same (sexual) misdeeds.[3]

The women's movement gained momentum over the next few decades as women witnessed doors opening to higher education and many professions.[4] Divorce laws were liberalized, and drastic changes in the legal status of married women evolved. By mid-century nearly all states had adopted legislation protecting married women's property, giving a married woman considerable leverage to establish her own economic base, and improving her legal position in child custody cases.[5] In 1920, women in the United States finally obtained the right to vote. By 1930 they were attaining higher education and entering the work force. Many of the legal, political, economic, and educational barriers that had restricted women were removed, and women stepped out into man's world with passion and zeal.

No one quite knows why — perhaps it was because of the war, or perhaps it was because the dream attained did not bring the satisfaction it promised — but within one generation, some women ceased to pursue the professional ends they had previously sought. They, and then their daughters, laid aside career and returned home to take up the profession of homemaker and wife. The fervor of the 1920s and 30s was lost, and the public cry for women's equality became dormant.

SIMONE DEBEAUVOIR

French philosopher Simone deBeauvoir broke the long silence about women's issues. Her book *Le Deuxieme Sexe* (*The Second Sex*) appeared in two successive volumes in 1949, and then was translated into English and introduced to America in 1953. The book was not an immediate success, but by the mid-1960s deBeauvoir's work was heralded as a manifesto for women's liberation. The first phase of the construction of *modern* feminist thought thus began.

In order to understand deBeauvoir's work, it is helpful to understand something of her training in academic philosophy and also to notice her association with a certain philosophic ideal. DeBeauvoir was an extraordinarily gifted student who studied philosophy at the Sorbonne, receiving first a degree in philosophy and then, by age twenty-two, the coveted *aggregation*.[6] The *aggregation* is the French qualification that allows its recipients to teach a particular subject in either a lycee or a university. It is more difficult and of far higher status than the Anglo-Saxon equivalent of a postgraduate teaching certificate or diploma.

During her studies deBeauvoir met the philosopher Jean-Paul Sartre. Sartre and deBeauvoir engaged in a fully consummated love affair, and although they encountered many trials and problems in their interpersonal relationship, their association continued throughout their lifetimes. Together, deBeauvoir and Sartre championed many causes, and together they embraced a common philosophy. Sartre had developed his philosophical ideals into a coherent conceptual system commonly described as existentialism: the term for various philosophical doctrines based on the concept that *the individual is entirely free, and must therefore accept commitment and full responsibility for his acts and decisions* in an uncertain and purposeless world. DeBeauvoir's education and her close association with Sartre shaped her analysis of the male-female relationship. In *The Second Sex*, she proposed a model for male-female interaction based upon existential philosophy.

WOMAN'S ROLE — "SECOND SEX"

DeBeauvoir's primary thesis, as the title of her book suggests, was that women as a group were assigned to second-class status in the world. Woman was "defined and differentiated with reference to man and not he with reference to her."[7] DeBeauvoir believed that the male sex comprised the prime measure by which the whole world — including women — were named and judged. Therefore, the world belonged to men. Women were the non-essential "other." DeBeauvoir argued: ". . . she is the incidental, the inessential as opposed to the essential. He is the Subject, he is the Absolute — she is the Other."[8]

DeBeauvoir noted this inequity of sex status in every area of society including economics, industry, politics, education, and even language:

Woman has always been man's dependent, if not his slave; the two sexes have never shared the world in equality . . . almost nowhere is her legal status the same as man's, and frequently it is much to her disadvantage. Even when her rights are legally recognized in the abstract, long-standing custom prevents their full expression in the mores. In the economic sphere men and women can almost be said to make up two castes; other things being equal, the former have the better jobs, get higher wages and have more opportunity for success. . . . In industry and politics men have a great many more positions and they monopolize the most important posts. In addition to all this, they enjoy a traditional prestige that the education of children tends in every way to support, for the present enshrines the past — and in the past all history has been made by men. . . . In actuality the relation of the two sexes is not quite like that of two electrical poles, for man represents both the positive and the neutral, as is indicated by the common use of man to designate human beings in general; whereas woman represents only the negative, defined by limiting criteria, without reciprocity.[9]

DeBeauvoir argued that it was a "man's world." Women were forced by men to conform to a mold that men had created for their own benefit and pleasure. This mold she named "the eternal feminine." According to deBeauvoir, it was a mold that caused women to be "frivolous, infantile, irresponsible and submissive."[10] She maintained that *the eternal feminine* corresponded to "the black soul" and to "the Jewish character"; women were shaped to occupy the lower, and men the higher of a master-slave/superior-inferior hierarchy. DeBeauvoir argued that the women of her day were not allowed or encouraged to do or become anything other than that which *the eternal feminine* dictated; they were trapped into a restrictive role of "*Küche, Kirche, und Kinder*": "Kitchen, church, and children" (Nazi Germany's official statement regarding the place of women). According to DeBeauvoir, women were to exist solely for the convenience and pleasure of men.

WOMAN'S DILEMMA — THE NEED TO TRANSCEND

DeBeauvoir viewed the dilemma of women in existential terms. Women, she pointed out, were autonomous beings with the need to "transcend" self, but this need was being suppressed by men. According to deBeauvoir, men had named and defined the world, and in doing so had identified all humanity as male, thus robbing women of autonomy.[11]

> Now, what peculiarly signalizes the situation of woman is that she — a free and autonomous being like all human creatures — nevertheless finds herself living in a world where men compel her to assume the status of the Other. They propose to stabilize her as object and to doom her to immanence since her transcendence is to be overshadowed and forever transcended by another ego (conscience) which is essential and sovereign. The drama of woman lies in this conflict between the fundamental aspirations of every subject (ego) — who always regards the self as the essential — and the compulsions of a situation in which she is the inessential.[12]

According to deBeauvoir, the dilemma for women was in being denied the right to autonomy, and therefore the right to transcend and develop. She viewed this right as the essence of human existence.

> There is no justification for present existence other than its expansion into an indefinitely open future. . . . Every individual concerned to justify his existence feels that his existence involves an undefined need to transcend himself, to engage in freely chosen projects.[13]

According to deBeauvoir, women's lack of autonomy condemned them to stagnation. She maintained that the women of her day were extremely unhappy in this situation, even though they were pronounced "happy" because they did not complain. DeBeauvoir argued that happiness did not consist in being at rest; rather individuals only achieved fulfillment through a continual reaching out toward other liberties. According to deBeauvoir, women were being denied this right.

WOMAN'S SOLUTION — COLLECTIVE ASSERTION

The philosophy of existentialism assigned responsibility for one's own destiny to oneself. Therefore, in formulating her theory, deBeauvoir blamed women for allowing the second sex status to be forced upon them: "If woman seems to be the inessential which never becomes the essential, it is because she herself fails to bring about this change."[14]

DeBeauvoir determined that the reason for woman's silence and apparent unwillingness to change was a lack of means of communication among women and a corresponding lack of organized corporate resistance.

> . . . women lack concrete means for organizing themselves into a unit which can stand face to face with the correlative unit. They have no past, no history, no religion of their own; and they have no such solidarity of work and interest as that of the proletariat. . . . They live dispersed among the males, attached through residence, housework, economic condition, and social standing to certain men — fathers or husbands — more firmly than they are to other women.[15]

DeBeauvoir declared that women needed to identify themselves as a group and collectively declare war on the second sex structure of their lives.[16] She believed that equality and liberation would be achieved only by destroying the male's superiority and refusing to succumb to a traditional role.[17] According to deBeauvoir, women were "imprisoned" by the roles of mother, wife, and sweetheart;[18] therefore, she maintained that "all forms of socialism, wresting woman away from the family, favor her liberation."[19] Her utopian ideal was one in which the collective state assumed responsibility for the maternal functions that burdened women and restricted their participation in the work force:

> A world where men and women would be equal is easy to visualize, for that precisely is what the Soviet Revolution promised: women raised and trained exactly like men were to work under the same conditions and for the same wages. Erotic liberty was to be recognized by custom, but the sexual act was not to be considered a "service" to be paid for; woman was to be *obliged* to provide for herself other ways of earning a living; marriage was to be based on a free agreement that the spouses could break at will; maternity was to be voluntary, which meant that contraception and abortion be authorized and that, on the other hand, all mothers and their children were to have exactly the same rights, in or out of marriage; pregnancy leaves paid for by the state, which would assume charge of the children. . . .[20]

DeBeauvoir viewed departure from the role of wife and mother and the establishment of economic and professional independence as the key to women's equality with men. Her model was socialist. It demanded the revolt of the "bourgeoisie" of women and encouraged state-regulated laws to overcome social mores and patterns of behavior.

Although containing some practical application, deBeauvoir's work was largely theoretical, dealing with the inequities of women's position and comparing the male-female relationship to that of the bourgeoisie versus the proletariat. Her existential and philosophical terminology did not appeal to the average North American woman. *The Second Sex* was therefore not widely noted in North America until after the appearance of a second manifesto, Betty Friedan's *The Feminine Mystique*.

BETTY FRIEDAN

In the early 1960s, an American journalist, Betty Friedan, transformed deBeauvoir's philosophical concepts into something more understandable for the average American woman. In 1957 Friedan had compiled a questionnaire for the female alumnae at her fifteen-year college reunion. She was determined to disprove the common notion that college education ill prepared women for the role of wife and mother. The results of her questionnaire surprised her. She found that her classmates were frustrated in their roles as wives and mothers. Friedan went on to ask whether the frustration was a result of education, or whether it was women's role itself that was at fault.[21] *McCall's* turned the article down, *Ladies' Home Journal* would not edit it to her satisfaction, and *Redbook* claimed the article would only appeal to the most neurotic housewife.[22] Friedan therefore decided to research and write a book that would thoroughly examine the role of the North American woman.

Friedan interviewed editors of women's magazines, surveyed articles and books, spoke with psychologists, anthropologists, sociologists and family-life experts, and finally interviewed eighty women in depth. She concluded that there existed a discrepancy between the reality of women's lives and the image to which women were trying to conform. Friedan named this image "the feminine mystique," and the phrase became the title of her book. *The Feminine Mystique* was published in 1963 and it, together with deBeauvoir's *The Second Sex*, formed the base for the development of the modern feminist movement.

WOMAN'S ROLE — "THE MYSTIQUE"

To support her case for a feminine "mystique," Betty Friedan pointed to a number of articles appearing in women's magazines in the late 1950s and early 1960s. These articles reported a "syndrome" that some women experienced. Its symptoms included feelings of "dissatisfaction," of "yearning," and of "emptiness." It became known as the "trapped housewife syndrome."[23] Friedan maintained that the feelings these women reported were not abnormal, but were in fact common to many women. Furthermore, she argued, their feelings arose as a result of society's expectations of women's role and behavior. Friedan argued,

> Fulfillment as a woman had only one definition for American women after 1949 — the housewife-mother. As swiftly as in a dream, the image of the American woman as a changing, growing individual in a changing world was shattered. Her solo flight to find her own identity was forgotten in the rush for the security of togetherness. Her limitless world shrunk to the cozy walls of home.[24]

Friedan echoed deBeauvoir's dismal assessment of women as limited to *"Küche, Kirche, Kinder."* She said that women had been convinced that in order to be "truly feminine," they should not want the careers, higher education, or political rights fought for by old-fashioned feminists.[25] According to Friedan, women of her day were taught to seek fulfillment only as wives and mothers. She argued that this mystique of feminine fulfillment left women acting "young and frivolous, almost child-like, fluffy and feminine; passive; gaily content in a world of bedroom and kitchen, sex, babies and home." They were "excluded from the world of thought and ideas," "denying their minds," and "ignoring questions of their own identity."[26] Friedan identified this mystique of feminine fulfillment as the "cherished and self-perpetuating core of contemporary American culture":

> Millions of women lived their lives in the image of those pretty pictures of the American sub-urban housewife, kissing their husbands goodbye in front of the picture window, depositing their station wagonsful of children at school, and smiling as they ran the new electric waxer over the spotless kitchen floor. They baked their own bread, sewed their own and their children's clothes, kept their new washing machines and dryers running all day. They changed the sheets on the beds twice a week instead of once, took the rug-hooking class in adult education, and pitied their poor frustrated mothers, who had dreamed of having a career. Their only dream was to be perfect wives and mothers; their highest ambition to have five children and a beautiful house, their only fight to get and keep their husbands. They had no thought for the unfeminine problems of the world outside the home; they wanted the men to make the major decisions. They gloried in their role as women, and wrote proudly on the census blank: "Occupation: housewife."[27]

Friedan claimed that women had a "problem of identity — a stunting or evasion of growth."[28] Women, Friedan claimed, had lost "the capacity to transcend the present and to act in light of the possible, the mysterious capacity to shape the future."[29] Friedan's ideas mirrored the existential philosophy proposed by deBeauvoir. Like deBeauvoir, she maintained that the only way for a woman to find herself and to know herself as a person was through creative work of her own.[30]

WOMAN'S DILEMMA — A PROBLEM WITHOUT A NAME

Betty Friedan believed self-fulfillment came from having a defined purpose and from shaping and contributing to the world in tangible and creative ways. Men could seek self-fulfillment, but women — curtailed by conformity to the role of wife and mother, and *the feminine mystique* — could not. This created a dilemma. On the one hand, women who devoted themselves fully to the feminine mystique were, according to Friedan, *un*happy and *un*fulfilled. On the other hand, society expected women to *be* happy and fulfilled in this particular role. Friedan argued that the inner frustration of women was seldom, if ever, discussed or open to debate. Women felt too ashamed to admit their dissatisfaction and were thus unaware of how many other women shared it.[31] Friedan called this dilemma "*a problem with no name.*"[32] It was caused by women trying to adjust to an image that did not permit them to become what they could be. It was the growing despair of those who had forfeited their own existence.[33]

Betty Friedan uncovered an emptiness, purposelessness, and frustration that was common to many women. She, together with Simone deBeauvoir, blamed this frustration on society's stereotyped expectation of the role of women. According to these early feminists, society had wrongly named and defined women. Woman's role, not women, was responsible for their unhappiness.

WOMAN'S SOLUTION — EDUCATION AND SERIOUS PROFESSIONAL COMMITMENT

Friedan saw education as a means to escape the impasse of *the feminine mystique*. But education was the key to changing the problem only when it was part of a new life plan and meant for serious use in society. Friedan maintained that educators at every college, university, junior college, and community college should see to it that women make a lifetime commitment to a field of thought and to a work of serious importance to society. According to Friedan, each woman would need to name herself by developing a vision for her own future. Furthermore, she pointed out, the fulfillment of a woman's vision necessitated the redesignation of her responsibilities. It was not possible for women to fulfill traditional roles as mother and wife and concurrently pursue their own visions; so society would have to adjust its basic ideas about employment, marriage, family and home:

There is only one way for women to reach full human potential — by participating in the mainstream of society, by exercising their own voice in all the decisions shaping that society. For women to have full identity and freedom, they must have economic independence. Breaking through the barriers that had kept them from the jobs and professions rewarded by society was the first step, but it wasn't sufficient. It would be necessary to change the rules of the game to restructure professions, marriage, the family, the home.

Friedan agreed with deBeauvoir that the liberation of women would require sweeping changes in society. Although her utopian vision was far less defined than deBeauvoir's socialist framework, her thoughts led in essentially the same direction.

SEARCHING FOR "SOMETHING MORE"

DeBeauvoir and Friedan determined that women of their generation were unfulfilled, unchallenged, aimless, frustrated, and searching for "something more." They pointed to the problem of male-female role interaction as being at the root of women's discontent. These second wave pioneers believed that inner wholeness could only be found through women leaving their traditional role in order to emulate men. They argued that women would only be fulfilled by joining the ranks of the professional and educated, contributing something more concrete to society than motherhood and wifehood. In order to transcend — to attain "something more" — women needed to take control of their own lives, name themselves, and set their own destiny.

NAMING THE PROBLEM — PATRIARCHY

Simone deBeauvoir's and Betty Friedan's writings began to gain popularity among North American women. Evidently, many women *were* experiencing inner feelings of frustration and discontentment, and many eagerly yearned for the "something more" proffered by these feminist pioneers. A problem had been exposed — feminists were convinced that it was *the* problem. And although they had not yet found a word to adequately describe it, they were confident that therein resided the cause of women's malaise.

In the late 1960s, feminist author Kate Millett used the term "patriarchy" to describe the "problem without a name." *Patriarchy* derives its origin from two Greek words: *pater*, meaning "father," and *arche*, meaning "rule." It was to be understood as "rule of the father," and was used to describe the societal dominance of the male, and the inferiority and subservience of the female. Feminists saw patriarchy as the ultimate cause of women's discontent. Adrienne Rich explained:

> Patriarchy is the power of the fathers: a familial-social, ideological, political system in which men — by force, direct pressure, or through ritual, tradition, law, and language, customs, etiquette, education, and the divi-

sion of labor — determine what part women shall or shall not play, and in which the female is everywhere subsumed under the male.[34]

The word *patriarchy* described the problem that deBeauvoir and Friedan had earlier identified. According to feminists, patriarchy was the power of men that oppressed women and was responsible for their unhappiness. Feminists reasoned that the demise of patriarchy would bring about women's fulfillment. Liberating women from patriarchy would allow women to become whole.

2

A Problem in the Church

Now the realization is growing among those who speak as Christians that the ancient role of women in religion and the Church is no longer adequate.[1]

About the same time Simone deBeauvoir was penning her *Second Sex* manifesto, a woman named Katherine Bliss was conducting a survey for the World Council of Churches entitled *The Service and Status of Women in the Church*.[2] The survey reported on the activities and ministries in which Christian women were commonly involved. Bliss noted that although women were extremely involved in the life of the Church, their participation was limited to auxiliary roles such as Sunday school and missions. Women were not participating in traditionally accepted leadership activities of teaching, preaching, administration, and evangelism, even though some appeared to be gifted in that manner. Bliss therefore called for a reevaluation of male/female roles in the Church — particularly with regards to the ordination of women. She argued that "we must begin to ask seriously what the will of God is concerning the diversity of gifts of men and women and concerning the spirit in which they are to serve together their common Lord."[3]

Although the report was completed in 1952, it did not receive substantial attention until 1961. When the Church's involvement in the pursuit of civil and political rights popularized the topic of personal rights, some Christians dusted off the ten-year-old survey to use as statistical ammunition against the Church. They, together with feminist women in secular society, were beginning to vocalize discontent with the differential treatment women received because of their sex.

In 1961, women's periodicals were reporting on the "trapped housewife syndrome." Also in 1961, a religious journal, the *Journal of Pastoral Psychology*, embarked on a series of articles on "Male and Female." The first article, "Women in the Church: Historical Perspectives and

Contemporary Dilemmas," by Dr. William Douglas, argued that women were assigned a lesser role in the Church:

> . . . in the Church as in society, men have tended to assign women to a completely subservient position, as the "weaker vessel," a form of property, a source of temptation away from the things of the Spirit. Both Judaism and Christianity have incorporated the dominant patriarchal attitude of the culture of their origins, and tended to maintain the culture's superstitious attitude toward feminine "uncleanness" and "wickedness." Though the Church has believed in a "new Adam," whereby the consequences of the Fall are set aside, it has been slow to accept the possibility of a "new Eve," free from her companion, the serpent.[4]

The problem, as Douglas saw it, was a quenching of women's giftedness and potential by relegating her to mundane service positions within the Church. Men could become ordained ministers, but women were barred from active ministry such as teaching, counseling, and pastoring. The division between "clergy" and "laity" necessitated by pervasive contemporary church structure had created a view of "the pastorate" or "the ministry" as a professional occupation. Inasmuch as the Church restricted women from the clergy role, it also effectively restricted them from the professional duties exclusively assigned to the clergy.[5] As Mary Daly observed, "A layman may be a member of the laity by choice; a woman is this of necessity."[6]

Douglas pointed out that ordained ministry simply was not an option for most Christian women. A woman, he argued, "might have the call to be a Christian, the inner call to ministry, and the providential call of talents and temperament suited to the task. But the ecclesiastical call, of official sanction and institutional opportunities for service, was lacking."[7] According to Douglas, women wanted to participate in religious life at a more meaningful level than sewing, or conducting bazaars, or putting on church suppers, or the other service and fund-raising endeavors usually assigned to them. They wanted to contribute *ideas* to the Church, as well as physical work.[8]

Douglas noted that women were, for the most part, relegated to a specific type of service position within the Church. If a woman did not fit into the "Women's Missionary Society" or "Women's Auxiliary" mold, she just did not fit. Doomed were the women who had pastoral vision, leadership, teaching or administrative skills, gifts of evangelism or prophecy.

Attention to the male/female role inequity within the Church became more intense as the secular women's movement gained momentum. The periodical *Christianity and Crisis* in 1962 demanded "fairness for the fair sex."[9] In 1964 an article in the *Union Seminary Quarterly Review* called for a "radical new order" for the vision of women in the life of the Church.[10] Later that year, the World Council of Churches issued a pamphlet *Concerning the Ordination of Women*, calling churches to a "re-examination of their traditions and canon law."[11] By 1967 an editorial in the *Journal of Ecumenical Studies* proclaimed "the status of women" *the* ecumenical question of the decade.[12] Other articles appeared: "Some Implications on Current Changes in Sex Role Patterns,"[13] "Where Is the Woman?"[14] and "The Church as Matriarchy."[15]

Catholic discussion of woman's role in the Church was also well underway. Gertrud Heinzelmann, Rosemary Lauer, Mary Daly, and Eleanor Schoen contributed articles to Catholic periodicals in preparation for discussion at Vatican II. And, although it took a little longer, evangelicals also joined the critical reappraisal. For example, in 1971 *Christianity Today* passed its judgment on the situation with an article by R. A. Schmidt in which Schmidt argued that women possessed "second-class citizenship in the Kingdom of God."[16]

Various denominations began to concur with Douglas that *Christianity had incorporated the dominant patriarchal attitude of the culture of its origin.*[17] Many Catholics, Methodists, Baptists, Episcopalians, Presbyterians, Congregationalists, and Lutherans agreed: Women in the Church needed liberation.

SETTING COURSE

The examination of the Church by Christian feminists revealed gross inequities in the role of male and female. Serious consideration needed to be given to the problem. William Douglas perceptively pointed out two possible courses of action in dealing with the dilemma. First, the Church could "reexamine the nature of the ministries of the Church, seeking to recapture the New Testament pattern which appears to be lost in contemporary Protestantism."[18] In other words, the Church could go back to its roots, reestablish the priesthood of all believers and dissolve the vast distinction between the clergy and laity, opening up ministry to all. Or, alternately, the Church could retain its current structure and simply open up the avenues of ordained ministry to women as well as men. Changing the way Church bureaucracies were structured, and changing ingrained perceptions regarding the pattern and function of Church leadership, would have been a formidable task. Furthermore, most believers did not associate the problem of women's involvement in the Church with a deeper problem of incorrect Church structure and function. The latter course of dealing with women's role inequity was thus chosen.

In the 1960s Christian feminists set themselves on a course parallel to that pursued by feminists in secular society. They — together with their counterparts — began to seek the de-differentiation of male/female roles. The dominant theme was that women needed to be allowed to name themselves. Feminists believed that women should be allowed to do everything that men could do, and in the same manner and with the same recognized status as men. This, they believed, constituted true equality.

Unfortunately, Christian feminists began to pursue the inclusion of women in leadership hierarchies without a clear analysis of whether or not the hierarchies themselves were structured and functioning according to Biblical pattern. They merely judged the Church to be sexist and implemented a course of action in response. Christian feminists, alongside their secular counterparts, began to demand "equal rights." They decided to seek androgyny in the Church by pursuing women's ordination and the obliteration of structured roles in marriage.

DEVELOPING THE ARGUMENT

The initial argument for role androgyny followed the same vein within both Protestant and Catholic circles. First, feminists disputed the historical analysis of the nature of women that had been presented by the early church fathers. They argued that these men had wrongly named and defined women. Second, they pointed out that the Bible supported the full worth and equality of women. According to the early feminist theologians, men had neglected this Biblical concept. Finally, proponents called attention to the rigidity of social customs and argued that these customs should not be an influence in the formulation of future Church practice. Feminists maintained that women ought to be free to name and define themselves with regards to their role. They developed the thesis that there is no immutable basis for role differentiation between the sexes. Therefore, they concluded, there is no basis for barring women from ordained ministry positions or for supporting hierarchically structured roles in marriage.

The Error of the Church Fathers:
Men Have Wrongly Named Women

In 1962, Dr. Gertrud Heinzelmann, a Swiss lawyer, dispatched a document to the Preparatory Commission of the Second Vatican Council. The Council's purpose was to re-analyze and reform Catholic church dogma. Dr. Heinzelmann and others were petitioning the Council to change the doctrine of the Catholic church forbidding women's participation in the diaconate and priesthood.[19] Heinzelmann's paper, *"Frau und Konzil":
Hoffnung und Erwartung"* ("Women and the Council: Hope and Expectancy"), attacked the Aristotelian-Thomistic tradition that Heinzelmann held responsible for the Catholic position on the role of women. She accused Aristotle of possessing a primitive, rationalistic view of biology with regards to women: "Woman, according to Aristotle, was not completely developed as a human being; she was a 'misbegotten' or defective male."[20]

According to Heinzelmann, Aristotle believed that only the male could pass on human nature to his offspring; the female functioned merely as a passive receptacle. Furthermore, she pointed out, Aristotle believed women were incapable of reason. Since the human species was characterized by rationality, she reasoned that Aristotle viewed women as less than fully human. According to Heinzelmann, defective Aristotelian biology, reinforced by an equally defective interpretation of Genesis, allowed Thomas

Aquinas to develop this ethical principle regarding the nature of the sexes: "Man is the principle and end of woman, as God is the principle and end of man. . . . Woman exists for the man, not man for the woman."[21]

Rosemary Lauer, who translated and rearticulated Heinzelmann's argument, pointed out that such notions were still taught to theology students. In one contemporary college, she said, students were informed that "the end of man is to know; the end of woman is to bear children."[22] Lauer proposed that — based on Aristotle and St. Thomas — "the only reason why nature would produce 'misbegotten males' is that they were somehow and unfortunately, necessary for the continuance of the human race."[23]

Both Catholic and Protestant feminist critics scrutinized church history and concluded that the founding fathers of the Church had possessed and promoted defective views on the nature of woman. Feminists critiqued Clement of Alexandria, Origen, Ambrose, St. Bonaventure, St. Bellarmine, and St. Chrysostom. They bristled at the insult contained in the prayer of the Jewish male in which he thanked God that he "had not been created female."[24] They pointed out that Thomas Aquinas believed that a "woman's voice and appearance constituted an invitation to unchastity," and that "woman lacked the required wisdom to be a teacher or preacher."[25] They additionally noted that Luther once had said:

> Men have broad and large chests and small hips, and more understanding than the women, who have but small and narrow breasts, and broad hips, to the end they would remain at home, sit still, keep house, and bear and bring up children.[26]

Feminists accused Tertullian of "ferociously misogynistic statements,"[27] and argued that Calvin "reaffirmed" woman's inferiority.[28] These church fathers had defined and named women, and some religious women were beginning to question the validity of their definitions. According to Christian feminists, men — and in particular, the church fathers — had wrongly named women.

Early Christian feminists used their critique of church history to buffer their case for the ordination of women and the obliteration of marital roles. They reasoned that women were kept out of authority positions because the church fathers viewed woman, in very nature, as inferior and less capable intellectually than men. Feminists argued, however, that advances in psychology, anthropology and genetics had challenged this early view of the nature of women. Therefore, since it had become evident that women were in no way inferior to men, the basis for their exclusion from ordained ministry and the basis for their subordination in marriage had disappeared.

The Bible Teaches Woman's Equality

Early Christian feminists charged that the account of woman's creation in Genesis was almost universally misinterpreted to teach the "God imposed inferiority and subjection" of women.[29] Feminists believed they were teach-

ing a new view of Genesis when they pointed out that woman, being flesh
of man's flesh and bone of his bone, in nature the same as he, was thus equal
to him.[30] According to Lauer, theologians tended to "interpret Scripture in
light of the thought of the day."[31] Therefore, since woman's inferiority was
accepted in society, she concluded that it was natural for theologians to read
the inferiority into the Genesis account and into the interpretation of the
rest of the Bible. Feminists claimed that the built-in bias of theologians had
caused them to overlook the underlying equality of women taught in the
Bible.

New Testament Scripture supporting the equality of women was also
cited by the early Christian feminists. Galatians 3:28, "In Christ there is neither male nor female," was held forth as the Biblical *magna carta* for
women. The example of Mary learning at the feet of Jesus; of Phoebe being
sent out as an ambassador to the churches; of the five daughters of Philip
who moved in prophetic ministry; of Priscilla, who instructed and discipled
Apollos together with Aquila — all the passages that demonstrated God's
high regard for women — were presented as evidence of the essential equality of women. Surely, feminists argued, if women were created in God's
image just as men were, then women were equal to men and just as capable as men to exercise authority.

Male theologians were accused by the early feminists of ignoring the
Bible passages supporting women's equality and twisting those serving their
own interests. The doctrine of Church leadership that excluded women
from ministry was therefore presented as a byproduct of a lopsided study
of Scripture.

Women Had the Right to Name Themselves

Christian feminists maintained that social custom restricted women to service roles in the home and in the Church. The fact that women's role had
always been structured in a hierarchy was not considered a valid argument
for maintaining that hierarchy, particularly with regards to Church leadership. Although feminists granted that women's exclusion from Church leadership may have been valid at one time, they viewed the extension of this
restriction to include all times and cultures as an extreme application of a
culturally relative practice. Lauer argued that "The cultural and historical
reasons for which women have been excluded no longer justify such an
exclusion. Moreover, there is undoubtedly much that women could contribute to the Church through the priesthood."[32]

Feminists argued that their role was based on culturally variable fac-
tors. In the past, they had been wrongly defined by men. Furthermore, men
had neglected the Biblical concept of women's equality. With an androgynous definition of equality in hand, early feminist theologians were able to
argue that they had the right to define their own roles, and that the rigidity
of "social customs" in the Church should not prevent them from doing so.

NO DIFFERENCE BETWEEN MALE AND FEMALE

The major thesis proposed by Christian feminists in the early 1960s was identical to the thesis of secular feminism. Feminists argued that as far as emotions, psyche, and intellect were concerned, there were no demonstrable differences between male and female. Any apparent differences resulted from cultural conditioning rather than biological fact. Women had been wrongly named by men and needed to correct the misperceptions. Lauer, for example, maintained that no differences between male and female had ever been proven, and that the differences attributed to the sexes were merely man's misperception of reality.

> To date, no one has ever produced this type of demonstration that any manner of acting, any particular degree of intellectual ability, or any special emotional makeup is "natural" to women. Indeed, such a demonstration is impossible, for women, as a matter of fact, (i.e. male claim) differ markedly in these characteristics. The statement frequently made, that women should act in accordance with their nature is one of those pious platitudes which satisfy the thoughtless, but it has no possible meaning. . . .[33]

Christian feminists disputed the concept of an "eternal feminine psychological make-up consisting of certain immutable traits of mind and personality."[34] They attributed the alleged fixed psychological differences to the effects of education and environment.[35] To support this view, Christian feminists drew heavily upon the work of anthropologist Margaret Mead who in the early 1930s had studied human behavior in various cultures and primitive tribes throughout the world. Mead, in *Sex and Temperament* (1935) and *Male and Female* (1949), contended that there was no fixed pattern of male-female interaction and roles. She concluded that differences between male and female were learned and conditioned by culture rather than set by nature.[36] Dennis Ashbrook, in an article in *Pastoral Psychology*, commented:

> Margaret Mead in her authoritative anthropological study, *Male and Female*, reminds us that there has been no single exclusive patterning of masculine and feminine roles in history. Cultural relativity is quite prevalent in this regard.[37]

Margaret Mead's work was so respected by Christian psychologists that she was invited to join the editorial advisory board of *Pastoral Psychology* magazine in early 1963 — a fact that undoubtedly affected the direction Christian feminism took. In the past two decades, most of Mead's analysis has been refuted; nevertheless, her research provided much of the foundation for the Christian philosophy of egalitarianism.[38] Feminists reasoned that since all people were the same (i.e., no differences between men and women), all people were entitled to the same rights. Therefore, because of the equality (i.e., "sameness") of the sexes, Christian feminists argued that women should be entitled to fill leadership positions within the home and Church equally with men. Lauer represented this line of reasoning in her statement: ". . . woman's soul does not differ from man's and therefore can receive the sacramental character of ordination as well as his."[39]

TOWARDS A NEW THEOLOGY — THE FIRST STEP

If it is true that our society is moving from a masculine to a feminine orientation, then theology ought to reconsider its estimate of the human condition and redefine its categories of sin and redemption. For a feminine society will have its own special potentialities for good and evil, to which a theology based solely on masculine experience may well be irrelevant. (Valerie Saiving Goldstein)

The ordination of women required the development of a new theology and Biblical hermeneutic. The first step towards this end was pioneered by theologian Valerie Saiving Goldstein, whose ideas were in many ways ahead of her time. Goldstein's article "The Human Situation — A Feminine Viewpoint" first appeared in the *Journal of Religion* in 1960.[40] It was republished in 1966 when the current of feminist thought in Christendom was well established.[41] Goldstein proposed that a theologian's sexual identity had bearing upon that person's theological views. At the time, it was radical to suggest that one's *gender* would affect one's interpretation of the Bible.

To support her contention, Goldstein cited the works of two contemporaries: Anders Nygren and Reinhold Niebuhr. These male theologians, in addressing the question of the human situation, had defined the basic sin of mankind as *pride* and had defined grace as *sacrificial love*. Goldstein contended that the human situation was quite different for *women*. She said that the sin of *men* may well indeed have been pride and the thirst for power, but that the sin of *women* was just the opposite. The sin of women, as she saw it, was the "underdevelopment or negation of the self . . . triviality, distractibility, diffuseness, dependence on others for one's own self-definition."[42] In sum, Goldstein claimed that the female perspective on sin was the antithesis of Niebuhr's and Nygren's definition. The sin of women was *too much* sacrificial love and *not enough pride* in themselves. She noted,

My purpose . . . is to awaken theologians to the fact that the situation of woman, however similar it may appear on the surface of our contemporary world to the situation of man and however much it may be echoed in the life of individual men, is at bottom, quite different — that the specifically feminine dilemma is, in fact, precisely the opposite of the masculine.[43]

Theologically, Goldstein proposed the idea that doctrinal interpretation of the Bible was different for the two sexes. She charged that the theology of the past had been male-oriented, and therefore unrepresentative of women and skewed in its conclusions: "the prevalent theologies today were created by men who lived amid the tensions of a hypermasculine culture."[44] Goldstein concluded that as society moved towards greater female orientation, theology would need to redefine itself in line with a feminine viewpoint. "[A] feminine society," she said, "will have its own special potentialities for good and evil, to which a theology based solely on masculine experience *may well be irrelevant.*"[45]

THE REVOLUTION IS UNDERWAY

To summarize, in the early 1960s, feminists began to seek de-differentiation between the roles of men and women in the Church. As in secular society, women's differences were regarded as being a result of culture and conditioning and thus a source of embarrassment. Feminists consequently desired to overcome their differences and name and define themselves to be *just like men.*

Christian feminists considered the ordained pastorate to be superior in spirituality, giftedness, intelligence and capability. These were characteristics which feminists felt they had been denied. Access to ordination was therefore the front on which they pursued equality within the Church. Katherine Bliss, and the others who struggled for the ordination of women, opened up the examination of male/female roles in the Church on a very visible, practical front. Valerie Saiving Goldstein, on the other hand, was much more theoretical, for she proposed the possibility of an entire new theology that would be based on women's experience and interpretation. New theological developments were necessary to support the ordination and "monolithic equality" (freedom without boundaries) that Christian women were beginning to seek.[46]

The immediate impact of these writings was not highly visible. However, just as Simone deBeauvoir's and Betty Friedan's books had laid the foundation for a major upheaval in secular society, so Katherine Bliss and Valerie Saiving Goldstein laid the foundation for a major upheaval within the Church. As William Douglas prophetically stated in 1961: "The place, the status, the opportunities for service of women within the Church are rapidly changing. A silent revolution is now under way."[47]

3

The Church and the Second Sex

Women do most of the work, while men exercise most of the authority. Such has been the common practice in the Christian Church. While few churchmen in modern times would openly profess St. Chrysostom's judgement of woman as "a necessary evil, a natural temptation, a domestic peril . . . ," "the second sex" retains second-class citizenship in most of Christendom.

Dr. William Douglas
Journal of Pastoral Psychology, 1961

White placards waved above the brightly dressed students crowded onto the steps in front of Gasson Hall. "Freedom of Speech!" "Stop Censorship!" "Women Need Liberation!" The scene at the Boston College administration building was like those staged on college campuses across the country during this season of demonstration for civil rights, black rights, student rights, and now women's rights.

College administrators had not been responsive thus far to the students' demands. Students therefore invited professors fired from other institutions to a seven-hour "teach in," and some protestors went so far as to deface Gasson Hall with brilliant red graffiti — all in an attempt to force the academy to reverse its decision to fire Mary Daly.

The academic senate called a meeting and elected a faculty review committee to investigate the case. Mary Daly had been issued a terminal contract — fired, in her opinion. The students were enraged. Students challenged the dismissal under the guise of "academic freedom," but the battle was on a much deeper level.

Mary Daly had recently published *The Church and the Second Sex* (1968) — a monograph that officially charged the Christian religion with the oppression of women. Jesuit-run Boston College where she taught had consequently served Daly with a terminal contract. The college felt that her ideas were incompatible with college philosophy. Following the student demonstrations and media fiasco, the college reversed its decision and granted Daly a promotion and tenure. The decision was more than a victory for freedom of speech, for the central issue behind the challenge was Daly's view regarding the Church's role in the oppression of women. Students viewed the reversal of the terminal contract as a victory for *women's rights* and a covert admission of guilt by the Church. Daly had accused the Church of being misogynistic. The Church had been tried and prosecuted. The Church as oppressor of women was "guilty as charged."

Mary Daly's work established a major phase in the construction of feminist theory within the Church. As the title suggested, *The Church and the Second Sex* drew heavily upon Simone deBeauvoir's book *The Second Sex*. Daly concurred with deBeauvoir's criticism of the Church; but contrary to deBeauvoir, Daly contended that the Church *was* redeemable. She explored the root of the problem of sexism in religion and proposed some theological solutions for women's equality in the Church.

THE CASE AGAINST THE CHURCH

Daly articulated a case against the Church based on Simone deBeauvoir's work. Although deBeauvoir had not specifically dealt with the Church's role in the oppression of women, she had mentioned the Church and religion frequently in passing. Daly extrapolated four major "themes" from deBeauvoir's remarks. She contended, along with deBeauvoir, that the church was guilty of:

1) causing women's legal oppression and deceiving women into enforced passivity.

2) teaching women's inferiority in its doctrine.

3) harming women through its moral teaching.

4) excluding women from Church leadership roles.

Oppression and Deception

To begin, Daly charged that the Christian religion had been an instrument for the oppression of women. For example, in the Middle Ages, she argued, the Church had upheld legislation that kept married women in a condition of servile economic and legal dependence. Even though modern society had emancipated women from the shackles of oppressive legislation, the Church "has only reluctantly gone along with this amelioration of her legal status."[1] According to Daly, the Church would have dearly loved to have kept women worldwide in a state of servitude because in their dependent condition, women were a "powerful trump in its hand."[2] As deBeauvoir had argued, "There must be religion for women; and there must be women, 'true women,' to perpetuate religion."[3]

DeBeauvoir argued that the oppressiveness of the Church towards women was masked by deception, namely, "the distraction of woman's attention from present injustice to promises of rewards in an afterlife."[4] Daly agreed that religion confirmed the social order by reinforcing the passivity of women: "Women need not *do* anything to save their souls — it is enough to *live in obedience*."[5] According to Daly, women's resignation to their inferior role was justified by giving them a hope of a better future in a sexless heaven.

Daly agreed with deBeauvoir that the Church was guilty of deceiving women by diverting their attention to bright rewards in a future life. She argued that it was also guilty of creating the delusion of equality already attained. The Church told women that the worth of their souls would be weighed in Heaven and not according to their accomplishments on earth. Therefore, Daly maintained, the Church "asked [a woman] in the name of God not so much to accept her inferiority as to believe that, thanks to him, she is the equal of the lordly male."[6] She noted that "even the temptation to revolt is suppressed by the claim that the injustice is overcome."[7] Women were degraded on the one hand, and exalted on the other. But, according to Daly, women's "exaltation" within the Christian faith was deceptive. It was really nothing more than a subversive glorification of men.[8] Daly believed that women's equality in the Church was a pseudo-equality — not a genuine acceptance of women.

Dogma versus Women

Daly echoed deBeauvoir when she accused the Church of conveying — via its doctrine — the idea that women were by nature inferior to men.[9] In pagan religions of antiquity, the mother-goddess was worshiped. DeBeauvoir argued that Christianity had reacted against this paganism by transfiguring the symbolism of the mother-goddess into the cult of the Virgin Mother of God. Women were encouraged to identify with the image of Mary as a passive, submissive mother. Therefore, the independent power of women, intrinsic to goddess worship, had been effectively enslaved by maternity. According to deBeauvoir, women — together with Mary — were glorified only in accepting the subordinate role of mother and housewife:

> For the first time in human history the mother kneels before her son; she freely accepts her inferiority. This is the supreme masculine victory, consummated in the cult of the Virgin — it is the rehabilitation of woman through the accomplishment of her defeat.[10]

Daly concurred with deBeauvoir that women were conditioned by Church doctrine — through teaching about Mary, and also through the interpretation of the epistles — to adore and serve men. According to Daly, the Church had formulated its doctrine to trap women in the restrictive, passive role of mother and housewife.

Harmful Moral Teaching

Third, Daly argued that certain aspects of the Church's moral doctrine were harmful to women. She believed that Hebrew tradition and Greek philosophy had shaped the moral teaching of the Bible. Furthermore, according to Daly, the Aristotelian-Thomistic teaching on the fixed natures of men and women had contributed to the idea of women's special sinfulness. Eve — the woman who succumbed to temptation in paradise — was viewed as morally inferior to Adam, whose demise she crafted. Because of this, Daly reasoned, women became the "devil's most fearsome temptation."[11] Man was the embodiment of pure spirit, while woman was the embodiment of the accursed flesh.

> And of course, since woman remains always the Other, it is not held that reciprocally male and female are both flesh; the flesh that is for the Christian the hostile Other is precisely woman. In her the Christian finds incarnated the temptations of the world, the flesh and the devil. All the Fathers of the Church insist on the idea that she led Adam into sin.[12]

Daly claimed that the Church was the promoter of the antisexual sentiments that cast women's body as sinful, thereby stifling women's sexuality. According to Daly, women could only overcome their special sinfulness by maintaining a perpetual virginal state. A double standard of morality therefore existed, wherein a woman had to be a virgin when she married, and thereafter was expected to remain eternally faithful to her husband. Her husband, on the other hand, had license to be promiscuous, both before and after marriage. Man suffered no disgrace as a result of his actions, whereas a promiscuous woman was punished with extreme penalties. Daly believed that this double standard reflected the Church's patriarchal view of "woman as man's property."

DeBeauvoir and Daly maintained that the Church, through its moral teaching on sexual behavior, had oppressed women for the sake of "perpetuating the family and keeping the patrimony intact."[13] To this end, they argued, the Church had also opposed abortion and the use of contraceptives. Women were destined to become pregnant and bear children against their wills, and were then enslaved in domestic servitude in the care and nurture of those children. A basic enmity existed, they argued, between much traditional Christian moral teaching and the personal aspirations of women. As deBeauvoir had noted, "Reduced to the condition of slavery to the species, instruments of reproduction, [women] cannot transcend their situation."[14]

Exclusion from Church Leadership

Finally, Daly decried the exclusive male hierarchy in Church leadership. She argued that the exclusion of women from these positions had contributed significantly to the inculcation of inferiority feelings in women. According to Daly, all God's representatives on earth — the pope, the bishop, the priest, the pastor — were male. She noted that the net effect of this was to "imbue girls with a sense of *specific* inferiority."[15] For it was futile for a girl "to aspire to such an exalted role no matter how great her talents and piety."[16] Daly argued that women were conditioned to believe they had an irremediably inferior nature to the exalted man. Furthermore, she reasoned, the exclusion of women from the Church hierarchy was linked with an idea of divinity as male. The fact that God was called Father, Christ was male, and the angels — though they were pure spirits — had masculine names, reinforced this tendency to equate the male sex with the divine. DeBeauvoir and Daly contended that the Church therefore led girls into a devastating self-mutilation: the only way to triumph over their debased natures was docility before men (who were closer to God and thus served as intermediaries between girls and a male God).

A GLIMMER OF HOPE

Nevertheless, Daly emerged with a positive message of hope for the Church. She firmly believed that the Church as an institution was guilty of oppressing women, but also maintained that the Church was capable of providing the needed condition for women to rise above the handicap of their sex. She believed that religion provided a means of transcendence for women, and that it was the vehicle that would bring about woman's liberation.

In *The Church and the Second Sex*, Daly accused the church of sexism. She then proposed theological changes she felt would help overcome the problem of patriarchy in the Church and would harmonize the concepts of feminism with religion. Five years later, in *Beyond God the Father*, she identified this as an insuperable pursuit. But for the time being, Daly was confident that changes in Church practice and doctrine would successfully merge the two philosophies and bring about liberation for women in the Church.

THEOLOGICAL MISTAKES — THE ROOT OF THE PROBLEM

Daly identified two major theological mistakes she thought were at the root of the problem of patriarchy in the Church. She maintained that patriarchy existed because of wrong concepts about God, and second, because of a wrong view of Biblical revelation.

Wrong Ideas About God

The Sex of God
The first misleading and harmful notion about God that Daly cited was the concept of God being male. Although she conceded that few theologians believed that God literally belonged to the male sex — God was Spirit and thus above sexual differentiation — she argued that the idea that God is male still lingered on in the minds of theologians, preachers, and simple

believers on a level not entirely explicit or conscious.[17] Furthermore, Daly argued, people took this idea of God as male and unconsciously extrapolated that the male is God — "Since God is male, the male is God"[18] — and therefore had bestowed a natural god-like superiority upon the male sex.

The Character of God

According to Daly the second harmful distortion of theology involved certain attributes traditionally ascribed to God's character. She argued that the concepts of "divine omnipotence," "divine immutability," and "divine providence" were due to an exaggerated influence of Greek philosophy upon Christian thought. They carried associations and images that alienated the peoples of modern Western culture.[19] Daly rejected an all-powerful, all-just God who evidently willed or, at least permitted oppressive conditions to exist. Moreover, she objected to the fact that this God was "changeless." Daly argued that in the face of such a God, man was "despairing and helpless."[20] She reasoned that humans would wonder why they should commit themselves to improving their condition or trying to bring about social justice if such a God existed:

> In fact, then, such notions can and do have the effect of paralyzing the human will to change evil conditions and can inspire callousness and insensitivity. This effect upon attitudes is reinforced by certain ideas of divine providence as a fixed plan being copied out in history. With such a frame of reference, there is a temptation to glorify the status quo, to assume that the social conditions peculiar to any given time and place are right simply because they exist.[21]

In order to harmonize feminism and religion, Daly found it necessary to reject the theology that presented God as omnipotent, immutable and providential, for she believed that this view discouraged women from seeking change. Furthermore, she viewed images of a jealous and vengeful God as projections and justifications for the role of "tyrant father in patriarchal society," rather than actual aspects of God's character.[22] The concept of an almighty, all-powerful, unchangeable, caring, providential God, jealous and demanding worship was, according to Daly, an "inadequacy in the conceptualization of basic doctrines which sustained and perpetuated androcentric theological teachings."[23]

Static Worldview — Ideas About the Bible

According to Daly, wrong concepts about God contributed to a static worldview described as a "changeless" view of reality. This static view conceived human biological nature to be part of a "natural order" sanctioned by God. Daly contended that a static view was not open to theological development and/or social change. Daly also considered a static view of the Bible — "the idea that divine revelation was given to man in the past, once and for all, and that it was 'closed' at the end of the apostolic age"[24] — inimical to healthy human development. She reasoned:

> . . . there can easily follow from this the idea that certain statements in the Bible represent descriptions of an unalterable divine plan, and that these statements must be accepted raw and forcibly applied even though the social context in which we find ourselves is vastly different from the situation in biblical times.[25]

Furthermore, Daly noted that the Bible illustrated the unfortunate, often miserable, condition of women in ancient times. "The authors of both the Old and the New Testaments were men of their times," she argued, and it would therefore "be naive to think that they were free of the prejudices of their epochs."[26] Daly concluded that it would be a "most dubious process to construct an idea of 'feminine nature' or of 'God's plan for women' from biblical texts."[27]

Daly wanted to discard the static worldview which regarded divine revelation as a closed event. Instead, she proposed a dynamic model of revelation that would respond to changes in culture and contain a "radical openness to the facts of contemporary experience."[28] According to Daly's experience, and the experience of other contemporary women, the Biblical text on the role of women was outdated and contained misogynistic dogma. Daly maintained that women in the Church had just as much right to direct current theology as the Apostle Paul did in his day. She believed the experience of women was calling them to act as prophets, naming themselves and guiding the Church in a new direction.[29]

THEOLOGICAL DEVELOPMENTS REQUIRED

Mary Daly believed that Christians could excise the root of patriarchy from the Church by correcting the two major theological "mistakes" — a wrong view of God and a wrong view of the Bible. However, she noted that these corrections would not be enough. Other theological developments would also be required because "The healing of theology's built-in misogynism is related to the advancement of doctrine on *many* levels."[30] Specifically, Daly mentioned ecclesiology (theology of the Church), Christology (theology of Christ), and soteriology (theology of salvation) as a few of those needing revision.

Daly stressed the importance of a "prophetic vision of the Church."[31] The Church needed to transcend its institutionalization and become more of a "movement in the world, concerned primarily with betterment of the human condition, and seeking to cooperate with all who are striving for this goal."[32] The mission of the Church, according to Daly, is the improvement of this world for the benefit of its people. In the area of Christology, Daly believed it was necessary to develop "an understanding of the Incarnation which goes beyond the regressive, sin-obsessed view of human life."[33] She implied that Christ was the paradigm for the transcendent condition that feminism pursued, rather than the Messiah who was sacrificed to redeem a fallen, sinful humanity. "Human progress on all levels," she contended, "continues the work of the Incarnation."[34] Finally, Daly challenged the literal interpretation of the Genesis account of the Fall and the doctrine of sin. She claimed that the literalist view perpetuated "a negative attitude toward sexuality, matter, and 'the world.'"[35]

> As long as theology is obsessed with a conception of human nature as fallen from a state of original integrity, and considers that state to have actually existed in the past, it must be pessimistic about the present and the future. It tends to see human life chiefly in terms of reparation and expiation. As long as this is the atmosphere of theology, Christianity cannot fully recognize itself to be what theologian Karl Rahner called it: "the religion of the absolute future."[36]

THE SECOND SEX AND THE FEMINIZATION OF THEOLOGY

Daly did not exhaustively develop the theological themes she outlined. Her purpose, rather, was to point out the broad areas of Judeo-Christian theology that were incompatible with feminist philosophy. Valerie Saiving Goldstein had initiated discussion by pointing out that theology needed feminization. Daly delineated some parameters for doing just that. She advanced the general feminist argument (women interpret Scripture differently than men, theology needs to consider woman's point of view) to a deeper level, identifying the specific doctrines that were abrasive to the feminist mind-set and which were thought to threaten the attainment of feminist equality.

The appearance of *The Church and the Second Sex* was timely and significant. Its publication coincided with increased secular attention to the women's liberation movement and with the advent of feminist consciousness-raising activity. Secular society was clearly identifying women as a sex class, a group of individuals suffering oppression because of their gender. Daly's book brought about the same sort of identification for women in the Church. Some Christian women began to identify themselves as a class of people within the Church who were being oppressed by the Church. In the Church — as in society — women were *the second sex*.

4

Biology Equals Destiny

Woman has ovaries, a uterus; these peculiarities imprison her in her subjectivity, circumscribe her within the limits of her own nature. . . .

Simone deBeauvoir

EXAMINING THE CAUSE OF PATRIARCHY

As the first phase of the construction of modern feminist thought progressed, secular feminist philosophers shifted the focus of their attention away from identifying the problem of patriarchy towards theorizing about the cause and origin of it. In doing so, they hoped to reveal the means by which to overcome patriarchy and to fill the emptiness plaguing so many women.

Four major books published in the late sixties and early seventies proposed theories regarding the cause and origin of patriarchy: *The Dialectic of Sex: The Case for Feminist Revolution*, by Shulamith Firestone, *Woman's Estate*, by Juliet Mitchell, *Against Our Will: Men, Women, & Rape*, by Susan Brownmiller, and *Sexual Politics*, by Kate Millett.

The Dialectic of Sex: The Case for Feminist Revolution — Shulamith Firestone

The heart of woman's oppression is her childbearing and childrearing roles.[1]

Shulamith Firestone borrowed heavily from Marx's books and philosophy when she wrote *The Dialectic of Sex*. Like deBeauvoir, Firestone identified women and men as relating within characteristic class distinctions — men being like the bourgeois (privileged class) and women being the proletariat (underclass, the serfs and slaves of men). Firestone believed that women's role in procreation was at the heart of this dualism.[2]

> The sexual-reproductive organization of society always furnishes the real basis, starting from which we can alone work out the ultimate explanation of the whole superstructure of economic, juridical and political institutions as well as of the religious, philosophical and other ideas of a given historical period.[3]

According to Firestone, biology determined social order. Therefore, the cultural oppression women experienced stemmed from women's reproductive capacity. To support her case, Firestone discussed what she called the "biological family" — the basic reproductive unit of male/female/infant. The biological family had certain fundamental characteristics: First, Firestone pointed out that women throughout history were at the continual mercy of their biological functions in menstruation, menopause, pregnancy, childbirth, wetnursing and care of infants — all of which made them dependent on males for physical survival. Second, the dependency of infants upon adults for physical survival restricted the adult female for an extended period of time, a fact compounded by the establishment of an artificial, self-perpetuating mother/child relationship. Finally, she noted the division of labor was based on the natural reproductive differences between the sexes. Men, for example, had to hunt for food because women could not leave nursing infants. Firestone argued that this division of labor had become stereotypically enshrined and self-perpetuating.[4]

Firestone claimed that these characteristics of the biological family caused psychosocial distortions in the human personality, evidenced by the existence of patriarchy.[5] She argued that patriarchy would only be overcome by re-ordering both culture and the natural sex differences that had determined culture.[6] She proposed that a "pansexuality" replace male and female sexual differentiation:

> The reproduction of the species by one sex for the benefit of both would be replaced by (at least the option of) artificial reproduction: children would be born to both sexes equally, or independently of either, however one chooses to look at it; the dependence of the child on the mother (and vice versa) would give way to a greatly shortened dependence on a small group of others in general, and any remaining inferiority to adults in physical strength would be compensated for culturally. The division of labor would be ended by the elimination of labor altogether (cybernation). The tyranny of the biological family would be broken.[7]

Firestone argued that women's reproductive biology accounted for their original and continued oppression, and not some sudden patriarchal revolution.[8] Therefore, she suggested that the goal of feminism should be to overcome the reproductive function that enslaved woman and to shatter all social structures inherent in the biological family. She argued that "unless revolution disturbs the basic social organization, the biological family — the vinculum through which the psychology of power can always be smuggled — the tapeworm of exploitation will never be annihilated."[9]

Woman's Estate — Juliet Mitchell

... her capacity for maternity is the definition of woman. ... Yet so long as it is allowed to remain a substitute for action and creativity ... woman will remain confined to the species, to her universal and natural condition.[10]

Juliet Mitchell was involved in the leftist movement in England. However, her writings were widely read by feminists in North America. Mitchell, like Firestone, proposed that patriarchy was caused by women's biological differences. She cited four structures in society, all based on women's biology, that she believed contributed to women's oppression.

The first structure Mitchell cited was *production*, the stereotyped division of labor based on anatomy which therefore assigned to men the occupations requiring greater physical (and mental) strength. Second, she listed the structure for the *reproduction of children*. According to Mitchell, women were entrapped by the very facts of their own childbearing function.[11] Moreover, the procreative function of women had evolved into a "cult of motherhood," an artificial idolization of a demeaning, restrictive role. Mitchell proposed that the third structure, *sexuality*, contributed to the oppression of women because men were allowed sexual freedom, but women were not (the double standard). Finally, she argued that the *socialization of children* had shaped youngsters into stereotyped male and female roles and thereby perpetuated the oppression of women.[12]

The solution Mitchell proposed was similar to Firestone's. She maintained that all oppressive cultural structures based on women's biological processes needed to be overcome through state control and legislation.

Sexual Politics — Kate Millett

... sex has a frequently neglected political aspect ... patriarchy is a political institution.[13]

Kate Millett was an American artist and civil rights activist. The bulk of Millett's book, *Sexual Politics*, was composed of a literary critique of four major male writers: D. H. Lawrence, Henry Miller, Norman Mailer, and Jean Genet. Millett chose these authors to expose the crude expression of power relationships depicted in the explicit sexual acts described in their books. According to Millett, the ideological implications of these fictional writings were precisely those of the power relationships between men and women. She maintained that the power relationship, in which the man is dominant and the woman subservient, was contained and expressed in the act of sex.

Millett sought to reveal the political nature of the relationships between men and women. She defined power and politics as "the intention to dominate." She argued that all women in a given society were kept subordinate via ideological, economic, psychological, anthropological, and legal means, but that this control, or power, was *ultimately exerted in the private, personal level, in the act of sex*. According to Millett, the sexual relationship between a man and a woman embodied a political dimension — namely, the domination and conquest of women by men. The act of sex, Millett concluded, was the primary means of social control exerted by men.

Against Our Will — Susan Brownmiller

> Man's violent capture and rape of the female led to . . . the full-blown
> male solidification of power, the patriarchy.[14]

Susan Brownmiller, an American journalist and civil rights activist, identified the act of rape and the subsequent development of a "rape culture" as the cause of patriarchy. According to Brownmiller, rape culture was the cultural atmosphere in which "the raping of women is taken to be normal, even expected, and in which male attitudes toward women, and those of women toward themselves and other women are colored by this assumption."[15]

Brownmiller observed that male physical anatomy allowed men to dominate women by force in the act of rape. She hypothesized that men discovered this ability early in history and had used it ever since for this advantage.

> . . . rape is man's basic weapon of force against woman, the principal agent
> of his will and her fear. It is nothing more or less than a conscious process
> of intimidation by which *all* men keep *all* women in a state of fear.[16]

Brownmiller acknowledged that all men were not rapists, but she argued that all men belonged to the portion of the human species capable of rape. She believed that men had thus developed a "mass psychology of the conqueror" — a mind-set that placed men above women because men could potentially conquer women. Furthermore, Brownmiller proposed that the fear of rape would cause a woman to associate herself with a male who would offer her protection from other males. This, according to Brownmiller, was the cause and origin of marriage and of all the societal structures of domination.[17]

> Female fear of an open season of rape, and not a natural inclination
> toward monogamy, motherhood or love, was probably the single
> causative factor in the original subjugation of woman by man, the most
> important key to her historic dependence, her domestication by protec-
> tive mating.[18]

Brownmiller hypothesized that man's violent capture and rape of the female led first to the establishment of a rudimentary male-protectorate and then sometime later to the full-blown male solidification of power, the patriarchy.[19] In her view, the act of rape was paradigmatic of male attitudes towards women, if not in practice, then at least in theory. She pointed out that this did not mean that all woman wanted to be raped, nor that all men wanted to rape women. But it did mean that, although rape was carried out as an actual act only by some men, all men in some sense benefited from their actions.[20]

BIOLOGY EQUALS DESTINY

The feminist authors in the late 1960s and early 1970s who theorized about the cause of patriarchy agreed that it was caused by the anatomical and biological differences between male and female. *One's biology determined one's destiny.* Some theorists, such as Firestone and Mitchell, focused on female anatomy — woman's capacity to bear children. Others, such as Brownmiller and Millett, focused on male anatomy: men's genitalia and physical strength were identified as weapons of power that had been used to intimidate women and keep them in the oppressed role. According to these theorists, biology was the basic cause, and culture the result and perpetuator of women's predicament. Human anatomy and physiology had given rise to the patterns of ideology and social organization inherently oppressive to women. As one feminist summarized:

> The reproductive function of a woman is the only innate function which distinguishes women from men. It is the critical distinction upon which all inequities toward women are grounded.[21]

Because feminists believed that patriarchy was caused by the biological differences between men and women, they thought that the way to overcome patriarchy was to overcome *all* distinctions between the sexes. Firestone wrote:

> And just as the end goal of socialist revolution was not only the elimination of the economic class *privilege* but of the economic class *distinction* itself, so the end goal of feminist revolution must be, unlike that of the first feminist movement, not just the elimination of male *privilege* but of the sex *distinction* itself: genital differences between human beings would no longer matter culturally.[22]

By overcoming — or at least minimizing — the distinctions between the sexes, feminists thought that the inequities would be overcome and that women would be freed to find meaning. "Sameness" would mean freedom, for biology would no longer determine destiny.

WOMEN'S DIFFERENCES AS WEAKNESSES

Feminists blamed women's differences for the existence of patriarchy. Therefore, in the first phase of the development of (second wave) feminist thought, women's differences were viewed as weaknesses. The goal of the first phase was thus to obliterate the differences which made women weak and vulnerable. The "burn the bra" marches of the late 1960s grew out of this view.[23] For example, one public demonstration centered around a "freedom trash can" into which bras, girdles, false eyelashes and other "instruments of female oppression" were tossed. These media spectacles symbolically expressed women's desire to overcome their differences in order to become *just like men*. Feminist women began to dress like men, to smoke, drink and swear like men, and to claim sexual freedom and participation in the work force on the same basis as men.

Many feminist organizations were founded in the first phase of the development of feminist theory.[24] They adopted agendas for changing women's role and for abating biological differences between the sexes. Their political blueprints for change were based upon the theories presented in the writings we have reviewed thus far. Shulamith Firestone, for example, presented the following structural imperatives for overcoming patriarchy:

1. The freeing of women from the tyranny of their reproductive biology by every means available, and the diffusion of the childbearing and childrearing role to the society as a whole, men as well as women.

2. The full self-determination, including economic independence of women.

3. The total and equal integration of women into all aspects of the larger society.

4. The freedom of all women to do what ever they wish to do sexually.[25]

These structural imperatives summarized the theory behind the activities of the newly established feminist groups — i.e., the quest for legalized abortion, national day care, affirmative action programs, pay equity, changes in education, and all other matters of their concern. Feminists wanted to overcome the biological differences they saw as responsible for patriarchy. These differences were a burden and a shame to them. They desired to strip away all distinction in order to transform the cultural roles of male and female into unisexual androgyny.

THE FEMALE EUNUCH — GERMAINE GREER

We know what we are, but know not what we may be, or what we might have been. . . . The new assumption behind the discussion of the body is that everything that we may observe *could be otherwise*.[26] (emphasis added)

The concept of women's differences as weaknesses was epitomized in another major feminist work: Germaine Greer's *The Female Eunuch*. Greer was an Australian who had studied literature and drama at Cambridge and then worked in England as a teacher and journalist. Because of *The Female Eunuch*, Greer was invited in 1971 to join in a debate in New York's Town Hall at the prestigious "Theatre of Ideas." Following the debate, Greer stayed in the United States and was recognized as a major figure in North American feminism. In *The Female Eunuch*, Greer theorized that women's bodily and psychological differences were *induced* characteristics imposed upon women to keep them subservient. She maintained, for instance, that woman's skeletal structure was greatly influenced by the role women were forced to occupy in society. Men were more vigorous than women, so their bones had more clearly marked muscular grooves that were more developed because of exercise. Furthermore, she argued that fashion and sex appeal had dictated the shape of the feminine skeleton through the posture women were expected to adopt (e.g., the sexually alluring sway-walk) and through high-heeled footwear that altered the alignment of their bones. Likewise, she proposed that women's curvatures and subcutaneous fat levels were dictated by the male's preference for "cuddlesome" women,[27] and that patterns of hair growth were influenced by male cultivation and female depilation of body hair. According to Greer, women's role and participation in coitus, her emotions, her character, her consumerism, her participation in education and the work force and her role in marriage were based upon a *false* perception of the biological differences between men and women. Greer conceded that some genital differences were obvious and undeniable, but argued that these differences had been exaggerated by the cultural roles women had been forced to occupy. According to Greer, men had shaped women into who they were. She argued that patriarchy had distorted both women's natural psychological and biological composition.

Greer proposed that all societal mores, structures, and institutions that falsely magnified the biological differences needed to be challenged and disassembled. She encouraged women to question and change the way they viewed male-female roles, the marital relationship, and even their own bodies.

OVERCOMING DESTINY

Secular feminists initiated the search for the cause of patriarchy and determined it to be biology and its resultant sociological structures. On that basis, they proposed social and political solutions they felt would minimize biological differences, disassemble societal structures, and ultimately overcome women's traditional destiny. Religious feminists also sought to uncover the cause of patriarchy. Mary Daly believed that the theological cause was a wrong view of God and a wrong view regarding revelation. But although Daly had determined the cause of patriarchy in the Church, she had not extensively developed a theology to correct it. Secular feminists had formulated a plan to eliminate patriarchy in society; feminist theologians, therefore, turned their attention towards developing a comprehensive theology of liberation for women that would provide the solution for the Church. They believed that solution would be found in a feminist form of liberation theology.

5

Feminist Liberation Theology

Just as the call for salvation from transitoriness to attain immortality could be heard in every corner of the ancient world, today a cry for liberation is shouted by the oppressed, the humiliated, and the offended in this inhuman world. . . . Whatever the language spoken, or the words used, the call for liberation is not just an empty slogan, but a cri de coeur. *It is a cry from the heart; a cry out of oppression; a cry for a new future, beginning now!*[1]

A massive banner conspicuously overhung the stage of the 1972 Grailville Conference of Women Exploring Theology. It portrayed a vividly colored butterfly stretching its wings in preparation for flight, remnants of an old cocoon encumbering its escape. Splashed across the banner was the slogan, "You can fly, but that cocoon has got to go!"[2] Such was the opinion of the theologians who had gathered to explore the question of feminist theology and women's liberation in the Church. They realized that in order to fully equalize the positions of male and female, the male-dominated theology of the past had to be shaken off and left behind. Women needed to take wing in navigating a woman-based theology for the future.

Two female theologians, Letty Russell (*Human Liberation in a Feminist Perspective: A Theology*, 1974) and Rosemary Radford Ruether (*Liberation Theology: Human Hope Confronts Christian History and American Power*, 1972), began to develop a theology specific to the liberation of women. They based their theology on liberation theology, newly introduced in Latin America. In order to understand why they chose liberation theology as their basic blueprint, we must investigate the phenomena of this theology in the Third World.

THE BEGINNINGS OF LIBERATION THEOLOGY

Liberation theology received its name from Gustavo Gutierrez's electrifying book of 1971, *A Theology of Liberation*. In his writings, Gutierrez, a Peruvian priest, initiated a new theological approach to the political problems of the Third World. He claimed that Latin America's ills were peculiar to that region, and were therefore seldom directly treated by European or North American theologians. The theology of the Western world was simply irrelevant to the social and political conditions of Third World countries such as Brazil, Argentina, Nicaragua, and Peru. Gutierrez's theology was an attempt to relate the eschatological message of freedom to the sociopolitical reality of Latin Americans.[3]

The movement towards a theology of liberation had actually begun a decade earlier with the birth of social conscience in the Church. During the Second Vatican Council (1962-1965), Latin American bishops from all regions had met together and resolved to attack the continent's socio-political problems head-on. They maintained that Christian teachings were relevant to life in this world, and that Catholic social thought thus had implications for the restructuring of unjust societies. Gutierrez worked among the poor peoples of Lima. His observations of that time led him to the conclusion that Peruvians had been trapped into a position of poverty and dependence by an oppressive political and economic system. In his opinion, Peruvians would only taste freedom from oppression when the system was destroyed and all distinctions between rich and poor were abolished. This task he saw as the job of the Church and even as the crux of the Christian message.

> I discovered three things. I discovered that poverty was a destructive thing, something to be fought against and destroyed, not merely something which was the object of our charity. Secondly, I discovered that poverty was not accidental. The fact that these people are poor and not rich is not just a matter of chance, but the result of a structure. It was a structural question. Thirdly, I discovered that poor people were a social class. When I discovered that poverty was something to be fought against ... it became crystal clear that in order to serve the poor, one had to move into political action.[4]

Gutierrez observed that Latin Americans were economically dependent on the rest of the world. He accused North America and Europe in particular of keeping Latin Americans in a position of servitude by exploiting the use of the region's raw materials. Furthermore, he equated the highly visible class inequalities between the rich and the poor to the class struggle posited by Marx between the proletariat and the bourgeoisie. Gutierrez's vision for the future was a classless society with no oppression, equality for all peoples, and power distributed among all. He proposed that a revolution based on the Biblical message of liberation would end the dualisms of rich/poor, oppressors/oppressed, bourgeoisie/proletariat. Liberation, the deliverance of the oppressed, therefore became the theme upon which Gutierrez built his theology. He claimed that he had rediscovered the messianic kernel of the gospel which was the very essence of the Biblical message.

The "cantus firmus of the liberating message" of the Bible is the good news of deliverance experienced by the Hebrew people, and the good news of the establishment of God's rulership as experienced by the early followers of Jesus Christ. These acts of deliverance are also the basis of traditioning into the present experience and future hope of those who seek liberation now.[5]

Gutierrez and other liberation theologians claimed that the truth of the Bible was found in its liberating potential, and that this truth was to be enacted by Christians through political and social *praxis* (action). So extreme was this position that liberation theologians claimed that socialism ("human life in society, liberated as far as possible from alienations") constituted the highest real value, that it was *the* theological crux of the Bible, and that to say otherwise reduced the gospel message to "no value at all."[6]

The end goal of liberation theology was the realization of full economic and social equality and participation of all peoples in a utopian, harmonic and peaceful society. It sought to build a new society, a new humanity, and a new future. Liberation theologians equated freedom from economic, social and political dependence with spiritual wholeness and the salvific promise of God. Gutierrez reasoned:

The liberation of our continent means more than overcoming economic, social, and political dependence. It means, in a deeper sense, to see the becoming of mankind as a process of the emancipation of man in history. It is to see man in search of a qualitatively different society in which he will be free from all servitude, in which he will be the artisan of his own destiny. It is to seek the building of *a new man*.[7]

Liberation theology focused on the Biblical message of God's mission to set humans free from bondage. In the light of oppression experienced by Third World people, it sought to communicate the good news of liberation — which it considered as the gospel — in such a way that people could "hear, understand, and accept this message of God's gift of freedom and salvation in their lives."[8] Liberation theologians claimed that the experience of the oppressed peoples of Latin America provided the axial point for a new Christianity, a new man, and a new future, and that Christianity had just reached its true identity in the identification of faith with revolutionary praxis towards the ending of all dualisms.[9]

Liberation theology provided a new model for Biblical theology, hermeneutics, and ultimately, for a revised worldview. Instead of looking at the newspaper through the lens of the Bible, liberation theologians viewed the Bible through the lens of contemporary experience and social events. They said: "This is a new way to do theology, with the newspaper in hand."[10]

LIBERATION THEOLOGY FOR WOMEN

Feminist theologians saw many parallels between the condition of the Latin American people and the condition of women. Like Third World liberation theology, feminist theology was written out of an experience of oppression in society. Feminist scholars claimed that the domination of women by men was "the most ancient and persistent form of the subjection of one human being to a permanent status of inferiority because of sex."[11] Furthermore, they argued that the distortion of man's relationship to woman was the root form of his alienation from his neighbor, "in the sense that it is from the estrangement of man and woman that other forms of human estrangement flow."[12] In other words, feminist theologians believed that sex discrimination was the root of all other forms of oppression. Feminists borrowed Gutierrez's analysis, but believed that the key to true liberation was deeper than mere social and political change. According to feminist theologians, the key to world liberation was the liberation of the world's largest oppressed class: women. Feminist theologians believed that the liberation of women would induce the end of poverty, racial discrimination, ecological destruction, and war. They argued that it would end all dualisms, usher in a new world order of peace, and witness the birth of a new humanity.

DUALISMS AS MODELS OF OPPRESSION

Rosemary Radford Ruether proposed that Christianity had inherited a system of dualisms that had distorted its "epistemological, moral, and ontological perceptions."[13] Ruether explained that a dualistic philosophy maintained that all phenomena in the universe could be explained in terms of two fundamental and exclusive principles of good or bad, right or wrong. She cited the gnostics, for example, as possessing an anti-material subject-object dualism that regarded the non-material universe as good, and the physical, material universe as bad. The gnostics, therefore, experienced salvation through repressing their sensual appetites and carnal feelings, and focusing instead on their inward, transcendent, spiritual selves.[14] According to Ruether, Christians adopted this Gnostic view, and Christian reality was thus split into a "non-material thinking substance" and a "non-thinking extension" or "matter."[15] She argued that Western Judeo-Christian culture operated out of a psychology that extended the same dualism of body and soul, subject and object into sociological alienation and oppression.

Ruether cited the male-female dualism as the primary social extension of subject-object dualism. Spirit, mind, soul, and man were linked with the "good" end of the polarity, while body, emotion, physical matter (earth) and woman were located on the debased, fallen end.

> Classical Christianity attributed all the intellectual virtues to the male. Woman was thereby modeled after the rejected part of the psyche. She is shallow, fickle-minded, irrational, carnal-minded, lacking all the true properties of knowing and willing and doing.[16]

Ruether argued that men used sexual dualism to justify the oppression of women by men. Furthermore, she argued that sexual dualism provided the basic model for class and racial oppression as well as earth exploitation. According to Ruether, aberrant dualistic spirituality was responsible for "self-alienation, world-alienation, and various kinds of social alienations in sexism, anti-Semitism, racism, alienation between classes, and colonialist imperialism."[17] Moreover, Ruether maintained that Christianity, "as the bearer of this culture of aberrant spirituality and its prime mover around the world, carried a particularly deep burden of guilt."[18]

Ruether believed that women and other oppressed groups would only be freed through the disintegration of dualistic polarities. "A perspective on liberation must emerge from a much more deeply integral vision which finds a new unity of opposites through transformation of values."[19] She, along with other feminist theologians, sought to create a new theology based on the "messianic gospel of liberation," which — like Latin American liberation theologians — they viewed as the crux of the Bible's message. In contrast to Gutierrez's theology, however, feminists saw the *male-female* relationship to be the primary dualism whose harmonization would end all others. In the feminist theologian's paradigm, the liberation of all peoples would only be achieved in and through the liberation of women.

THE GOALS OF FEMINIST LIBERATION THEOLOGY

Letty Russell outlined the goals of feminist liberation theology. According to Russell, the first feminist goal of liberation was *freedom*. She argued (using Paul's picture of the whole universe groaning for freedom — Romans 8:22-23) that liberation was the ultimate pursuit and goal of history. Russell used this text, and the Biblical story of Israel's exodus from slavery, to advocate the contemporary pursuit of women's liberation on a personal and social level.

> Remembering the Biblical story of liberation in the exodus and the resurrection, we can look together at how groaning for freedom, discovery of freedom and horizon of freedom appear to be happening in the experience of women in today's world.[20]

Although freedom was feminism's ultimate goal, Russell and other feminist theologians found it difficult to define the term. Generally, they agreed that freedom referred to a feeling of "wholeness," "autonomy," or a "world-transcending spirit."[21] Ruether summarized the essence of freedom as consisting of "integral personhood."[22] As Russell explained:

> Freedom is a journey with others and for others toward God's future. Freedom can never be defined once and for all. Freedom defined is freedom no longer, because it always transcends all our definitions or concepts. It can be experienced and celebrated only as it breaks into our lives as new awareness of hope in God's future, and new confidence in the growing ability to experience and share love with others.[23]

Feminist theologians viewed freedom as a *process* that rested within the individual. It was realized through experience, yet had an elusive "never-totally realized" quality. Russell explained that: `

> . . . the promises of liberation, like the promises of God, are not fully known except as they are experienced, and then they always have an "overspill" of longing that points to the next fulfillment.[24]

Letty Russell proposed that the experience of Biblical freedom for women led to a new responsibility to serve. Women were being set free for service (*diakonia*) to others.[25] According to Russell, this service was threefold. First, women were called to *curative diakonia* — the "healing of the wounds of those who have become victims of life; providing help to the sick, the hungry, and the homeless." Second, they were to be involved in *preventive diakonia* — "attempting to curtail developments that might easily lead to restriction of full freedom for life."[26] Finally, and most importantly, Russell stated that women tasted Biblical freedom in order to practice *prospective diakonia* — "attempting to open the situation for a future realization of life; helping those who are outcasts from the dominant culture or society to participate fully in society or to reshape that society."[27]

According to Russell, *diakonia* therefore meant "a genuine struggle to see that the church takes steps to support prospective action on the part of those groups and movements working for their own liberation and development."[28] Curative and preventive *diakonia* were always needed, but were not adequate. Russell argued that those who themselves had experienced a groaning and longing to be free needed to face up to "the risky business of advocating human liberation in the process of working out better ways for expressing solidarity with others."[29] In sum, Russell viewed liberation as an ongoing process of intervention on behalf of others. According to Russell, "liberation is a long journey. It is a never-ending struggle by people to find out who they are and what they must become. . . . It is the calling of men and women to stay on that road toward freedom and to *keep the freedom rumor going*."[30]

Russell's first goal of liberation (self-realized freedom for the oppressed) led to her second goal, a new communal social ethic. According to Russell, as individuals experienced freedom for themselves, they were called to participate in the freeing of other oppressed groups.

> Insofar as we have a small foretaste of God's gift of freedom, we are also led to see more clearly that this gift is intended by God for all women and men . . . our heightened restlessness and longing, brought about by this foretaste, can only direct us toward participating in God's solidarity with humankind.[31]

Ruether agreed with Russell. She believed that "development toward a new planetary humanity goes hand in hand with the revolt of every oppressed group, in demands for national, class, racial, and sexual integrity and identity. [Humans] can move closer together only on the basis of each group's self-realization."[32]

Feminist theologians believed that individual freedom would eventually produce a corporate society of justice and *shalom* wherein all would be free.[33] They argued that when women and men were no longer polarized, but interacting on a pattern of mutuality, a new cooperative social order would arise that would ultimately end all dualities. Ruether summarized the second feminist goal of a new communal social ethic:

> We need to build a new cooperative social order out beyond the principles of hierarchy, rule and competitiveness. Starting in the grass-roots local units of human society where psycho-social polarization first began, we must create a living pattern of mutuality between men and women, between parents and children, among people in their social, economic and political relationships, and finally, between mankind and the organic harmonies of nature.[34]

The final and ultimate goal of liberation that Russell cited was the realization of a new humanity. Feminist theologians had a vision for a new age and a paradisal renewal of earth and society. They believed that "God with Us" and the "return of Christ" would occur when humanity achieved a reconciliation of soul and body and thereby ushered in a "new creation." Ruether noted that the "revolution of the feminine . . . sought to reclaim spirit for body and body for spirit in a messianic appearing of the body of God."[35] According to Russell, the messianic appearing of the body of God would occur when all humans learned to exist together harmoniously, free from the dualisms of oppression. She concluded:

> In its state of mortality and decadence all the universe longs for the fulfillment of God's new creation when all the parts will be born again in harmony, when the New Age promised by God and begun in Jesus Christ will be fulfilled. . . . When the end and goal of this action is completed, Christ will hand himself and all things back to God.[36]

THE THEOLOGICAL SOLUTION

Feminist theologians Ruether and Russell modified Gutierrez's liberation theology into a feminist theology of liberation for women. They accepted his proposal that the liberation of the oppressed was the crux of the Biblical message, but shifted his focus from those who were economically oppressed to those who were oppressed because of their gender. Ruether and Russell argued that the Bible supported the liberation of women. The Bible pointed toward the freedom and integral personhood of woman. It advocated a new communal social ethic in which those who had already experienced freedom would struggle on behalf of other groups who had not yet experienced it. Ruether and Russell believed that the Kingdom of God would be realized when people achieved a new planetary humanity by harmonizing all dualisms.

Ruether and Russell believed that a feminist liberation theology — which viewed liberation as the crux of the Bible — was the theological solution for the equality of women. However, in choosing *liberation* and more specifically the *liberation of women* as the lens through which to interpret the Bible and contemporary events, they claimed the right to name themselves. Instead of deciding what *liberation* and *freedom* meant, according to the Bible, they interpreted the Bible according to their preconceived definitions of those terms. Ruether and Russell determined that *all* Biblical interpretation needed to align with *their* vision for the liberation of women. They further claimed that the Bible supported social and political action not only for the liberation of women, but for the eventual liberation of all of creation. The butterfly motif of the 1972 Grailville Conference of Women Exploring Theology thus began to be transferred into reality. Feminist theologians had claimed the right to name themselves. They had broken out of the cocoon of traditional methods of Biblical interpretation, spread their wings, and left the cocoon far behind.

6

The Personal Becomes Political

What a misfortune to be a woman! And yet the misfortune,
when one is a woman, is at bottom not to comprehend that
it is one.

Søren Kierkegaard

A few years before secular and religious feminists had formulated comprehensive theories as to the solutions for patriarchy, isolated feminists had begun channelling their theories into political and social action. This impetus intensified through the formation of the National Organization for Women (NOW). NOW was a small women's civil rights organization inaugurated to lobby the Equal Employment Opportunity Commission (EEOC)[1] on sex discrimination in employment. NOW's presentations to the EEOC received minimal attention, but the organization's visual demonstrations did arouse the media's interest. Members of NOW picketed outside the *New York Times* building in opposition to the male/female segregated help-wanted ads run by the *Times*; they organized demonstrations against the firing of stewardesses;[2] and they demonstrated on Madison Avenue against TV soap operas. In March of 1968, the *New York Times Magazine* responded to the demonstrations with an article by Martha Weinman Lear entitled "The Second Feminist Wave — What Do These Women *Want*?" The public's attention was again directed towards feminism when actress Valeria Solanis, a self-identified "women's-libber" and author of "The SCUM (Society for Cutting Up Men) Manifesto" shot the famous artist Andy Warhol in the stomach. But despite all the protests and legislative lobbying and scandal, most North Americans were only vaguely aware of an organized women's movement.

In the autumn of 1968, that changed. On September 7, a splashy protest of the Miss America contest danced across nearly every television screen in the country. The feminist protest was an attention grabber that garnered, in the *New York Times* alone, ten times the space allotted to the actual winner of the popular beauty contest.

Over one hundred women had responded to an angry mimeographed flyer calling for "No More Miss America." The TV cameras caught the protesters marching down the boardwalk, singing, shouting, and holding up placards.

"No More Beauty Standards — Everyone Is Beautiful."
"Welcome to the Miss America Cattle Auction."
"I am a Woman — Not a Toy, a Pet or a Mascot."

The random parade of women in jeans and mini-skirts, braless under T-shirts, had continued toward the pageant site. There, women filled the "Freedom Trash Can" with objects of women's oppression: dishcloths, girdles, false eyelashes, bras, copies of *Playboy*, *Vogue*, and *Ladies Home Journal*. They auctioned off an eight-foot-high, voluminously bosomed Miss America dummy resplendent in spangles. They trotted out a live sheep with a big bow strapped to its tail, draped it with a banner, and crowned *it* Miss America.

The pageant proper began at 8:30, and a few of the protestors, followed watchfully by a contingent of security officers, entered the convention hall. Two hours later, flashbulbs popped and television cameras zoomed in to record the coronation of the new queen. As the pretty young woman began to speak, shouts burst out in the hall.

"Down with Miss America!"
"Freedom!"

And then . . . a huge, white bedsheet floated slowly down from the balcony. The cameras wheeled around, and there millions (undoubtedly for the first time) saw suspended on that wavy banner an unmistakable message: "WOMEN'S LIBERATION."[3]

Thus began a feminist media extravaganza. The public watched in fascination as feminists tossed Colgate-Palmolive products in a toilet bowl to protest stereotyped advertising and as demonstrators staged an eleven-hour sit-in in the office of the *Ladies Home Journal* editor-in-chief. They watched as feminists picketed the New York City Marriage License Bureau, saw the arrest of the women's libbers who broke into a pornographic publishing house, and witnessed the famous Plaza Hotel Oak room invasion.[4] Magazines, newspapers, television, radio — every medium of public communication became preoccupied with the activities and philosophy of this movement. "Women's Lib" became a household term and a hot topic of conversation at nearly every gathering.

Although awareness of the women's movement was spreading, allegiance to the feminist perspective was still not widespread. Women's libbers were, for the most part, portrayed by the media humorously, as discontented, raving, ugly, placard-waving spinsters. Therefore, those who embraced feminist philosophy were most often regarded by society as discontented, maladjusted oddities. Feminists were openly mocked, ridiculed, and belittled. Betty Friedan herself endured much antagonism. One caller to a radio talk-show demanded that this "destroyer of womanhood" be taken off the air. The struggles and ridicule that women's libbers encountered convinced them that even though they had unveiled a problem common to all women, the majority of women were not personally aware of this problem and therefore were not supportive of the radical social changes that the feminist movement championed. Feminist theorists concluded that women as a whole needed enlightenment, and feminists needed a tool to show women how bad their condition really was.

Quite inadvertently, feminists unearthed the tool that would serve to educate and convince the average woman of her plight and would further ignite revolutionary fervor in her mind. They discovered the principle that *collective bitterness and anger give way to collective political expression.* The most effective way to instill in individual women a collective bitterness and unity of purpose was to expose women to other women in the context of small feminist discussion groups. By the process of group dynamics, small sparks of personal unhappiness could be fanned into an inferno of corporate discontent and political action. Large numbers of women would thereby reconceptualize their personal problems as having corporate and political origins. This process of reconceptualization, "consciousness raising," was seminal to the furtherance of the feminist movement, and was the vital building block that completed the first phase of the construction of modern-day feminism.

SPEAKING BITTERNESS:
THE STORY OF CONSCIOUSNESS RAISING

> *Speak bitterness to recall bitterness.*
> *Speak pain to recall pain.*
> Mao Tse-tung

Consciousness raising was a political technique used in the late 1940s by the revolutionary army of Mao Tse-tung in its invasion of North China. To assist in purging the villages of Japanese and Kuomintang control, the political revolutionaries called the townswomen to gather in the town squares to recite the crimes their men had committed against them. The women were encouraged to "speak bitterness and pain." Initial reluctance gave way to collective anger as woman after woman recounted stories of rape by landlords, of being sold as concubines, and of physical abuse by husbands and fathers-in-law. As the women vented their bitterness they experienced a newfound strength and resolve that empowered them to corporate action. Local associations were formed to provide support for women who acted against the oppression they now felt they shared. For example, in one village, a peasant, Man-ts'ang, was called before a gathering of the local women's association to answer for beating his wife. Almost all of the women in the village were present. The confrontation exploded into violence as an unrepentant Man-ts'ang was physically pummelled and attacked by the entire group.[5] Speaking bitterness was said to have been the salvation of Man-ts'ang's wife. Together with other women, she had found the strength to confront her situation and had found the resolve to be active in forcing change. This was a truly revolutionary act.

Consciousness raising was the North American expression of the Chinese "speak bitterness" meetings. Its goal was to show women the commonality of their oppression and to provide support for acting against it. Formal consciousness-raising groups began in the United States in the late 1960s as female political activists abandoned male-dominated organizations to join the quest for women's liberation. One such activist, Kathie Sarachild, a film editor and veteran of the civil rights movement, helped found the New York Radical Women, a women's liberation organization. At its inaugural meeting, Sarachild proposed that her group study the political and social roots of female oppression by discussing their own experiences as women. In April, 1968 the group engaged in a rap session, "Woman as Child," during which participants discussed prenatal prejudices — preferences parents had about the sex of their children even before the children were born. They also talked about differences in expectations, and differences in how male and female children were raised. The initial discussion led to others on subjects such as sex and sexuality, motherhood, marriage, women in the work force, and domestic work.

By the middle of 1968 Sarachild was convinced that she had struck upon something extraordinary. She organized a guide and manifesto to consciousness raising (CR) and presented it to the first Women's Liberation Conference, held in Chicago in November of 1968.[6] The paper, entitled "A Program for Feminist Consciousness Raising," was reprinted in many feminist anthologies and spurred the establishment of CR groups all over the United States. By 1970, it was hard to find a feminist group anywhere in North America that did not engage in this practice.

Using consciousness raising to develop feminist theory and prompt feminist action met with resistance from some thinkers in the women's liberation movement. Betty Friedan, for instance, denounced CR as "navel gazing."[7] But as time wore on and the effectiveness of this method was demonstrated, Sarachild's position prevailed. The practice of consciousness raising grew, and members of the early groups translated their CR discussions into the basic theoretical documents of feminism. Pat Marinardi, for example, an artist and member of the New York Radical Women, transformed a discussion on women and housework into an article, "The Politics of Housework." Alix Shulman was so stimulated by discussions on marriage that she wrote a marriage contract for herself and her spouse. The contract was later reprinted in *Redbook* and was the subject of an article in *Life*.[8] Anne Koedt expanded discussions from her CR group into a paper, "The Myth of the Vaginal Orgasm." As well as stimulating theoretical work, CR also sparked political demonstrations such as those held in opposition to the Miss America contest. While Sarachild's rules and directives for CR were modified, and methodologies amongst groups varied, feminists agreed that consciousness raising, or "speaking bitterness," was the most potent, effective tool in the mobilization of the feminist movement.

THE CONSCIOUSNESS-RAISING GROUP

Consciousness raising, or reconceptualization, was best accomplished in small groups made up of seven to twelve women brought together through informal or formal means. Ideally, these groups involved women with no prior involvement in feminism as well as at least one experienced member of the feminist movement who helped guide discussions. The meetings generally took place once a week in one of the participants' homes.[9]

In the course of the meetings, participants extensively discussed topics related to their position as women. Emphasis was placed on openly sharing and discussing personal experiences and feelings. As meetings continued, the leader challenged each participant to think over a series of provocative questions. Why, for example, do you dress the way you do? Are fashionable but uncomfortable clothes, elaborate hair styles, and make-up necessary? Are you catering to men? Why should you go to such trouble? Is it a wife's responsibility to devote herself primarily to caring for her husband? Should you cook all his meals, clean the house, wash his clothes, type his term papers, type his thesis, and eventually type his book in return for an acknowledgment that includes the words "love" and "without whose help"? Should women have to sacrifice more than men for the sake of companionship and the intimacy of marriage? Is it the mother's responsibility to care for and raise children? Should women refrain from being assertive and aggressive? Why do they characteristically lack self-confidence? Ought almost all the enterprising occupations be male-dominated and almost all the care-giving, nurturing ones female? Do you like sex? Do you have orgasms regularly? Do you give in to sex even when you don't feel like it? Do your partner's sexual needs take precedence over your own? Do you like other women?

A range of topics was introduced, and many personal experiences exchanged. Through lengthy discussions group members discovered that they, as women, shared very similar "problems." Members began to question the entire role of women, which until that time, many had taken for granted. Finally, the group leader guided the group into acceptance of feminist ideology and involvement in the feminist movement. Maren Lockwood Cardin, author of a widely used feminist textbook, described the process of consciousness raising and conversion to feminist ideology that occurred in the CR group:

> Women who are eventually to become committed to the feminist ideology as members of Women's Liberation do not accept that ideology as

soon as they hear of it. They join a [consciousness-raising] group because feminist ideas interest them and because the group offers the opportunity to talk about and perhaps resolve the role-related problems which worry them. In the course of participation, they achieve a changed perspective on these problems and on their identity as women.[10]

The essence of consciousness raising was reconceptualization or re-education of one's normative patterns of thought. While this process occurred in varied ways and over varied periods of time, consciousness raising within a small group followed a single general pattern. First, a woman was invited to join a discussion or support group to talk about women's issues. In the course of group discussion, she was encouraged to share personal hurt and anger. As more and more women in the group "spoke bitterness," they were led to see that the source of their discontent commonly stemmed from their relationship or interaction with the men in their lives, be it fathers, employers, colleagues, spouses, teachers or other men. Bitterness grew as the participants concluded that men were responsible for women's unhappiness. Group members were then challenged to question and rethink their old conceptions of womanhood and their role as women. They were, at that point, susceptible to conversion to a feminist perspective. Cardin explained:

> Once a group member has evaluated her own life experiences and has begun to ask general questions, she is in a position to be "converted" to the new feminist perspective. The conversion is a matter of a conscious shift of thought processes from acceptance of the status quo to seriously questioning it.[11]

Jo Freeman, author of *The Politics of Women's Liberation*, agreed with Cardin. She maintained that CR groups were "created specifically for the purpose of altering the participants' perceptions and conceptions of themselves and society at large."[12]

Cardin acknowledged that consciousness-raising groups assisted women to adopt a new perspective on the feminine role and further convinced them to become active in the feminist movement. However, she pointed out that many members required further consciousness raising in order to understand the full manifestation of the women's liberation perspective.[13] According to Cardin, a continuum of raised consciousness existed. Individuals began the process by questioning the role of male and female in society. As they ascended to a higher level, they not only questioned their own role, but began to question and discard all values and beliefs subscribed to in the past. In essence, the fully-raised consciousness demanded giving up the Judeo-Christian paradigm in exchange for a feminist worldview. But even though fledgling CR members may not have grasped the magnitude and implications of the raised feminist consciousness, they became committed to the ideology in the same way. Cardin observed:

> They exchange accounts of personal experiences, identify shared problems, and interpret these problems in terms of the movement's ideology. Having examined all aspects of their lives from this new perspective, they eventually reconceptualize their thinking *and accept that perspective* [i.e., feminism] *as the correct way to interpret women's experience.*[14] (italics and comments mine)

Indeed, it was the consciousness-raising group, a method which relied heavily on emotional group dynamics and pressure, which was most instrumental in convincing women that the feminist perspective was "the correct way to interpret women's experience."

THE PERSONAL IS POLITICAL

After having her consciousness raised, a woman was ready to assume an active role in feminism. Feminists encouraged her to change her behavior patterns, to make new demands in her interpersonal relationships, to insist on her own rights, to convince other women of their oppressed status, and to support the women's movement, thereby consummating her new awareness with personal and political action. According to feminist historian Hester Eisenstein, a crucial function of CR was to "constrain women to connect the personal with the political."[15] Juliet Mitchell observed:

> At first it [the CR group] is the means of bringing women into close personal solidarity and friendship with each other. In the final stage, many small groups see themselves as revolutionary collectives, whose task is to analyze the nature of women's oppression and thereby work out a strategy. The transition marks the changing awareness that as women's problems are not private and personal, so, neither is their solution; or, to put it another way, it reflects the change from personal self-awareness to group-consciousness or the oppressed person's equivalent to "class-consciousness." The small group permits the transition from the personal to the political and simultaneously interrelates them.[16]

Mitchell noted that women's liberation was crucially concerned with that area of politics that was experienced as personal. She said that women first came into the movement suffering from an unspecified personal frustration. Through the CR group, however, they found that what they thought was an individual dilemma was actually a social predicament and therefore a political problem. According to Mitchell, "the process of transforming the hidden, individual fears of women into a shared awareness of the meaning of them as social problems, the release of anger, anxiety, the

struggle of proclaiming the painful and transforming it into the political —
this process is consciousness-raising."[17]

WOMEN AS SEX CLASS

In January, 1968 a newly formed group calling itself the New York Radical
Women staged a torch-lit parade in protest of the Vietnam War. The group
distributed leaflets implying that America's involvement in the war was
indicative of a national battle fought clandestinely — that of men against
women. The policies and problems of America, they claimed, began at
home. To turn the country around, women had to raise their own consciousness, recognize their own oppression, and stand united in solidarity.
The handbill contained a slogan which was to activate thousands across the
country: "Sisterhood Is Powerful." By 1970, the slogan graced an anthology of feminist essays, poems and manifestos[18] and also splashed across a
New York Times article which explained the women's movement.[19]

Sisterhood? . . . women's liberation? . . . a *movement*? After years of
ridicule and lassitude the public sat up to take notice. Could it be that this
was a topic to be taken seriously? A contributing editor and political colum-
nist for the *New York Times* thought so. She had for many years been an
avid social activist: anti-war, Black Power, the welfare movement — all the
churning rebellions of the sixties had incurred her sympathies. It was
shortly following the "Sisterhood Is Powerful" article that she decided to
lend her patronage to women's liberation. Her name: Gloria Steinem.
"After Black Power, Women's Liberation" was her inaugural address. The
article won a Penney-Missouri Journalism Award, and because of it,
Steinem became identified as spokeswoman for the burgeoning feminist
movement. Gloria Steinem — attractive, articulate, and listed among "the
Beautiful People" — gave credibility to an otherwise unconventional social
front. On August 16, 1971, Steinem's picture graced the cover of
Newsweek, and an article proclaimed her the personification of women's
liberation. A few months later, *McCall's* named her Woman of the Year.
Gloria Steinem's alignment with women's lib escalated public interest in the
movement. Because of her, sisterhood became more than powerful, it also
became chic.

Women, feminists insisted, were a sisterhood. Or, as Shulamith
Firestone had specified — a *sex class.* This concept was foreign to most people, but in the course of time — and with incessant exposure — a subtle shift
occurred in people's minds. They began to view the condition of being
female as a defining characteristic, cutting across differences of class and
race.[20] Issues of abortion, pornography, wife abuse, and women's participation in the work force were no longer owned by society as a whole, but
were assigned to women as specific concerns which applied to their *class.*
By the mid-1970s, the public had accepted feminist theory to the point of
identifying "women" as a distinct group of oppressed people, and broad

terms such as "women's issues" and "women's concerns" had come to identify a uniquely feminist agenda.

Consciousness raising and the ensuing cultural perception of women as
a sex class catapulted the women's movement into its second phase.
Women, as a group, were given a new awareness of the commonality of
their experience. The effect was an internal, personal legitimization of the
differences found in women. Thus, whereas the first phase of the movement
viewed women's differences as *weaknesses*, the second phase viewed
women's differences as a *source of pride and confidence*. This shift in mind-
set was epitomized in Helen Reddy's Grammy-winning song which topped
the North American pop charts in 1972: "I am strong, I am invincible . . .
I AM WOMAN!" Feminists were putting their bras back on and were
becoming proud of being women. Subsequently, *women's lib* with all its
negative bra-burning connotations began to be replaced with a term that
recognized and rejoiced in women's differences, in women's *femininity*. The
term *women's liberation* was changed to *feminism* as women began to celebrate and explore the differences they had once shunned.

NAMING SELF

Neither secular nor religious feminists liked the traditional role which had
been assigned to women. They claimed this role had been determined by
men and that it was oppressive to women. Feminist women rejected the
right of men to regulate women's lives. As the first decade of the women's
movement ended, women all across the continent began to claim the right
to name and define themselves. By August 26, 1970, on the fiftieth anniver-
sary of women's suffrage in America, twenty thousand women marched
proudly down New York's Fifth Avenue, identifying themselves as part of
the women's liberation movement. Friedan summed up the tenor of the
movement when, at the conclusion of the march, she blazed:

> In the religion of my ancestors, there was a prayer that Jewish men said
> every morning. They prayed, "Thank thee, Lord, that I was not born a
> woman." Today . . . all women are going to be able to say . . . "Thank
> thee, Lord, that I was born a woman, for this day. . . ."
>
> After tonight, the politics of this nation will never be the same
> again. . . . There is no way any man, woman, or child can escape the
> nature of our revolution. . . .[21]

PART TWO

Naming the World

7

Woman-centered Analysis

Suddenly there was a new reference group and an alternative authoritative voice which was constructing a very different interpretation of the world. . . .[1]

Dale Spender

Up until about 1972, it would have been possible for an individual to claim to have read *all* the contemporary feminist books; after 1972 such a claim would have become increasingly preposterous. The middle years of the decade witnessed an explosion of feminist books, pamphlets, newsletters and courses. These revealed an emerging feminist worldview.

Feminism supposed that men had secured power for themselves by claiming the authority to decree meanings. History, anthropology, sociology, psychology, religion, medicine, art, culture — all of life's meaning was arbitrarily defined by men. Therefore, as the philosophy of feminism spread, it challenged society to make *women's* experience a reference point for determining life's meaning. A particular field of study, Women's Studies, was developed to encourage the formation of that analysis. *Woman-centered analysis*, as it was called, viewed the female experience as the major focus of study and the source of dominant values for the culture as a whole. It provided a uniquely feminine way of looking at the world.

Woman-centered analysis was a broad-scale effort of feminist women to name not only themselves, but also the world. It challenged and redefined every niche of human existence. While it is beyond the scope of this book to explore its every detail, it will be helpful to paint in broad brush strokes some of the concepts of woman-centered analysis that shaped the flow and direction of the feminist movement in the 1970s.

LANGUAGE AND LITERATURE

The method of liberation, then, involves a castrating of language and images that reflect and perpetuate the structures of a sexist world. It castrates precisely in the sense of cutting away the phallocentric value system imposed by patriarchy, in its subtle as well as in its more manifest expressions. As aliens in a man's world [we] are now rising up to name — that is, to create — our own world. . . .[2]

Women's studies contended that society had been constructed with a bias favoring males. Feminist linguists argued that this bias could be located in language, in both syntax and semantics. In 1975, linguist Robin Lakoff attempted to show that male and female use of language pointed to the nature and extent of sexual inequity. Lakoff suggested that women experienced linguistic discrimination in two ways: in the way they were taught to use language, and in the way general language use treated them. Both tend "to relegate women to subservient functions," Lakoff said.[3] Language used women as much as women used language.[4]

Lakoff suggested that the sexes were socialized to speak in uniquely "boy language" or "girl language." She argued that women's speech varied from men's in several significant ways. For instance, Lakoff claimed that women were typically tentative and unassertive in speech. They "hedged" and asked "tag questions" rather than outrightly expressing their opinions. Hedging used lexical qualifiers that weakened the force of a statement: "It's *sort of* hot in here"; "I'd *kind of* like to go"; "*I guess* . . ."; "It *seems like* . . ."; and so on. Tag questions were utterances halfway between a declaration and a question and were supposedly a means whereby the user could make a declaration without being assertive. "It's a nice day, isn't it?"; "John is here, isn't he?" Women were also guilty of using empty adjectives such as "divine, charming, cute, sweet, adorable, and lovely." Furthermore, they were restricted from using expletive swear words, choosing instead, to use trivial particles like "Oh dear" or "Oh fudge!" Lakoff believed that in allowing men stronger means of expression than were open to women, language further reinforced men's position of strength in the real world. She reasoned that people listened with more attention to strongly and forcefully expressed opinions, and that a speaker unable — for whatever reason — to be forceful in stating his views was much less likely to be taken seriously. Other forms of speech, such as the tendency to intonate a declarative statement as a question, were also noted by Lakoff as being peculiar to women. For example, in response to the question, "When will dinner by ready?" an answer like "Around six o'Clock?" was given (as though seeking approval and asking whether that time would be alright).

The second point cited by Lakoff was the way in which general language usage treated women, relegating women to a lesser status than men. Lakoff claimed there was a much greater incidence of derogatory epithets for women. The terms *lady* and *girl*, for example, often could be a frivolous or condescending way to refer to women. Furthermore, she noted that pairs of parallel male and female terms, such as master/mistress and bachelor/spinster, did not bear parallel connotations. People respected the male term, but the female one carried negative images. In addition, Lakoff pointed out, there was a lack of parallelism in men's and women's titles. Referring to men as *Mr.* did not identify his marital status, while referring to a woman as *Miss* or *Mrs.* immediately identified her according to her relationship with man. She argued that women were further debased by relinquishing their own name in marriage. Not only did they give up surnames, but were also socially identified by their husbands' first names, losing their own identity altogether. For example, introducing "Mrs. John Jones" was socially proper, yet introducing a man as "Mr. Sally Smith" was unthinkable. Lakoff pointed out that occupational descriptors were also indicative of social disparity. Terms such as *chairman, repairman,* and *policeman* inferred that these positions were reserved for men. Finally, Lakoff cited the universal use of the masculine pronoun *he* to refer to the entire human race as the most blatant linguistic evidence of sexual discrimination.

Lakoff argued that language effectively relegated women to an inferior status in society:

... the overall effect of "women's language" — meaning both language restricted in use to women and language descriptive of women alone — is this: it submerges a woman's personal identity, by denying her the means of expressing herself strongly, on the one hand, and encouraging expressions that suggest triviality in subject matter and uncertainty about it; and, when a woman is being discussed, by treating her as an object — sexual or otherwise — but never a serious person with individual views. Of course, other forms of behavior in this society have the same purpose; but the phenomena seem especially clear linguistically.[5]

Lakoff believed the distinction between men's and women's language was a symptom of a problem in our culture, not the problem itself. She argued that language reflected the fact that men and women were expected to have different interests and different roles, hold different types of conversations, and react differently to other people.[6]

The linguistic discussion, initiated by Robin Lakoff, was furthered by many other feminists, including Casey Miller, Kate Swift and Dale Spender.[7] Lakoff's assumption that women's language was inferior to men's was quickly modified by her successors who said it was not woman's, but *man's* language that was inferior. Furthermore, feminists expanded the preliminary analysis of language to include the critique of literature. Feminists, such as Elaine Showalter, concentrated on exposing the misogyny of literary practice — i.e., the stereotyped images of women in literature as angels or monsters, the literary abuse or textual harassment of women in classic and popular male literature, and the exclusion of women from literary history.[8] Feminists thus established gender as a fundamental category for the analysis of both language and literature.[9] Feminists claimed that women had been wrongly "named" by men. They wanted to claim the right to name and define themselves. They viewed the creation of a new language structure as essential for women's liberation. As Dale Spender pointed out:

> As soon as we hear words we find ourselves outside them This makes us aliens. This makes us silent. This makes us vulnerable. We need a language which constructs the reality of women's autonomy, women's strength, women's power. With such a language we will not be a muted group.[10]

Mary Daly had insisted that "to exist humanly is to name the self, the world, and God."[11] Through women-centered analysis, feminists sought to draw attention to the sexual inequities of language and to change social attitudes and practices through the changing of language. They encouraged women to claim power for themselves in claiming the right to name.

PSYCHOLOGY

All forms of oppression encourage people to enlist in their own enslavement. For women, especially, this enlistment inevitably takes psychological forms and often ends in being called neuroses and other such things.[12]

Psychologist Phyllis Chesler in *Women & Madness* (1972) used a woman-centered analysis to challenge the validity of the traditional definition of mental health. What was necessary, she argued, was a completely new way of describing and explaining mental health which accurately considered women's point of view. Chesler believed that psychology and psychiatry were blatant instruments of oppression against women and were used by the male elite to ensure their own power. She believed that what was often diagnosed as mental illness in women was simply a *healthy response* to a patriarchal environment. Chesler argued that far from helping women, clinical psychology and psychiatry constituted a means of punishing women.

Chesler's most essential and dramatic thesis in *Women & Madness* was that women were defined by men, and that this ensured their vulnerability as victims of the mental health weapon. She argued that psychiatry contained a double standard of mental health favoring men and male power. What society viewed as a mentally sick man, she explained — someone who was dependent, passive, lacking in initiative and in need of support — was precisely society's view of a mentally healthy woman. Conversely, she reported that psychology regarded a woman who displayed some of the valued characteristics of the healthy male — self-reliance, confidence, and independence — as sick. Chesler argued that women's position of inferiority encouraged her to develop unhealthy psychological traits:

> ... the position of inferiority encourages development of personal psychological characteristics which are pleasing to the dominant group. These characteristics include: submissiveness, passivity, docility, dependency, lack of initiative, inability to act, to decide, to think, and the like. In general, this cluster of personality traits includes qualities characteristic of children — immaturity, weakness, and helplessness. If women as subordinates adopt these characteristics for themselves they are considered well-adjusted.[13]
>
> However, when subordinates show the potential for, or even more dangerously have developed other characteristics — let us say intelligence, initiative, assertiveness — there is usually no room available within the dominant framework for acknowledgement of these characteristics. Such people will be defined as at least unusual, if not definitely abnormal.[14]

According to Chesler, the assignment of human characteristics according to gender led to a pervasive male reality in which the male was the norm and woman, the other, was deviant and *mad*. In fact, Chesler believed that madness applied to all women. Women who had transferred their frustration with the traditional female role into clinical psychiatric symptoms — women who did in fact react *normally* to their predicament — were outrightly labeled as mad by the medical establishment. Those who had rejected the male-defined woman's role were labeled mad because of their deviance. Furthermore, she maintained that "normal" women — although labeled normal — were essentially *mad* in that they repressed their true nature to conform to patriarchal expectations. Their madness consisted of being defined as *other*. According to Chesler, it was a no-win situation. Thus, Chesler concluded, "the role of a mental patient is often the *only* resolution (cure) for having been born female."[15] She argued that both psychotherapy and marriage "enabled women to express and defuse their anger by experiencing it as a form of emotional illness, by translating it into hysterical symptoms: frigidity, chronic depression, phobias, and the like."[16]

Chesler understood madness in terms of "oppression" and "conditioning." Women who were labeled *mad* were either being punished for rejecting their sex-role stereotype or for embracing it in too deadly a manner. In contrast, women who were labeled *normal* had been intimidated into that role by the threat of mental health treatment — drugs, shock-therapy — and by severe cultural conditioning. Chesler's theory of psychology was reiterated and refined by Dr. Jean Baker Miller in *Toward a New Psychology of Women*. Miller, like Chesler, believed that society's definition of the normal female had perpetuated and reinforced a situation of inequality for women. According to Miller, this subordinate position had forced women into a state of psychological conflict in which they were unable to recognize and meet their own needs:

In a situation of inequality the woman is not encouraged to take her own needs seriously, to explore them, to try to act on them as a separate individual. She is enjoined from engaging all of her own resources and thereby prevented from developing some valid and reliable sense of her own worth. Instead, the woman is encouraged to concentrate on the needs and development of the man.[17]

Miller believed that women paid a price for demanding equality with men; namely, terrible isolation or severe conflict not only with men, but with all social institutions and with the inner image of what it meant to be a woman.[18] She believed most women were unwilling or unable to pay that price; therefore they were either diverted from exploring and expressing their needs, or they were forced to "transform" their own needs (to perceive them as being identical to those of men and children). According to Miller, women who managed this transformation *deceived* themselves into feeling comfortable and fulfilled, but it was a most precarious transformation. It left the psyches of women hanging, as it were, by a delicate thread, susceptible to severe psychological trouble.[19] Therefore, Miller argued that women's "psychological problems were not so much caused by the unconscious as by deprivations of full consciousness."[20]

Chesler and Miller proposed a new psychology of women and mental health. In the years to follow, mental health practitioners who adopted this model identified themselves as "feminist" therapists, counselors, or psychologists. And indeed, they counseled women from a perspective that deviated markedly from traditional counseling procedure. Feminist therapists guided women to realize that their negative emotions and frustrations were attributable to the false role that *men* had forced upon them. They believed that patriarchy — and not some unseen internal process — was responsible for women's dilemma. Feminist therapy was a form of one-on-one consciousness raising. It sought to usher the client into a "new reality" and into a new space within a feminist frame of reference.

HOLISTIC MEDICINE

Patriarchal man created — out of a mixture of sexual and affective frustration, blind need, physical force, ignorance, and intelligence split from its emotional grounding, a system which turned against woman her own organic nature, the source of her awe and original powers. In a sense, female evolution was mutilated, and we have no way now of imagining what its development hitherto might have been; we can only try, at last, to take it into female hands.[21]

In 1973, Barbara Ehrenreich and Deirdre English began to question the role of the male in relation to women's health. Two pamphlets, *Complaints and Disorders: The Sexual Politics of Sickness* and *Witches, Midwives and*

Nurses: A History of Women Healers, marked the beginnings of an entirely new perspective on women's health. Whereas Phyllis Chesler had discovered a male ethic of mental health, Ehrenreich and English proposed in *Complaints and Disorders* that the ethic of health per se was male, and that this had enormous implications for the diagnosis and treatment of women's illnesses.[22]

Ehrenreich and English began *Complaints and Disorders* by pointing out that the medical system was strategic to women's liberation because it was "the guardian of reproductive technology" and "held the promise of freedom from hundreds of unspoken fears and complaints." But, they added, the medical system was also strategic to women's oppression, because medical science was a "primary and powerful source of sexist ideology." Theories of male superiority "ultimately rested on biology."[23]

Witches, Midwives, and Nurses: A History of Women Healers traced the roots of the medical profession back to the witch burnings of the late Middle Ages and followed its rise in Europe and later in the United States. The authors maintained that the new medical profession had suppressed and discredited the widespread and effective practice of medicine and healing by women, most serving as herbalists, nutritionists, and midwives to the common people. They also noted that the medical profession had created a rigid institutional pyramid in which men were concentrated at the top as the all-powerful, highly-respected diagnosticians and decision-makers, and women at the bottom as obedient, low-status caretakers. Ehrenreich and English argued that just as psychology had labeled *normal* women as sick, so medicine's prime contribution to sexist ideology had been to describe women in general "as sick, and as potentially sickening to men."[24] According to Ehrenreich and English, doctors viewed the unique functions of women as they did any other pathological disease. They maintained that doctors regarded pregnancy, childbirth, menstruation, menopause, and all the other functions unique to women as problematic rather than natural, and that doctors therefore chose intrusive medical treatment such as drugs and surgery over the natural regulation and treatment of women's functions.

Through the woman-centered analysis of the medical profession, Ehrenreich and English encouraged women to return to a de-institutionalized, natural view of their bodies. Their feminist analysis contributed to the proliferation of health stores, herbalists, nutritionists, and non-medical healing practitioners. Natural childbirth methods surfaced, women returned to feeding their infants from breast rather than bottle, and midwifery — which had assisted women in childbirth up until the advent of institutionalized medicine — once again became a respected profession.

Another major publication reflecting the woman-centered analysis of health and medicine was *Our Bodies, Our Selves,* compiled by a women's group, the Boston Woman's Health Collective. This book has been revised, updated, and reprinted a number of times. *Our Bodies, Our Selves* familiarized women with basic female anatomy and sexual response. It discussed

conditions and medical procedures specific to women and suggested preferred and alternate courses of treatment. The members of the Boston
Collective advocated nutritional, herbal, and natural methods of maintaining and/or restoring women's health. Furthermore, they encouraged women
to become intimately familiar with their own bodies. To this end, they
encouraged women to explore their own bodies and sexual responses
through masturbation and provided advice for lesbian relationships. They,
like Ehrenreich and English, also advocated a return to the ancient art of
healing practiced by Eastern mystics and witches. According to these feminist authors, the witches of the Middle Ages were not evil sorcerers, but
merely women who had a knowledge of healing. They were burned as
witches *because they were women* and because they possessed a power to
heal that was unacceptable to the male establishment. Ehrenreich and
English argued,

> . . . many witches were midwives and doctors, whose knowledge of
> painkillers, abortion, and herbal or "faith healing" threatened the
> Church's anti-scientific, anti-sexual, and anti-female doctrines . . . by aid-
> ing the weak, the witch tended to undermine the established hierarchy of
> dominance — of priest over penitent, lord over peasant, man over woman
> — and herein lay the principal threat of the witch and is why the Church
> set out to crush her.[25]

Feminists encouraged a de-institutionalized practice of medicine and
encouraged women to trust their own experience and perceptions regarding their own bodies. Furthermore, they advised women to trust the wisdom and experience of women of the past and return to ancient female
methods of healing and wholeness. Feminists therefore advocated that
women return to self-awareness, imagery, ritual, reflexology, acupuncture,
auras, gemstones, magic, and any other modality of treatment or preven-
tion that had been, in the past, practiced by women. Feminists determined
that the ancient methods were acceptable solely because other women had
accepted them. Feminists thereby established women's experience as the
new litmus test for the validity of medical practices.

MOTHERHOOD

> The Institution of Motherhood has alienated women from their bodies
> by incarcerating them within . . . motherhood as intuition has ghettoized
> and degraded female potentialities.[26]

> There is for the first time today a possibility of converting our physical-
> ity into both knowledge and power.[27]

A woman-centered analysis of motherhood is closely related to the field of medicine. Adrienne Rich attacked the institution of motherhood in her book *Of Woman Born*.[28] Rich claimed that the institution of motherhood, which she defined as "the socially accepted form of bearing and raising children within the structure of marriage," was oppressive. In her eyes, this institution reflected one of the major bastions of male supremacy and control. "Patriarchy has always dictated to women whether or not and under what circumstances to produce children,"[29] she asserted.

Rich argued that both maternity and sexuality had been channeled to serve male interests. As a result, any behaviors that threatened the institution (adultery, illegitimacy, abortion, and lesbianism) were considered by society to be deviant or criminal.[30] According to Rich, women's careers and day care were also viewed as threats to maternity and therefore discouraged. She maintained that the male-defined institution of motherhood had exploited women's sexual, reproductive, and other capacities. It had alienated women from themselves and enslaved them to the family unit. According to Rich, the institution of motherhood required the "underemployment of female consciousness . . . maternal instinct rather than intelligence, selflessness rather than self-realization, and relation to others rather than the creation of self."[31] Rich believed that under patriarchy, female possibility had "been literally massacred on the site of motherhood."[32]

Rich was careful to distinguish between the institution of motherhood and the motherhood experience. She did not view the institution of motherhood as identical with bearing and caring for children.[33] Rich exalted the fact that it was women, and not men, who were able to bear children. She regarded the reproductive capacity of women as the *elemental* source of women's power. According to Rich, women's power was not a power *over* others, but a "transforming and creating power," which, she argued, was "the only true significant and essential power."[34] Rich said that it was this power, in prepatriarchal society, that women knew for their own. She reasoned:

> The images of the prepatriarchal goddess-cults tell women that *power, awesomeness, and centrality are theirs by nature*, not by privilege or miracle; *the female is primary*. The male appears in the earliest art, if at all, in the aspect of a child, often tiny and helpless, carried horizontally in arms, or seated in the lap of the goddess, or suckling at her breast.[35]

According to Rich, patriarchy had turned the essential creative power of a woman's body against her. By domesticating maternal power, men had transfigured and enslaved women. The womb — which Rich viewed as the ultimate source of power — was itself made into a source of powerlessness.[36] Rich argued that men had dictated the rules, the parameters, and the framework for sexuality and reproduction. They had therefore stolen the power that was woman's by natural right.

Rich believed that women's plight would be alleviated when they reclaimed their bodies. This, according to Rich, would destroy the *institution* of motherhood. But she restated that to destroy the institution was *not* to abolish motherhood. It was, rather, "to release the creation and sustenance of life into the same realm of decision, struggle, surprise, imagination, and conscious intelligence, as any other difficult, but freely chosen work."[37] Rich argued that each individual woman had the right to determine when, where, and how to become a mother. According to her, women should have the right to engage in sex when and with whom they pleased and the choice to abort a child if their actions resulted in unwanted pregnancy. Furthermore, women needed to be freed from the societal structure of bearing children within the context of marriage. Rich proposed that children be cared for by society as a whole so the responsibility would not restrict women in any way.

Rich portrayed a mystic interaction between women's capacity for motherhood and the elemental power of the universe. According to Rich, the capacity of women to produce life attested to woman's "intrinsic importance, her depth of meaning, her existence at the very center of what is necessary and sacred . . . her body possesses mass, interior depth, inner rest, and balance."[38] Rich believed that the physical power to create, which was inherent in every woman, harnessed the mystic, elemental, creative power of the universe. Furthermore, she proposed that controlling motherhood harnessed that power. She argued that patriarchal man had stolen this power from woman, and that woman needed to reclaim it for herself. In this way, Rich said, women would "convert [their] physicality into both knowledge and power."[39] According to Rich, reclaiming the right to control their own bodies was the primary means of women's liberation:

> The repossession by women of our bodies will bring far more essential change to human society than the seizing of the means of production by workers. . . . We need to imagine a world in which every woman is the presiding genius of her own body. In such a world women will truly create new life, bringing forth not only children (if and as we choose) but the visions, and the thinking, necessary to sustain, console, and alter human existence — a new relationship to the universe. Sexuality, politics, intelligence, power, motherhood, work, community, intimacy will develop new meanings; thinking itself will be transformed. This is where we have to begin.[40]

SOCIOLOGY

> . . . a more fundamental source of discrimination lies in the realm of social attitudes and beliefs. The reality of women's situation is daily constructed out of these attitudes: women are, in part, the way they are because of the way they are thought to be. (Ann Oakley)

Ann Oakley was to the woman-centered analysis of sociology what Phyllis Chesler and Jean Baker Miller were to woman-centered psychology.

In 1971, Oakley conducted a sociological study of housewives and their attitude towards housework. Rather than treating housework as an aspect of the female role in the family — as a part of women's role in marriage, or as a dimension of child-rearing — Oakley undertook to study housework as a job, analogous to any other kind of job in modern society. This perspective, she maintained, had been totally neglected in the male-dominated discipline of sociology. According to Oakley, the sociological neglect of housework reflected the wider issue of bias against women in sociology as a whole.

The starting point of Ann Oakley's book *The Sociology of Housework* (1974) was a critique of the biased nature of sociology itself. Oakley maintained that sociology as a discipline had defined women out of existence. In family and marriage literature women were entirely encapsulated within the feminine role. She argued that sociology had defined them as wives and mothers to the virtual exclusion of any other role. Oakley hoped to reveal the hidden sociological assumption — and the hidden societal assumption — that men were more important than women:

> In much sociology women as a social group are invisible or inadequately represented: they take the insubstantial form of ghosts, shadows or stereotyped characters. . . . Sociology is sexist because it is male-oriented . . . it exhibits a focus on, or a direction towards, the interests and activities of men in a gender-differentiated society.[41]

Oakley pointed out that in choosing its topics of study, sociology defined the things that were powerful in the shaping of society: social stratification, political institutions, religion, education, deviance, the sociology of industry and work, the family and marriage, and so on. According to Oakley, the broad subject-divisions current to sociology only *appeared* to be logical and non-sexist. But Oakley claimed that these divisions *automatically* neglected women's concerns:

> The male focus, incorporated into the definition of subject-areas, reduces women to a side-issue from the start. For example, a major preoccupation of sociologists has been with the cohesive effect of directive institutions through which power is exercised — the law, political systems, etc. These are male-dominated arenas; women have historically been tangential to them. The more sociology is concerned with such areas, the less it is, by definition, likely to include women within its frame of reference. The appropriate analogy for the structural weakness of sociology in this respect is the social reality sociologists study: sexism is not merely a question of institutional discrimination against women, but the schema of underlying values is also implicated.[42]

Oakley claimed that by studying the institutions of power, sociology had virtually confined itself to the study of men — thus circularly proving and reinforcing the primary importance of men. She pointed out that men at the workplace were studied *ad infinitum*, and that the few studies that were undertaken on the 36 percent of the women in the work force treated women's presence there as problematic. ". . . they were asked why they worked."[43] Working women were not studied in terms of their lives, but in relation to the difficulties they created for their husbands and families. Oakley also objected to sociology's stratification of members of society into hierarchical order: the status of the family being determined by its head — the man. By this means, she argued, the men gained preeminence and the educational, occupational and financial resources of women were completely denied.

Ann Oakley could not locate any sociological research that analyzed the major facet of women's role: housework. She believed that the omission of the topic of housework from both family sociology and the sociology of work blatantly demonstrated the male bias inherent in sociological study. According to Oakley, sociology had denied the reality of women's situation. Oakley thus sought to explore the sociological concept of woman as a worker in the home. She endeavored to statistically reveal the appalling nature of women's working conditions — arduous work, for long hours, in isolation, with little or no pay, no compensation, no pension, no relief, no time off, no paid holidays, and no basis for negotiation for improved conditions.[44] In classifying women in the home as workers, Ann Oakley hoped to expose men as exploitative employers and to give the gross injustices against women sociological significance.

In the course of her study, Oakley discovered many contradictions between women's analyses of their jobs and their reported satisfaction with the role of housewife. In spite of their admissions of the repetitive, monotonous nature of their tasks, and in spite of their concessions that they didn't really enjoy housework, Oakley found that many women were committed to the housewife role. In fact, many defended the role and claimed to enjoy it. Ann Oakley concluded that housewives were socialized into accepting an otherwise unacceptable, oppressive job. Women themselves, she deduced, were party to their oppression.

Oakley believed that her woman-centered sociological study of housework demonstrated that women needed to be educated regarding their oppressed condition and brought to see how that oppression was personally internalized and accepted. According to Oakley, a feminist revolt would not be accomplished until women realized they were oppressed: "A major — perhaps the major — tool of feminist revolt is a comprehensive understanding of the way in which women 'internalize their own oppression.'"[45]

Oakley sought to statistically prove that the role of housewife — in housework and child care — was exploitive and oppressive. Moreover, women's apparent satisfaction with this role reinforced the fact that women had been socialized, shaped and defined by men. Oakley argued that patriarchy had forced women into an oppressed role and had kept them there by covertly convincing them that they were satisfied. Oakley used a woman-centered sociological analysis to argue that women needed their consciousness raised to the reality of their bitter situation and needed to be convinced that they should *not* be satisfied with the traditional woman's role.

SEXUAL RELATIONSHIPS — THE "WOMAN-IDENTIFIED-WOMAN"

What is a lesbian? A lesbian is the rage of all women. . . . She is the woman who acts in accordance with her inner compulsion to be a more complete and freer human being than her society cares to allow her. (Radicalesbians 1970)[46]

Following the sexual revolution of the 1960s, feminists agreed that women ought to have the freedom to have sexual relations with whomever they wanted, whenever they wanted. What was not clear — and what had been a taboo of discussion up until that point — was the matter of sexual relationships *between women*. In the early 1970s the issue was forced, and a woman's choice of sexual partners became much more than a personal choice — it became a political statement. A lesbian — a woman who had sexually disentangled herself from involvement with men — became the symbol of women's liberation. Because a lesbian did not define herself in relation to a man, some feminists called her a "Woman-Identified Woman." This identification, they argued, truly set her free.

Kate Millett's *Sexual Politics*, published in 1970, intertwined the two eternally fascinating themes of sex and power.[47] It scornfully, relentlessly, and unmercifully attacked four of the literary giants of the century. The bastions of the literary establishment (male critics and media personalities) embraced the book with uncharacteristic zeal. In August, just a few months after the book's publication, a formidable portrait of Kate Millett was unveiled in newsstands, supermarkets, and drugstores. "The Mao Tse-tung of Women's Liberation," *Time* called her.[48] Glowing reviews and extraordinary critiques concealed — for the moment — the controversy that was to follow.

In the fall of 1970, Millet spoke at Columbia University on the topic of sexual liberation. Following the lecture several students asked questions. Then someone shouted, "Kate . . . KATE! Are you a lesbian?"

Silence.

The voice loudly and venomously persisted. "Say it. Are you? Are you a lesbian? Say it!"

The crowd waited for her reply, and Millet weighed in her mind what the consequences of her answer would be. Many feminists feared that the taint of homosexuality could destroy the progress the woman's movement had made. If Millett, now heralded far and wide as the new leader, was to publicly "confess" lesbianism . . .

But Millet had to answer, so with slow determination she forced out her confession:

"Yes, I am a lesbian."

Kate Millett — *the* Kate Millett — a lesbian? Shock reverberated through the centers of media power. Bisexuality they could — with some difficulty — manage, but lesbianism was *too* radical. The American public would not readily condone such deviance. *Time* recanted. By December 14, they offered readers "A Second Look at Women's Lib." "Kate Millet's disclosure," spouted the article, "is bound to discredit her as a spokeswoman for her cause, cast further doubt on her theories and reinforce the views of those skeptics who routinely dismiss all liberationists as lesbians."[49]

Would the movement survive? The issue had been forced. Lesbianism — Women's liberation/Women's liberation — lesbianism: What was the connection? The subject of lesbianism had only incidentally surfaced in feminism. Never, certainly, in public. Private discussions were always volatile, and — as those involved in inner circles were painfully aware — deeply divisive. But now feminists needed to respond. A few days later — to the consternation of some and wild applause of others — the feminist movement revealed its new color.

At a women's march in New York — organized in support of abortion and child-care centers — a dabbling of pale purple became evident amidst the crowd. The color spread as lavender armbands were distributed to the entire group. "ALL women," the proponents explained, "are wearing lavender lesbian armbands today."[50]

The leaflet that was passed out stated, "It is not one woman's sexual experience that is under attack. It is the freedom of all women to openly state values that fundamentally challenge the basic structure of patriarchy. If they succeed in scaring us with words like 'dyke' or 'lesbian' or 'bisexual,' they'll have won. AGAIN. They'll have divided us. AGAIN. Sexism will have triumphed. AGAIN. . . . They can call us all lesbians until such time as there is no stigma attached to women loving women. SISTERHOOD IS POWERFUL!!!"[51]

Less than a week later, on December 18 in the Washington Square Methodist Church, came the famous "Kate Is Great" press conference. Journalists and members of various women's organizations came forth to publicly support and exonerate Kate Millett. Many would remember Millett sitting at a table in front of about fifty supporters. Gloria Steinem, her streaked-blonde hair flowing over her shoulders, sat directly beside Kate holding her hand.

In a quiet voice which often trembled, Kate Millett read her statement:

Women's liberation and homosexual liberation are both struggling towards a common goal: a society free from defining and categorizing people by virtue of gender and/or sexual preference. "Lesbian" is a label used as a psychic weapon to keep women locked into their male-defined "feminine role." The essence of that role is that a woman is defined in terms of her relationship to men. A woman is called lesbian when she functions autonomously. Women's autonomy is what women's liberation is all about.[52]

"Lesbianism," the National Organization for Women (NOW) reluctantly admitted, "is indeed a legitimate concern of feminism." In the years that immediately followed NOW's proclamation, lesbianism became much more than "a legitimate concern" of feminism. For those within the inner circles of feminism, it became a water-shed issue — the acid test of one's allegiance to the feminist cause. Sexual intercourse with men was equated with male power over women. Many feminists argued that by rejecting sexual liaisons with men women would become entirely independent from men.

A document published by the New York based Radicalesbians presented the first major statement of lesbian feminist theory. Entitled *The Woman Identified Woman*, the paper urged women to forge their identities in terms of one another's needs, experiences, and perceptions.[53] They argued that lesbians identified themselves with reference to women and not in relation to men. Accordingly, as Jill Johnston stated, "a woman who seeks and receives validation from other women is not hostage to male approval."[54] Feminists proposed that by participating in the lesbian experience, a woman freed herself from patriarchy in order to know and experience her true self. As summarized by the Radicalesbians:

> Until women see in each other the possibility of primal commitment which includes sexual love, they will be denying themselves the love and value they readily accord to men, thus affirming their second-class status.[55]

Prominent feminist figures supported and reinforced the concepts put forth by the Radicalesbians. Jill Johnston in *Lesbian Nation* proposed that lesbianism was much more than sexual preference, "it [was] also a *political* commitment signifying activism and resistance."[56] Charlotte Bunch labeled heterosexuality as "*a cornerstone of male supremacy*"[57] — a means whereby men forced their way into women's lives and gained power and control over them. According to Bunch, heterosexuality as "institution and ideology" was a primary factor in the oppression of women. Adrienne Rich also viewed compulsory heterosexuality as a "political institution which guaranteed women's continued subordination."[58] Rich went on to justify and provide credibility for lesbian practice by citing an "extensive continuum" of lesbian experience in the past and present. She pointed out that lesbianism, "like motherhood, is a profoundly *female* experience."[59] Citing numerous studies regarding the mother-daughter bond, Rich argued that lesbianism was the *normative* experience between women. Heterosexuality, on the other hand, was a system *imposed* upon women by men out of fear of losing women. It was neither natural nor innate.[60] Martha Shelley urged that the lesbian should be seen as the model of the independent woman. She believed that "in a male-dominated society, Lesbianism is a sign of mental health."[61] Finally, Anne Koedt gave *pragmatic* shape to lesbian theory in an influential article ("Loving Another Woman") in which she interviewed a feminist who had recently discovered her lesbian potential. Koedt's case study gave personal credibility to the daily outworking of the lesbian concept.[62]

Within a year of Kate Millett's disclosure, many feminists covertly regarded lesbians as the only *true* feminists within the women's liberation movement. One New York feminist group went so far as to insist that no more than one-third of their members be married or living with a man. Most feminist theorists viewed lesbianism as a necessary perspective in shaping the future of the feminist movement. Ti-Grace Atkinson believed that by virtue of their ties to other women, and therefore of their freedom from conventional heterosexual commitments, and particularly marriage, lesbians set themselves in a sociological situation of great freedom. She maintained that the common stereotypes regarding women were overthrown and rejected by lesbians' blatant sexual/social choices.[63] Atkinson argued that only lesbian women could think radically and profoundly about the possibility of social change, free from the shackles of heterosexual gender assignments. Her perspective was, for a while, shared by many. Julia Penelope reasoned, "It is the primacy of women relating to women, of women creating a new consciousness of and with each other which is at the heart of women's liberation, and the basis for the cultural revolution."[64] Jill Johnston proclaimed, "the lesbian is the key figure in the social revolution to end the sexual caste system."[65]

Lesbianism was a controversial issue within the feminist movement. Not all feminist women agreed with the precepts advocated by the proponents of lesbianism. However, even though they did not condone lesbianism, members of the women's movement were eventually persuaded to accept it as an alternate lifestyle for women. Even Betty Friedan, the most vocal opponent of lesbianism, publicly accepted lesbianism at NOW's Houston convention in 1977 — "for unity's sake."[66]

It took a number of years before the centrality of the question of lesbianism in the woman's movement diminished. Nonetheless, the issue had tested a major precept underlying feminist theory. If women's experience was a legitimate source of meaning, would the experience of some — even those who countered traditional standards of behavior — be esteemed so highly as to put aside all previous norms of morality? The question was raised again a decade later when prostitutes demanded their rights within the feminist movement, and the answer was necessarily the same. The only boundaries within feminism were those which feminist women themselves held to be true. Since feminism gave women the right to name themselves and their worlds, standards and boundaries were arbitrary and could be challenged and changed at any time. Lesbianism bore witness to the value feminists placed on women's experience. According to feminism, women had the right to name themselves and their world in whatever way they deemed appropriate.

OTHER AREAS OF WOMAN-CENTERED ANALYSIS

Many other areas of society came under the scrutiny of woman-centered analysis. In politics, for example, some feminists reasoned that women were more capable than men to lead the human race:

> Man is the enemy of nature: to kill, to root up, to level off, to pollute, to destroy are his instinctive reactions to the unmanufactured phenomena of nature, which he basically fears and distrusts. Woman, on the other hand, is the ally of nature, and her instinct is to tend, to nurture, to encourage healthy growth, and to preserve ecological balance. She is the natural leader of society and of civilization, and the usurpation of her primeval authority by man has resulted in the uncoordinated chaos that is leading the human race inexorably back to barbarism. . . . Today . . . women are in the vanguard of the emerging civilization; and it is to the women that we look for salvation.[67]

Women-centered analysis also became evident in the visual and performing arts. Feminists devoted themselves to women's art which attempted to make a statement about women's lives in some manner, be it the oppression of women by men, the celebration of women's bodies, or women's mystic connectedness with nature. Judy Chicago, for example, displayed a massive feminist artwork at the San Francisco Museum of Modern Art entitled *The Dinner Party*. It consisted of a triangular dining table, along the sides of which were placed symbolic representations of thirty-nine women: pre-Christian goddesses, historical figures such as Sappho and Boadaceia, and more recent women like suffragist Susan B. Anthony. The mythological goddesses were symbolized through renderings of clitoral and vaginal imagery — silk and satin vaginas trimmed with white lace. The ceramic tiles, pottery, weaving and hand-stitched articles that were part of the display were also highly symbolic of women's history. All told, over one thousand women were symbolically represented. Chicago's work made a statement regarding the oppression and invisibility of the women of the past.

DIFFERENCES SOURCE OF PRIDE AND CONFIDENCE

Law, economics, anthropology, science — woman-centered analysis included all realms of human existence. As woman-centered analysis progressed, the feminist belief underlying the critique was strengthened. Women were different from men, but this fact was not a source of shame, but rather a source of pride. Feminism taught that women ought to be proud of their different bodies and their different perceptions. The "male" interpretations of the past were therefore boldly rejected and replaced with interpretations reflecting a feminist definition of reality. The feminist view was so widely accepted in some circles that *it* became the mode and norm for truth. Women had not only claimed the right to name themselves, but also the right to name and define the world around them.

Two important points should be noted from this overview of woman-centered analysis. First, the presupposition that provided impetus to the phenomenon was the philosophy of women's differences as a source of pride, confidence, and ultimately as the source of truth. Second, one should be left with an impression of the breadth of the phenomenon. Through woman-centered analysis, *every* area of human existence was examined and redefined. Woman-centered analysis was both a systematic analysis of the past and an attack on the values that shaped that past. More importantly, it provided a new paradigm for a massive restructuring of society for the future.

8

Woman-centered Analysis of Theology

In patriarchal theology, woman not only fares badly in the doctrines of God, creation, and sin, but little better in the doctrines of redemption. . . . Feminist theology arises at the point where this sexist bias of classical theology is perceived and repudiated.

Rosemary Radford Ruether[1]

As secular academics began to examine every academic discipline through feminist eyes, so feminist theologians began to fill in the details of a feminist theology based on the foundation of liberation theology. Letty Russell and Rosemary Radford Ruether had established that it was necessary to interpret the Bible with a view toward the liberation of women. They viewed *liberation* as the essential crux for Scriptural interpretation. Their theology was based upon their perception of the oppressed condition of women. It was a *woman-centered* analysis of theology that placed women and women's experience at the center of the theological process. Feminist women in the Church had begun their feminist journey by naming and defining themselves and their role in the Church. In the second phase of feminist theological development, they began to name and define the world around them by using their own experience as the new norm for theology and Biblical interpretation.

As cited in Chapter Five, feminist liberation theology pursued altruistic goals such as wholeness, liberty, freedom, peace, harmony, community, love, and the coming of God's new age. These pursuits certainly appealed to the Christian ear, for they contained familiar elements of Biblical truth. However, the feminist theology proposed by Ruether and Russell deviated markedly from traditional Biblical doctrine and methods of interpretation.

This was evident in their explanation of the presuppositions, methodology, perspectives, themes, and definitions of feminist theology.

PRESUPPOSITIONS OF FEMINIST THEOLOGY

Ruether and Russell adopted Mary Daly's presupposition regarding the dynamic nature of revelation. They believed that liberation occurred as a result of human reflection on, and interaction with, the Biblical message of freedom. In other words, the Bible was not regarded as a guidebook full of directives for all time, but rather as a tool that assisted people to understand how God had worked throughout history to free the oppressed. According to Ruether, only the Biblical texts that spoke to women's contemporary quest for liberation were valid.[2] As Russell pointed out, "interpretations of the gospel are tested by the experience of Christian communities working with others in society."[3] If, according to an individual's experience, a certain interpretation of the Bible did not ring true — if it did not seem applicable — then that particular interpretation could be challenged and revised. Feminist theologians therefore had liberty to discard the passages of the Bible that did not agree with their vision of sexual equality. They either dismissed the text as outdated — relative only to a particular time and culture — and the author of the text as misogynistic, or they reinterpreted it and assigned it a meaning different than that which the author intended. The dynamic view of the Bible which feminists adopted allowed them to adjust Biblical interpretation in order to make the Bible relevant to the problems and perspectives of women in contemporary culture. Feminist theologians argued that Biblical interpretation could and should change.

METHODOLOGY OF FEMINIST THEOLOGY

Based on the presupposition of the dynamic nature of Biblical revelation, feminist theologians used a methodology that Russell called "critical reflection."[4] It was the process by which feminist women analyzed the Bible based on their personal experience, and then began to formulate doctrine applicable to their current situation. Letty Russell maintained that this was true "*theo-logy.*" She reasoned that feminists should "utilize their *logos* (their mind) in the perspective of God (*theos*), as God was known in and through the Word in the world."[5] The methodology for Biblical study that Russell described could perhaps more accurately be named "*logy-theo,*" for she ascribed more value to women's personal interpretation of God than to God's recorded revelation in the Word. Nevertheless, her approach to theology was congruent with the dynamic model of revelation that she had adopted as her presupposition.

According to Russell, the feminist method of critical reflection was inductive and hence experimental in nature. It was a "process of seeking out the right questions to ask and trying out different hypotheses that arise."[6]

Russell noted that it was "a theology of constantly revised questions and tentative observations about a changing world."[7] She explained:

In general, women, along with other liberation theologians, stress an inductive rather than a deductive approach. In the past much theology was done by deducing conclusions from first principles established out of Christian tradition and philosophy. Today many people find it more helpful to do theology by an inductive method — drawing out the material for reflection from their life experience as it relates to the gospel message. Here stress is placed on the situation-variable nature of the gospel. The gospel is good news to people only when it speaks concretely to their particular needs of liberation.[8]

Russell stated that the purpose of an experimental, inductive theology was *praxis*, "action" that was "concurrent with reflection or analysis" and which led to "new questions, actions, and reflections."[9] According to Russell, the purpose of doing theology was not to order the discoveries and conclusions into an overarching plan, but rather to "apply the discoveries to a new way of action to bring about change in society."[10]

PERSPECTIVES OF FEMINIST THEOLOGY

Biblical Promise

Letty Russell identified two major motifs or themes of the Bible, *liberation* and *universality*.[11] First of all, she viewed God as the ultimate liberator — the one who set people free. Russell did not believe that the Bible taught an immutable plan for liberation for people of every age, at all times, and for all nations. She believed, rather, that messages of liberation that were current to our culture could be "drawn out" of the Bible. She said that feminist theologians "aren't in the slightest claiming that their reading of the Bible is valid for all times. But they say it is the right one for the society we live in today — and that is all that matters."[12]

The second Biblical theme presented by Russell was that of *universality*. She believed that God's plan for the world provided an eschatological perspective concerning the future of humanity that promised God's utopia to *all*.[13] According to Russell, Christians were but one of the groups who participated in God's work of liberation. "No longer are lines drawn between Christian and non-Christian, or between one confession and another. Instead, Christians join with all those involved in the revolution of freedom, justice, and peace."[14] Feminist theologians did not see divisions between sinner and saint, between redeemed and condemned, as applicable. They argued that God's promise of liberation would come to *all* people in the realization of an ecumenical new humanity, a new social order, and a new age.

World as History

Russell noted that in the feminist perspective, both humanity and the world were to be understood as historical, as both "changing and changeable."[15] World history was viewed as a series of meaningful events moving toward the fulfillment of God's plan and purpose of salvation, namely, a utopic new age of peace and harmony. Feminists believed that God had promised them an open future, not a "blueprint." According to Russell, God had not provided an exact knowledge of how liberation would be accomplished nor of how it would look.[16] Therefore, she explained, feminists saw the Christian purpose as advocating the rights of the oppressed: "To view the world as history is to become involved in the development of ideologies or sets of ideas that can be used to change and shape this reality."[17]

Salvation as a Social Event

To the feminist, *salvation* was viewed as a social as well as an individual event. According to Russell, salvation had traditionally been considered an individual event that would be consummated in the afterlife by the corporate redemption of the people of God. She, however, saw salvation as "a present corporate event . . . a condition of shalom or wholeness and total social well-being in community with other."[18] Russell defined salvation as *the realization of personal power and corporate responsibility to change the world for the better.* She argued that in a historical view of the world, salvation was not an escape from fated nature, but rather "the power and possibility of transforming the world, restoring creation, and seeking to overcome suffering."[19]

THEMES OF FEMINIST THEOLOGY

Humanization

Russell presented the first major theme of feminist theology as *humanization*. She claimed that oppressive relationships were inhuman — that they existed contrary to true human nature. Russell said that the longing to experience humanity in its fullness was integral to all people. "In situations of broken community, of oppression, of defuturized minorities and majorities there is a constant longing to be a whole human being."[20] According to Russell, the quest of feminist theology was to realize a new humanity. She observed,

> . . . the goal beyond — or rather through — the struggle against misery, injustice, and exploitation is the creation of a new man [and woman]. . . .
> This aspiration to create a new humanity is the deepest motivation in the struggle for liberation.[21]

Feminists had discussed at length the question of what it meant to be human. Although they did not settle on any one definition, feminists agreed that humanization entailed self-discovery, acceptance of the individual into a community, and the freedom to make one's own choices. Russell defined humanization as the "setting free of all humanity to have a future and a hope."[22] According to Russell, women and men needed full personal and social well-being as well as the power to participate in shaping the world in order to realize their own humanity.[23]

> Although there is no one definition of what it means to be human, it seems clear that some of the key factors are to be discovered in the area of human relationships of love, freedom, and respect. Human beings need support communities in order to find out who they are. The task of finding who they are can only be done by themselves. They are the ones who must build their own house of freedom.[24]

Conscientization

Russell noted that a second theme prevalent in feminist theology was that of *conscientization*. She defined it as the process of coming to self-awareness. It was the theological version of the secular process of consciousness raising. In conscientization, people become aware of the oppressiveness of the human situation and begin to take personal initiative for the Biblical liberation of humanity. Russell explained,

> If human beings have responsibility for shaping their own individual and social history, then they need a process of coming to self-awareness that helps them to learn their own potential for action in shaping the world. This process of coming to new consciousness and new ability to take action has become popularly known as *conscientization*.[25]

Feminist theologians viewed conscientization as an intentional, circular action-education process.[26] Russell maintained that it entailed "the interrelation of self-awareness which leads to action and action which leads to new awareness which constitutes a permanent, constant dynamic of our attitude toward culture itself."[27] Freire, a Latin American theologian, described the dynamic process of conscientization in a typology of stages of historical awareness and action: *doxa* (historical awareness); *logos* (critical awareness); *praxis* (commitment to action-reflection); and *utopia* (the vision of trust which makes possible a transformed self and world).[28]

Conscientization, like its consciousness-raising counterpart, involved a radical reorientation of the psyche. In consciousness raising, the participant was encouraged to discard traditional views for *new* understandings. Likewise, the goal of conscientization was to imbue Christian women with an awareness of the misogynistic bent of the Bible's authors and to free them to interpret the Bible's meaning according to their own experience. Feminist theologians reported that a woman's new awareness would lead her into new understandings, and the new understandings, in turn, would lead to new experiences. As Russell pointed out, "in conscientization there is a whole new understanding of the meaning of life which leads to rebirth as a new person."[29]

Dialogue and Community

The final theme embodied in feminist theology was the process of dialogue in the pursuit of a new community. Unlike some of their secular counterparts, Christian feminists did not want to alienate the oppressors (the men); rather, they wanted to educate and dialogue with them in order to free them into a new consciousness as well. As Ruether noted, "One cannot dehumanize the oppressors without ultimately dehumanizing oneself, and aborting the possibilities of the liberation movement into an exchange of roles of oppressor and oppressed."[30]

According to feminist theologians, in order to liberate the oppressors, true dialogue between the oppressors and the oppressed needed to take place. However, Ruether saw this as an impossibility until there was an end to "vertical and horizontal violence." She explained that in vertical violence hierarchical inequality was expressed between oppressors and oppressed: men and women, rich and poor, white and black. In horizontal violence, oppressed groups expressed their own frustrations and their low opinion of *themselves* by putting one another down and accepting the image of inferiority projected on them by the status quo.[31] According to Russell, there would not be true dialogue in the Church "until the structures of oppression were confronted and transformed into a situation of true partnership."[32] She believed that true dialogue between men and women could only happen if women were granted the same rights, responsibilities, and privileges as men in the Church. Ruether and Russell argued that with the structures supporting role equalization in place, dialogue could occur between all peoples, and the realization of true community would then be induced.

NEW DEFINITIONS OF FEMINIST THEOLOGY

The themes which characterized feminist theology were extrapolated from the Bible. However, the definitions of their words were revised significantly. As Russell pointed out:

> In another age we might have talked more about salvation instead of the process of *conscientization* and conversion; of incarnation instead of the search for *humanization*; or of communion instead of *dialogue and community*. Now we must talk of our common faith and our common world in whatever way that illuminates our common task together as women and men in a Christian context.[33]

Ruether claimed that the destruction of the traditional dualisms of classical Christian theology demanded a transformation of the semantic content of religious symbols. The key Christian symbols of incarnation, revelation and resurrection needed to be revised so that they ceased "pointing backward to some once and for all event in the past, which has been reified as a mysterious salvific power in the institutional Church," and become, instead, "paradigms of the liberation which takes place in people here and now."[34] Feminist theologians believed they had a mandate to develop doctrine that affirmed their current experience as an oppressed class and that pointed towards their own liberation. In doing so, they systematically examined all doctrine and theology of the past. If they found doctrines to be incongruent with feminist philosophy, they discarded them in lieu of a new "life-shaping faith." Russell explained:

> In trying to develop new models for thinking about God in a Christian context, women discover a vast quantity of questions addressed to Biblical and church tradition and to the concepts of creation, redemption, sin, salvation, and incarnation. The experimental nature of this inductive theology leaves no doctrine unchallenged in the search for a faith that can shape life amid rapid, and sometimes chaotic, change.[35]

According to Ruether, the doctrines of God, Jesus, salvation, redemption, sin, ecclesiology, and eschatology were "no longer taken so much as answers than as ways of formulating the questions."[36] She and other feminist theologians questioned these doctrines and found them to be incompatible with the feminist paradigm of liberation and equality. They therefore revised traditional doctrinal definitions in order to harmonize them with the feminist vision. In this way, Christian feminists began to name their world.

God
Biblically, Christians believed that humans existed to serve and bring glory to their Creator, God. Feminist theology, however, shifted the emphasis: God's purpose was to assist *humans* to realize liberation, wholeness, and utopia for *themselves*. As Russell reasoned, "our human hopes as Christians are always based on the perfect freedom of God. It is God's perfect freedom which is exercised in being for us. . . . 'God is not our utopia, but we are God's utopia.'"[37]

Jesus
Jesus Christ, as God's son, was viewed by feminists as an image of full and true humanity. Rather than being God incarnate, Jesus represented a deitic humanity — a "foretaste of freedom" — promised to all.[38] Russell explained that:

> In him [Jesus] we trust that God has made known the beginnings of the love, obedience, and true humanity which is the destiny of a restored creation. For women and men alike, Jesus embodies in his life, death, and resurrection what a truly human being might be like. One who would love and live and suffer for love of God and for others. He was not just

a male; he was for us all, a real live child of God! He was the second humanity (Adam) and showed both parts of humanity, male and female, both the cost and promise of freedom.[39]

According to Russell, Jesus was not to be viewed as the *one who saves*, but rather as the primary *example* of God's salvation, which is liberation. Christ was "the first object and bearer of all salvific tradition."[40] Russell believed that "the Christ event initiated [woman's] freedom in such a way that [they] are drawn with all creation into the horizon of God's freedom by participating in the action of God on behalf of human liberation."[41]

Sin
Feminists argued that the traditional definition of sin was aligned with classical dualities of right and wrong and was thus unacceptable. They redefined sin as "a situation in which there is no community, no room to live as a whole human being."[42] Feminist theologians viewed sin as the opposite of liberation — oppression. According to Russell, sin was "the dehumanization of others by means of excluding their perspectives from the meaning of human reality and wholeness."[43]

Salvation
Feminist theologians defined salvation as a journey toward freedom from sex class oppression and as a process of self-liberation in community with others.[44] They saw salvation as "humanization and reconciliation with the earth."[45] Russell argued:

> The message of salvation as expressed in the Bible and heard among the nations today cannot be reduced to one simple formula. . . . Salvation has to do with new joy and wholeness, freedom and hope that is experienced in the lives of individuals and communities as a gift of God. This message of liberation is good news to those of our age who are searching for freedom, for meaning, for community, for authentic existence as human beings.[46]

Because salvation was viewed as the process of liberation, feminists defined "a child of God" as "one who had been set free." They drew an analogy between coming to consciousness (conscientization) and coming to faith or trust in God through Jesus Christ. Therefore, God's children were not only those who believed in Jesus; rather, all those who were working for equality were the children of God:

> . . . *everyone* who is working and longing for freedom is eagerly longing to catch a vision of what "it means to be free." For to be set free is to become real live children of God and to be part of a universe inhabited by these real live children! . . . Because we are all on this journey toward

freedom together, we do not know exactly what children of God look like.[47]

Church

Feminist theologians also changed the traditional understanding of the Church. They viewed the Church as that "people of God" whose reason for existence was to be the servant and midwife of the process of liberation and the overthrower of the oppressive orders of society. Ruether believed that the Church did not exist for itself, but "to serve the revolution."[48] Feminists therefore viewed ecclesiology — church structure and function — as open-ended. According to Russell, there were a "variety of possible shapes the church might take in order to participate in God's liberating activity."[49] She maintained that the Church was "called to become *open to the world, to others*, and *to the future*."[50] Therefore, she saw the Church not as a religious assembly, temple, or synagogue, "but as a part of the world where it joins God's action in becoming a pressure group for change."[51] According to Russell, the Church was only "one of the signs of cosmic salvation," and not the exclusive mediator of that salvation.[52]

Eschatology

Feminist theologians also changed traditional doctrines of the end-times. They believed that through experiencing and pursuing liberation for people on the earth, humans themselves would usher in a new humanity and witness the "new age" promised by God. According to Russell, the realization of liberation for all would enable the condition of "God with us" to occur.[53] In sum, feminist theologians believed that a utopian society of Heaven on earth, justice, peace, and freedom were achievable by humanity.

EXPERIENCE AS NEW NORM FOR THEOLOGICAL STUDIES

Feminists within the Church in the early 1970s formulated a new theology based on women's perspective. In spite of the drastic deviance from traditional theology, feminist theologians did not see themselves as deviating from Biblical truth. With a presupposition of dynamism — that is, the evolutionary, developmental nature of revelation, Ruether and Russell saw their theology merely as a *furtherance* of truth.

Ruether's and Russell's work in theology mirrored the development of feminist philosophy in secular society. At the time when women in society had begun to view their differences as a source of pride and confidence rather than a source of shame, these church women began to take pride in their own experience and perspectives in the interpretation of the Bible and formulation of Christian doctrine. They regarded women's experience as the new norm for theological study. Russell encouraged all Christian women to become involved in theology, for she regarded theology as the basis of liberation:

. . . women will have to *do their homework* and be willing to take concrete actions for social change based on their *own* new consciousness of
the social and theological issues at stake. For Christian women in this situation "doing theology" is not just an added luxury after developing
expertise in other disciplines. Doing theology is itself an act of freedom!
It is a critical means of searching out the right questions about the Bible
and ecclesial tradition, about God and faith. Instead of accepting a certain text delivered from the "fathers," serious questions must be raised
in order to try to discern what it means to be real live children of God.[54]

Russell wanted women to contribute to the meaning of faith and theology from their own experience in order to make theology "more complete." According to Russell, this action formed the basis of feminist
theology.

In a Christian context [feminists] reflect on the way in which theology can
become more complete, as all people are encouraged to contribute to the
meaning of faith from their own perspective. Such action and theory form
the basis of *feminist theology*. It is "feminist" because the women
involved are actively engaged in advocating the equality and partnership
of women and men in church and society.[55]

The advent of feminist theology in the Church replicated the development of feminist philosophy in secular society. Secular women had analyzed
the world through women's perspective and judged the knowledge of the
world to be skewed and incomplete. Similarly, women in the Church
judged the truth of the Bible by their experience. If a doctrine or text did
not agree with woman's experience of oppression and quest for liberation,
then it was freely revised in order to make it agree. Ruether and Russell
developed many themes that had been earlier identified by Mary Daly as
problematic to women's liberation in the Church. Their major contribution
was to provide women a new paradigm from which to view the Bible and
Biblical revelation. Feminists identified the *crux interpretum* of the Bible as
the message of God's liberation to all people. For those who had felt ostra-
cized by the "misogynism" in the Church, this brought a glimmer of hope.
Feminists proclaimed not only that women had a place in God's plan; they
proclaimed that women, and not men, had the right to name themselves and
their religious world.

9

The First Sex

In nature's plan the male is but a glorified gonad. The female is the species.

Elizabeth Gould Davis

Women-centered analysis led to a new understanding of the condition of women in society. Women's experience had become a crucial component used by secular women to interpret art, sociology, medicine, and the like, and by religious feminists to interpret the Bible. But some feminists were not content to restructure their own disciplines. These feminists were interested in searching the ancient past for clues to the origins of patriarchy and evidences for women's superiority. Prominent among these feminists was Elizabeth Gould Davis. In her book *The First Sex* she sought to establish the primacy of women by exploring prehistory. She argued that women possessed an evolutionary primacy testified to by their superior biological and sexual attributes. According to Davis, women were once supreme but lost that supremacy when men — who were genetic mutations of women — formed into bands and overthrew the peaceful matriarchies, inventing rape and other forms of violence.

THE GREAT LOST MATRIARCHY

Davis wrote of a great worldwide civilization preceding the Dark Ages in the time of "prehistory." She testified to a *golden age* — a gynocratic (woman-ruled) civilization that endured for untold millennia, up past the dawn of written history.[1] According to Davis, in this civilization, woman was civilizer, craftsman, industrialist, agriculturalist, engineer, inventor, and discoverer. Humans were pacific herbivores, unacquainted with warfare and violence. Furthermore, she argued that earth was a semiparadise of peace and tranquillity, presided over by an omnipotent goddess.[2]

Davis based her theory on four pieces of evidence. First, she pointed to a decreasing complexity of language structure. Latin, Greek, and Sanskrit were less complex than the common Indo-European language from which she said they evolved. According to Davis, the latter languages appeared to derive from a more sophisticated language. Davis believed that language was the "true image and organ of the degree of civilization attained."[3] Therefore, she reasoned that the complex languages of Indo-Europe were remnants of an even more complex universal language of some great and untraced civilization of the past.[4] Second, Davis referred to the archaeological discovery of complex ancient maps that appeared to have been drawn with the help of highly sophisticated instruments. According to Davis, the maps suggested the existence of a great civilization that, ten thousand years before the Christian era, mapped the world with an accuracy never again achieved until the twentieth century. Scientific knowledge within that lost civilization, she concluded, equalled that found in contemporary society. Third, Davis cited a "wonderful stranger tradition" among many of the world's primitive peoples; she noted that the folklore of many lands included stories of a red-haired celtic race of people of advanced technological knowledge who visited from afar.[5] Fourth, she argued that archaeological discoveries, such as ancient iron nails and fine gold threads, added credence to the theory of the existence of a prehistoric, highly advanced technological civilization. According to Davis:

> The only rational supposition remains that there must have been a great original nation, now utterly extinct, and of whose history no document remains, who had advanced to a very high degree of perfection in the sciences and the arts; who sent colonies to the other parts of the world; who, in fine, were the instructors, and communicated their knowledge to peoples more barbarous than they.[6]

Davis hypothesized that the leaders of the ancient civilization had become deities and demi-deities, heroes and heras as their deeds were passed down from generation to generation. She maintained that the mythology of today was but the history of yesterday, records of real events experienced by the human race.[7] According to Davis, mythology reflected the memory of the civilization that once was. She proposed that in mythology, women could find the truth of the past.

According to Davis, the most ancient mythology spoke of goddesses, of women who created and ruled and who were revered as all-powerful. Ancient mythology had a female deity at the helm of creation, creating the world of her own accord without a male partner. Davis pointed out that the deity was originally female (as in the mythologies of Metis, Tanit, Tiamat, Gaia, and Anat). But she noted that by the time of mythological Orpheus, the creative deity was depicted as bisexual. Finally, Davis reported that in classical times, this Creator — who was once recognized as female — was transformed into an all-male God.[8]

. . . myth supports the idea . . . that there is an original Great Goddess who creates the universe, the earth, and the heavens, and finally creates the gods and mankind. Eventually she bears, parthenogenetically, a son who later becomes her lover, then her consort, next her surrogate and finally, in patriarchal ages, the usurper of her power.[9]

Davis concluded that the progression of mythology reflected the actual progression of the evolution of the human race. She believed that humans were female and matriarchal in their original evolutionary state. In this state, according to Davis, they had attained lofty levels of art and technology. As history progressed, however, mutant men changed traditional mythology to include themselves in the creative process. Davis hypothesized that men finally resorted to violence and overthrew the matriarchies to claim sole omnipotence. According to her theory, civilization was, at that time, thrown into "the dark ages" and the glory of the matriarchies was lost.

BIOLOGICAL AND SEXUAL PRIMACY OF WOMEN

In order to substantiate her "great lost matriarchy" theory, Davis sought to establish the original female condition of all human beings. She proposed that women's reproductive organs were far older than man's and were far more highly evolved. Furthermore, she argued, women had a greater sexual capacity than men. Davis concluded that women were "the first sex," possessing a foundational primacy and superiority in biology and sexuality.

Davis drew attention to the fact that all mammalian embryos, male and female, were anatomically female during the early stages of fetal life. In humans, the differentiation of the male from the female was accomplished by the action of a fetal hormone, androgen. This process began about the sixth week of embryonic life and was completed by the end of the third month. Female structures developed autonomously without the necessity of hormonal intervention. In other words, Davis argued that the state of "femaleness" was normative, but male genitalia only developed upon the *addition* of hormones. Furthermore, Davis pointed out that females developed in utero more quickly than males and that this acceleration in growth was maintained by the female throughout childhood.

Davis' second evidence for the biological primacy and superiority of the female was genetic. She explained that there are two types of sex chromosomes in the human body, commonly referred to as "X" and "Y." The Y chromosome is much smaller than the X — comprising only one-fifth of the volume of the X chromosome. Gender is determined by the presence of X and Y chromosomes. Females possessed two X chromosomes, while males possessed one X and one Y chromosome. Davis borrowed from Ashley Montague in hypothesizing that the presence of two X chromosomes was normative, and that the Y chromosome, which determined maleness, was a mutation or genetic anomaly. Montague had considered the Y chromosome as:

> . . . an undeveloped X-chromosome or perhaps as a remnant of an X-chromosome. It is as if in the evolution of sex a fragment at one time broke away from an X-chromosome, carrying with it some rather unfortunate genes, and thereafter in relation to the other chromosomes was helpless to prevent them from expressing themselves in the form of an incomplete female, the creature we call the male! This "just-so" story makes the male a sort of crippled female, a creature who by virtue of his having only one X-chromosome is not so well equipped biologically as the female.[10]

Montague and Davis appealed to the presence of X and Y chromosomes to provide evidence that females were the original, normative sex, and males, mere accidents of nature. Davis regarded the male Y chromosome to be a deformed and broken mutation of the female X chromosome. She stated:

> . . . the Y chromosome that produces males is a deformed and broken X chromosome — the female chromosome. All women have two X chromosomes, while the male has one X derived from his mother and one Y from his father. It seems very logical that this small and twisted Y chromosome is a genetic error — an accident of nature, and that originally there was only one sex — the female.[11]

To further support her claim, Davis cited clinical symptoms of genetic XY chromosomal abnormalities. She argued:

> The suspicion that maleness is abnormal and that the Y chromosome is an accidental mutation boding no good for the race is strongly supported by the recent discovery by geneticists that congenital killers and criminals are possessed of not one but two Y chromosomes, bearing a double dose, as it were, of genetically undesirable maleness. If the Y chromosome is a degeneration and a deformity of the female X chromosome, then the male sex represents a degeneration and deformity of the female.[12]

Davis also pointed out that the Y chromosome was linked with many genetic disorders such as color-blindness and hemophilia.[13] The male, who was sole possessor of the Y chromosome, was reported by Davis to be much more susceptible to genetic defects. Davis also maintained that the extra X chromosome in females accounted not only for the greater freedom of girls from birth defects and congenital diseases, "but also for the superior physiological makeup and the superior *intelligence* of women over men."[14] Davis argued that other female traits also supported the biological supremacy of the female, such as woman's capacity for reproduction, her greater resistance to disease, her increased longevity and her excellent metabolic efficiency. Women, Davis concluded, were far superior to men biologically.

Davis believed the male was a genetic mutation of the female — a freak accident of nature. But the question arises, why did the male being continue to exist and to multiply? Davis found the answer in the unbounded sexual capacity of woman. According to Davis, man's body — his phallic organ — was found to be sexually pleasurable to the woman. He thus survived because of his sexual use to her. "Man," Davis explained, "was made expressly to please woman."[15]

Davis and her posterity claimed that women possessed a "biologically determined, inordinately high, cyclic sexual drive"[16] and were capable of numerous, repeated orgasms.[17] Davis believed that precivilized woman enjoyed full sexual freedom and was often totally incapable of controlling her sexual drive.[18] The capricious appearance of the male organism was explored sexually and found to be pleasing. According to Davis, men were therefore kept to serve women sexually.[19] Eventually, she reasoned, man usurped the matriarchies and coercively suppressed woman's sexuality, inhibiting the trait that had once confirmed his very existence.[20]

In sum, Davis presented the state of being female as normative and the state of being male as abnormal. She believed that women possessed an evolutionary primacy and superiority that was evidenced by their biological and sexual composition. According to Davis, man was merely an imperfect female:

> . . . the first males were mutants, freaks produced by some damage to the genes caused perhaps by disease or a radiation bombardment from the sun. Maleness remains a recessive genetic trait. . . .[21] *Women are the race itself — the strong primary sex.* Men are the biological afterthought.[22] Man is but an imperfect female.[23] (emphasis added)

Davis pointed out that the female (according to naturalists, biologists, and human geneticists) had been given the protective covering, the camouflaged plumage, the reserve food supply, the more efficient metabolism, the more specialized organs, the greater resistance to disease, the built-in immunity to certain specific ailments, the extra X chromosome, the more convoluted brain, the stronger heart, and the longer life. According to Davis, in nature's plan the male was but a "glorified gonad. . . . *The female is the species"*[24] (emphasis added).

WOMAN THE DIVINE

Davis hypothesized that in the matriarchy of precivilization, woman's superiority was recognized by the genetically deficient male vassal. She believed that early man respected and acknowledged women's innate wisdom, power, and ability to procreate. According to Davis, woman by her nature was considered to participate in the divine, for it was women who had given the first mighty impulse to the civilization of the human race. From women sprang poetry, music and all the arts; she held the secrets of nature, and she was the only channel through which flowed the wisdom and knowledge of the ages.[25] Davis reasoned:

> This superiority of intellect [of women] exerted a strong influence on primitive man. Men could not help but believe that woman was closer to the deity than was man and that she had a superior understanding of the laws of nature — laws that baffled his dimmer perceptions and rendered him dependent on woman as the interpreter between man and man and man and deity.[26]

Davis theorized that women dominated men in the golden civilization. According to Davis, woman was a "fascinating magician before whom his soul trembled."[27] Davis noted that all the qualities that embellished contemporary man's life were known by feminine names — justice, peace, intelligence, wisdom, rectitude, devotion, liberty, mercy, intellect, nobility, concord, gentleness, clemency, generosity, kindliness, dignity, spirit, soul, freedom — all feminine — a fact that she said was not a free invention of accident, but an expression of historical truth. According to Davis, the accord between historical facts and the linguistic phenomenon was evident.[28] Davis argued that woman was the originator of all noble qualities. Woman, by virtue of her sex, had participated in deity and exhibited character of godlike glory.

THE GREAT USURPATION

Davis believed that the original matriarchies lived in colonies sustained by agriculture. The settlements were pacific and herbaceous — unacquainted with violence against either humans or animals. She theorized that the male mutants who had been accepted into the gynocratic colonies aided the women in agricultural pursuits and were expected to conform to the communal standards of peace. But, she reasoned, because of their genetic structure, men were not innately pacific — as were the women. When violent tendencies surfaced, men were banned from the civilized communities and sent into wilderness exile. Davis suggested that bands of marauding males became killers, devouring raw animal flesh out of desperation.

According to Davis, meat-eaters have larger sexual organs than vegetarians. Therefore, the wild habits and raw meat diet of undomesticated males led to their gradual sexual development and, Davis argued, to their eventual conquest of the matriarchs. The wandering, defiant men became more sexually attractive to women than those who had chosen to remain at home under female supervision. Davis argued that this development may have proved irresistible to the sexually insatiable women.[29]

In their newfound physical status, Davis theorized that men violently oppressed women as they sought to wipe out all traces of their former condition of servitude.[30] Men feared, resented, and hated women's natural superiority and therefore began to revolt. Davis argued that this retaliation had extended throughout history into modern existence:

> The implacability with which Western man has since retaliated against woman serves only to confirm the truth of her former dominance — a dominance that man felt compelled to stamp out and forget.[31]

Davis believed that the patriarchal revolution was born out of a severe case of womb envy reflected by male initiatory rites and sex customs among primitive peoples consisting entirely in men pretending to be women: penis mutilation, castration, mock menstruation and childbirth.[32] Man was covetous of female power and therefore overthrew the matriarchy to claim power for himself. Davis argued that,

> . . . the female principle is primary in nature. Woman possesses a power that no man can ever have: the capacity to give birth to new life, as well as the ability to experience an unlimited amount of pleasure in the sexual act. She is the creator of life, while his role in conception is, at best, a secondary one. Patriarchy is based on the "phallacy" that the male is creator. Man's original awe and envy of woman becomes, under patriarchy, resentment and hostility. The only way man can possess female power is through woman, and so he colonizes her, suppressing her sexuality so that it serves him rather than being the source of her power.[33]

Davis proposed that male envy of the female led to patriarchal revolt and repression of the natural order of society. She also maintained that men had since repressed and belittled women — even to the point of denying the essential femaleness of the creative deity.

> . . . it is man's fear and dread of the hated sex that has made woman's lot such a cruel one in the brave new masculine world. In the frenzied insecurity of his fear of women, man has remade society after his own pattern of confusion and strife and has created a world in which woman is the outsider. He has rewritten history with the conscious purpose of ignoring, belittling, and ridiculing the great women of the past. . . . He has devalued woman to an object of his basest physical desires and has remade God in his own image — a God that does not love women.[34]

RETURN TO MATRIARCHY — SOCIETY'S ONLY HOPE

The rot of masculist materialism has indeed permeated all spheres of twentieth-century life and now attacks its very core. The only remedy for the invading and consuming rot is a return to the values of the matriarchies, and the rediscovery of the nonmaterial universe that had so humanizing an influence on the awakening minds of our ancestors.[35]

According to Davis, men had usurped female power, and all the ills of our world stemmed from that fact. She argued that the "rot of masculist patriarchy" had corroded all true human (female) values, morals and ideals. Davis maintained that characteristically masculine thinking squeezed out human and emotional considerations and enabled men to kill (people, animals, plants, natural processes) with free consciences.[36] In her view, patriarchy promoted destructive, death-oriented behavior as opposed to the holistic, multiple perspective afforded by the feminine. Davis saw the only solution — the only hope — in a renunciation of patriarchal concepts and values and a return to a natural gynocentric worldview. According to Davis, only the holistic, spiritual vision of the female could lead the world in a life-affirming direction.[37]

In the new science of the twenty-first century, not physical force but spiritual force will lead the way. Mental and spiritual gifts will be more in demand than gifts of a physical nature. Extrasensory perception will take precedence over sensory perception. And in this sphere woman will again predominate. She who was revered and worshiped by early man because of her power to see the unseen will once again be the pivot — not as sex but as divine woman — about whom the next civilization will, as of old, revolve.[38]

Davis called for radical revision within society. She presented a vision of utopia that would ensue when women were reinstated to their true position — a position innately superior to men. Davis regarded women as the hope, the future, and the true and natural possessors of wisdom, power and divinity.

The ages of masculism are now drawing to a close. Their dying days are lit up by a final flare of universal violence and despair such as the world has seldom before seen. Men of goodwill turn in every direction seeking cures for their perishing society, but to no avail. Any and all social reforms superimposed upon our sick civilization can be no more effective than a bandage on a gaping and putrefying wound. Only the complete and total demolition of the social body will cure the fatal sickness. Only the overthrow of the three-thousand-year-old beast of masculist materialism will save the race.[39]

THE DREAM OF MATRIARCHY

Elizabeth Gould Davis's book *The First Sex* was the first feminist work to present a comprehensive argument for the existence of a universal "golden" gynocratic era. The work was certainly controversial. Not all agreed with her assessment of prehistory and the actual existence of a matriarchal society. Nonetheless, even though many aspects of her work were disputed, feminists incorporated her concluding theme into feminist ideology. Davis presented a model of a world ruled by the feminine in which the feminine principle was powerful and dominant. In such a society, she postulated, humans would exist in absolute peace and harmony with nature and spirit. Ecological problems, war and violence, abuse, rape, and poverty would not exist, and physical and mental illness would be minimal. All peoples would be valued and discrimination would be unheard of. Davis proposed that society would rise to new heights as females were encouraged to realize their full potential.

Davis may not have convinced historians as to *what was*, but she certainly inspired feminists with a vision of *what could be*. Davis believed that in demolishing patriarchy and establishing a world centered around feminine values, humans would once again find themselves entering into a glorious reality that would satisfy their deepest longings.

With the publication of Davis's work, feminists began to murmur subtly: "Women *are* different than men and women should be *proud* of these differences, for the differences themselves attest to the value of women." And, underlying all the equality rhetoric was the hint of an idea that perhaps — just perhaps — woman was a bit *more* than equal to man. For if the original creative force of nature was feminine, and if the life-sustaining flow of the universe was feminine, then it could be reasoned that woman — because of her very nature — possessed within her inner spirit an apportion of divinity itself.

10

Herstory

A feminist who loves the Bible produces, in the thinking of many, an oxymoron. Perhaps clever as rhetoric, the description offers no possibility for existential integrity. After all, if no man can serve two masters, no woman can serve two authorities, a master called scripture and a mistress called feminism.

Phyllis Trible

Elizabeth Gould Davis and other secular feminists studied history to uncover remnants of a usable past for women. They argued that the prehistoric past provided a model of matriarchy which was important for feminists. Similarly, religious feminists began to search their Judeo-Christian roots for "a usable past." They wanted to find seeds of hope which would justify their loyalty to Christianity. Not all religious feminists, however, felt they could stay in the Church. Mary Daly, in *Beyond God the Father*, wrote of her disillusionment with the God of the Bible. Her hope for the liberation of women within the boundaries of institutionalized religion had, in the five years since the publication of her first book, totally vanished. The transition was dramatic. Daly spurned God and called for a spiritual women's revolution that would be "Antichurch" as well as "Antichrist."[1] She had come to the realization that altering images of God and the Bible left her outside the boundaries of the Christian religion. Instead of forcing Christianity to change, Mary Daly decided to leave. According to Daly, the Judeo-Christian God was antithetical to the liberation of women. God and the Bible were beyond all hope.

Daly's retreat did not cause a mass exodus of feminists from the Church. It did, however, encourage feminists to carefully analyze their reasons for staying within the Christian tradition. Daly's lack of hope challenged Christian feminists to justify their own hope. The next step in the development of religious feminism, therefore, sought to explain why, and how, and for what purpose to use the Bible. It embarked on a full-scale woman-centered analysis of the canon of Scripture.

Phyllis Trible, in *God and the Rhetoric of Sexuality*, argued that the female dimension of faith — containing female imagery and motifs — had been lost through centuries of Biblical male authors and interpreters. She likened the search for a usable past to that of the ancient housekeeper of the New Testament.[2] This woman, while possessing nine coins, searched for the tenth which she had lost. Trible maintained that feminists likewise, having identified the dominance of the male in the writing and interpretation of Scripture, needed to light a lamp, sweep the house, and seek diligently for the precious coin of the feminine dimension in Christianity.

Feminists embarked on a search for the part of the Bible and Christian tradition that would be "usable" in their quest for liberation and inner wholeness. As Letty Russell pointed out:

> Women are voicing their search for liberation by rejecting oppressive and sexist religious traditions that declare that they are socially, ecclesiastically, and personally inferior because of their sex. They are digging deeper into their traditions, raising questions about the authority of the church "fathers," and searching out the hidden evidence of the contributions of the church "mothers" to the life and mission of the church. They are looking for truly authentic and liberating roots as they search for a *usable past.*"[3]

According to Russell, the struggles of Christian women, by and large, remained invisible in an androcentric Church and culture. Yet by searching back into Biblical and ecclesiastical history, women could unveil the "tradition of God" — the liberation of the oppressed — as their own tradition. Russell observed that as women searched back into Biblical and ecclesiastical history, they found increasingly that they were not entirely invisible. Russell marveled that somehow the tradition of God had *broken through* the traditions of men to provide clues of the hidden presence of the oppressed and forgotten members of the human family, women.[4]

Feminists regarded women as an oppressed and forgotten group within the ecclesiastical community. They therefore embarked on a woman-centered analysis of the Bible in order to recover *her*story, the story about women and for women, hidden in the text. Elisabeth Schüssler Fiorenza, a German scholar and professor of New Testament Studies and Theology at the University of Notre Dame, wrote:

> Since Biblical texts are rooted in a patriarchal culture and recorded from an androcentric point of view, a careful analysis from a feminist perspective might unearth traces of a genuine "her-story" of women in the Bible. It is very important that teachers and preachers point out these instances of a genuine "her-story" again and again, so that women in the

church become conscious of their own "her-story" in the Biblical patriarchal history.[5]

CRITICAL INTERPRETATION OF THE BIBLE

Feminists had chosen the *liberation of women* as their *crux interpretum* for the Bible. They did not, therefore, accept any interpretation of Scripture that did not support the liberation of women. In this manner, feminists established some guidelines on how the Bible could *not* be used. But what had not been established, to this point, were clear ways in which the Bible *could* be used. Fiorenza summarized four structural elements essential for a feminist Biblical interpretation: a hermeneutic of suspicion, remembrance, proclamation, and creative actualization.[6]

Hermeneutic of Suspicion

Fiorenza advocated a *hermeneutic of suspicion* rather than one of *consent and affirmation*. She did not presuppose the authority and truth of the Bible, but accepted the feminist assumption that Biblical texts and their interpretations were androcentric and that they served to reinforce patriarchy. Feminists reasoned that since the Bible was written by men, and since it was most often interpreted by male theologians, it could not be trusted. A hermeneutic of suspicion allowed the reader to raise questions regarding the validity of the Biblical authors' interpretation of events. J. Ellen Nunnally, an Episcopal priest, interpreted the story of Jezebel, for example, in a way that differed significantly from the narrator's point of view.

According to the account in 1 Kings, King Ahab of Israel married a foreign woman named Jezebel, daughter of the King of the Zidonians. Ahab and Jezebel served Baal, the fertility god of Canaan, and his consort, Asherah, a mother-goddess and fertility deity. They set up an altar for Baal and erected poles in the image of Asherah for the people to worship. Four hundred prophets of Asherah and four hundred and fifty prophets of Baal were regularly fed at Jezebel's table. According to the Bible, God was "exceedingly provoked" and sent Elijah to confront the couple.

Jezebel, angered by the judgment Elijah conveyed, murdered hundreds of the prophets of the Lord. The events culminated several years later in the challenge on Mount Carmel. The prophets of the gods of Baal and the goddess Asherah gathered with Elijah and all of Israel to witness the event. They placed a sacrificed bull upon wood on an altar and proceeded to call on their deities to bring fire. For hours the prophets of Baal called on their gods to no avail. Elijah then called on the God of Israel, and fire fell from heaven to consume not only the offering, but also the altar and the water entrenched around it. The people of Israel fell on their faces crying, "The Lord, He is God; the Lord, He is God!" The prophets of Baal were seized and killed, the rain came, and the famine ended.

Not long afterwards, Jezebel plotted the death of Naboth the Jezreelite in order to secure Naboth's vineyard for Ahab. Again, Elijah was sent to confront the couple. He relayed the word of the Lord which condemned Ahab and his sons to the same fate as Naboth. They were appointed to die in destitution; their bones were to be eaten by dogs and picked clean by birds. Jezebel faced the same fate. The Lord decreed that dogs would eat her by the wall of Jezreel. Several years after the death of Ahab, Jezebel was killed in a political war. She was thrown out a window by her own servants, trampled in the street by horses, and eaten by dogs.

The story of Jezebel, Ahab and Elijah is one of intrigue, power, violence and evil, and for centuries Jezebel has been labeled a wicked woman, her name a synonym for evil. But Nunnally, employing a feminist hermeneutic of suspicion, questioned this judgment:

> While we cannot claim Jezebel to be without fault, we can at least credit her for being the daughter, wife, and mother of kings, and perhaps not as barbarous as she often appears. And we can also raise some curious questions: what makes her so alien? What makes her so feared? Wherein lies her power? . . .
>
> Jezebel, then, is to be feared, for she is a powerful force with a strong following. *The writer of the narrative would naturally wish to cast her in a disparaging light,* for her very presence threatens the heart of Israel. This is not to say Jezebel's character is sterling, for she is as political and as ruthless as the next, but *it is to call into question the basis for her condemnation.* Female symbols for God, female Goddesses, and female rulers appear to evoke deep-seated resistance in the minds of some, and it is this which needs to be examined.[7] (emphasis mine)

Nunnally implied that the writer of 1 Kings condemned Jezebel and her female deities out of misogynistic jealously and fear. In her view the 1 Kings account reflected the Biblical writer's patriarchal prejudice against women and the power of woman. Furthermore, she accused, the judgment against the worship of Asherah was merely a male ploy to retain the reins of power. Therefore, according to Nunnally, goddess worship may indeed have been valid. She argued that it could not be dismissed because of its denouncement by this male writer.

Hermeneutic of Proclamation

The second aspect of feminist Biblical interpretation cited by Fiorenza was the hermeneutic of proclamation, namely, that those portions of the Bible which proclaimed liberation for the oppressed women of contemporary culture should be proclaimed, and those which did not should be attributed to historical patriarchal structure and therefore rejected. Fiorenza explained:

> Faithfulness to the struggle of women for liberation requires an evaluative theological judgement and insistence that oppressive patriarchal texts and sexist traditions cannot claim the authority of divine revelation.

Such oppressive texts and traditions must be denounced as androcentric articulations of patriarchal interests and structures. . . .

. . . a feminist hermeneutics of proclamation has, on the one hand, to insist that all texts that are identified as sexist or patriarchal *should not be retained* in the lectionary and be proclaimed in Christian worship or catechesis. On the other hand, those texts that in a feminist critical process of evaluation are identified as transcending their patriarchal contexts and as articulating a liberating vision of human freedom and wholeness should receive their proper place in the liturgy and teaching of the churches.[8]

The feminist hermeneutic of proclamation espoused by Fiorenza would allow Galatians 3:28 to be included in authoritative canon, but would leave out 1 Corinthians 11. It would set forth John 8:36, but would not mention Ephesians 5:22. It would loudly herald Romans 16:1, but scoff at 1 Timothy 2:11. It would embrace only those portions of the Bible that were comfortable to feminists and aligned with their vision for women's liberation.

Hermeneutic of Remembrance

The third feminist hermeneutic was a hermeneutic of remembrance that encouraged women to explore the suffering of women in the Bible and to draw feminist meaning from it. Rather than abandoning the memory of women's sufferings and hopes, a hermeneutic of remembrance *reclaimed* their sufferings and struggles in and through the "subversive power of the remembered past."[9] According to Fiorenza, this remembrance would bring about a universal sisterhood for the present and future of women in religion.

Nunnally, in *Fore-Mothers: Women of the Bible*, systematically examined the lives of women with a feminist hermeneutic of remembrance. Here are some examples of how she used this hermeneutic:

. . . when Abraham laughs at the announcement of a son, when he further rolls on the ground in mirth, nothing happens. God ignores the outbreak and continues conversation. When Sarah chuckles over the thought of having a son, and that behind a tent flap, God is immediately incensed. Abraham is, at most, corrected, but Sarah is plainly punished. Why this disparate behavior on the part of the Lord? Once again, we would attribute this to the mind of the narrator, rather than the Lord.[10]

Women are rarely named as tribal figures or national heroines, yet Miriam seems to carry a good deal of influence in her community. It is of great interest, then, that Miriam is the one to receive leprosy in the minor mutiny against Moses, while Aaron remains untouched. Perhaps this suggests the kind of power Miriam held, and perhaps to the storyteller this seemed dangerous.[11]

We note further the namelessness of the daughters and wife. Whereas sons, uncles, and fathers are usually named, the women are not. Lot's wife and daughters remain anonymous to us, as do Noah's wife and daughters, and countless more.[12]

Like Nunnally, Phyllis Trible, in *Texts of Terror*, used a hermeneutic of remembrance to focus on abused and disparaged women of the Bible: Hagar, Tamar, an unnamed woman, and the unnamed daughter of Jephthah. She forcibly pointed out the misogynistic attitudes and behavior that were inherent in these Biblical accounts. Trible argued:

> While the establishment prefers to forget its use and abuse of women, feminism wrestles with the meaning of it all. To accord these stories happy endings would be preposterous; yet to succumb to their suffering would be destructive. The demanding task is to retell them on behalf of the victims. In undertaking this project, I have endeavored not just to expose misogyny and certainly not to perpetuate crime, but rather to appropriate the past in a dialectic of redemption. Reinterpretation remembers in order not to repeat. Its memorial calls for repentance.[13]

The goal, or at least the end result, of a feminist hermeneutic of remembrance, was to heighten women's bitterness, anger and disillusionment with God and the Bible. It served much the same purpose as the selective statistics and information presented in secular consciousness-raising sessions and women's studies courses. Fiorenza's "subversive power of the remembered past" sounds hauntingly similar to Mao Tse-tung's "Speak bitterness to recall bitterness," and the results were much the same. Through a hermeneutic of remembrance, women harnessed their anger and claimed the right to define themselves and the Bible. Furthermore, they were incited to harbor anger and bitterness toward man. Finally, they were encouraged to join the quest for women's equality and liberation in the arena of religion in order to vindicate their foresisters' sufferings.

Hermeneutic of Creative Actualization

Fiorenza did not believe the hermeneutics of suspicion, proclamation and remembrance were adequate in themselves. She maintained that in order to truly ensure the liberation of women in the Church, these first three hermeneutics would need to be supplemented with creative actualization, that process whereby feminist theologians read into, embellished, or augmented the Biblical text. It expressed the "active engagement" of women in the ongoing Biblical story of liberation.

> While a feminist hermeneutics of remembrance is interested in historical-critial reconstruction, a feminist hermeneutics of creative actualization allows women to enter the biblical story with the help of historical imagination, artistic recreation, and liturgical ritualization. . . . Such a

hermeneutics of creative actualization seeks to retell biblical stories from a feminist perspective, to reformulate biblical visions and injunctions.[14]

According to Fiorenza, a hermeneutic of creative actualization reclaimed for Church women the same imaginative freedom, popular creativity, and ritual powers that the male prophets and apostles had possessed. She argued that feminist creative actualization should therefore incorporate new, woman-centered stories and rituals into the Judeo-Christian religion:

Women today not only rewrite biblical stories about women, but also reformulate patriarchal prayers and create feminist rituals celebrating our ancestors. We rediscover in story and poetry, in drama and liturgy, in song and dance, our biblical foresisters' sufferings and victories. . . . In ever new images and symbols we seek to rename the God of the Bible and the significance of Jesus. . . . We not only spin tales about the voyages of Prisca, the missionary, or about Junia, the apostle, but also dance Sarah's circle and experience prophetic enthusiasm. We sing litanies of praise to our foresisters and pray laments of mourning for the lost stories of our foremothers.[15]

According to feminist theologians, the Biblical story of liberation was an ongoing, ever-occuring process. Feminist women were therefore allowed to "dream new dreams and see new visions" in anticipation and quest of their liberation. They were allowed, by feminist theology, to add to the Biblical text whatever was appropriate to their personal vision of freedom.

One of the first texts to which feminist theologians applied creative actualization was the Genesis account of creation. Following is a feminist narrative on "Lilith and Eve," composed by Judith Plaskow and others at the Grailville Conference on Women Exploring Theology.[16]

In the beginning the Lord God formed Adam and Lilith from the dust of the ground and breathed into their nostrils the breath of life. Created from the same source, both having been formed from the ground, they were equal in all ways. Adam, man that he was, didn't like this situation, and he looked for ways to change it. He said, "I'll have my figs now, Lilith," ordering her to wait on him, and he tried to leave to her the daily tasks of life in the garden. But Lilith wasn't one to take any nonsense; she picked herself up, uttered God's holy name, and flew away. "Well, now, Lord," complained Adam, "that uppity woman you sent me has gone and deserted me." The Lord, inclined to be sympathetic, sent his messengers after Lilith, telling her to shape up and return to Adam or face dire punishment. She, however, preferring anything to living with Adam, decided to stay right where she was. And so God, after more careful consideration this time, caused a deep sleep to fall upon Adam, and out of one of his ribs created for him a second companion, Eve.

For a time Eve and Adam had quite a good thing going. Adam was happy now, and Eve, though she occasionally sensed capacities within herself that remained undeveloped, was basically satisfied with the role of Adam's wife and helper. The only thing that really disturbed her was the excluding closeness of the relationship between Adam and God. Adam and God just seemed to have more in common, being both men, and Adam came to identify with God more and more. After a while that made God a bit uncomfortable too, and he started going over in his mind whether he might not have made a mistake in letting Adam talk him into banishing Lilith and creating Eve, in light of the power that had given Adam.

Meanwhile Lilith, all alone, attempted from time to time to rejoin the human community in the garden. After her first fruitless attempt to breach its walls, Adam worked hard to build them stronger, even getting Eve to help him. He told her fearsome stories of the demon Lilith who threatens women in childbirth and steals children from their cradles in the middle of the night. The second time Lilith came she stormed the garden's main gate, and a great battle between her and Adam ensued, in which she was finally defeated. This time, however, before Lilith got away, Eve got a glimpse of her and saw she was a woman like herself.

After this encounter, seeds of curiosity and doubt began to grow in Eve's mind. Was Lilith indeed just another woman? Adam had said she was a demon. Another woman! The very idea attracted Eve. She had never seen another creature like herself before. And how beautiful and strong Lilith had looked! How bravely she had fought! Slowly, slowly, Eve began to think about the limits of her own life within the garden.

One day, after many months of strange and disturbing thoughts, Eve, wandering around the edge of the garden, noticed a young apple tree she and Adam had planted, and saw that one of its branches stretched over the garden wall. Spontaneously she tried to climb it, and struggling to the top, swung herself over the wall.

She had not wandered long on the other side before she met the one she had come to find, for Lilith was waiting. At first sight of her, Eve remembered the tales of Adam and was frightened, but Lilith understood and greeted her kindly. "Who are you?" they asked each other, "What is your story?" And they sat and talked not once, but many times, and for many hours. They taught each other many things, and told each other stories, and laughed together, and cried, over and over, till the bond of sisterhood grew between them.

Meanwhile, back in the garden, Adam was puzzled by Eve's comings and goings, and disturbed by what he sensed to be her new attitude toward him. He talked to God about it, and God, having his own problems with Adam and a somewhat broader perspective, was able to help him out a little — but he, too, was confused. Something had failed to go according to plan. As in the days of Abraham, he needed counsel from his children. "I am who I am," thought God, "but I must become who I will become."

And God and Adam were expectant and afraid the day Eve and Lilith returned to the garden, bursting with possibilities, ready to rebuild it together.

TOWARDS A USABLE FUTURE

Russell suggested that feminists in the Church needed a usable future as well as a usable past. Through the hermeneutics of suspicion, proclamation and remembrance, feminist theologians extracted a usable past from the Bible. Moreover, the hermeneutic of creative actualization enabled them to open up the door for a usable feminist *future*. Feminist theologians concluded that they did not need to leave the Church, as Mary Daly had, for with appropriate feminist hermeneutic tools in their hands, they could make a space for themselves within the Christian tradition. Feminists shaped a usable feminist history into a "living and evolving past" in order to dictate and name the shape of the Christianity of the future. Russell reinforced that feminists needed to shape the past and the future in such a way that man would no longer be the measure:

> Awareness of their own history and struggles is frequently nonexistent among women as a group. Yet it is toward such a search for a usable history that they must turn *to build a still living and evolving past in order to shape their future as partners in society.* "We create a history in which man is no longer the measure. . . ."[17] (emphasis added)

Naming the World

The development of feminist theology in the Church followed a similar path to the development of feminist philosophy in secular society. Women's differences came to be viewed as a source of pride and confidence, and the feminist experience became the normative standard for naming the world, even *their* world of Scriptural interpretation and theological study. In Letty Russell's terms, women were entering into a "household of freedom." According to Russell, in the liberation of their souls, women would be free to name theology, free to name the Bible, and free to "interpret the world in terms of possibility and future."[18] Religious women were standing in the doorway, on the threshold, ready to enter. Feminism had turned the key and had opened up rooms full of possibility.

11

Women's Studies

And the glory was that the world was transformed. Without guns, without strikes, and without bloodshed.

"The Sisterhood," Marcia Cohan

Secular feminists had used consciousness-raising groups to communicate feminist theory to the average woman in society. But although these groups were effective, they reached a limited part of the population. Feminists found that by sponsoring women's studies courses at colleges and universities, they could effectively reach a large number of younger women.

Women's studies was the study of the world based on women's own perceptions and experiences. The Hunter College Women's Studies group defined women's studies as "the study of women which places women's own experiences in the *center* of the process. . . . It examines the world and the human beings who inhabit it with questions, analyses, and theories built directly on women's experiences."[1] Although women's studies was very similar to woman-centered analysis, it went further than analysis, for it involved communicating feminist theory to others. The National Women's Studies Association noted that it was an *educational strategy*, "a breakthrough in consciousness and knowledge which will transform individuals, institutions, relationships, and, ultimately, the whole of society."[2]

Therefore, although women's studies encompassed and furthered a woman-centered analysis of society, it was more concerned with the *dissemination* of that information. It sought to impart feminist knowledge and facilitate "a breakthrough in consciousness" for individuals, institutions and organizations, and eventually, for society at large.

HISTORY OF WOMEN'S STUDIES

The first ideas for women's studies courses were initiated by Sheila Tobias at a Women's Conference at Cornell University in 1969. Tobias outlined a vision for communicating the feminist perspective to students in post-secondary institutions of learning. Tobias's proposal was timely, for many colleges and universities had begun, in response to the movements of the fifties and sixties, to offer studies of civil and student rights. It was not long, therefore, before courses sprang up across the country exploring the rights of women, their status in society, the discrimination they experienced in public roles and private lives, as well as the gender bias prevalent in culture, literature, and learning.[3] These courses were initially offered as interdisciplinary courses, then as a separate course of study called women's studies.

In the United States, a 1970 *Guide to Current Female Studies* listed approximately one hundred women's studies courses; the second edition, published one year later, included over six hundred. By the late 1970s, the number of women's studies courses had mushroomed to well over thirty thousand. Furthermore, 301 women's studies *programs* were in operation on college campuses in all but nine of the fifty states. By 1979, eighty programs offered B.A. degrees in women's studies, twenty-one the M.A., and five the Ph.D. or equivalent.[4] A similar development occurred in Canada. A women's studies teaching collective was founded in 1971 at the University of Toronto and a women's studies program in 1972. Women's studies, both in interdisciplinary course offerings and in separate programs, multiplied until programs were present in every institution of higher learning. In 1977, the National Women's Studies Association (U.S.A.) was founded to promote and sustain the educational strategy of women's studies with its final view toward the "transformation of society."[5] Its northern counterpart, The Canadian Women's Studies Association (CWSA), was formed in 1982.

Publishers supported the new discipline of women's studies with fervor. From 1970 to 1976 an unprecedented number of feminist publications flooded the market. Journals such as *Feminist Studies, Women's Studies, Signs, Quest, Sex Roles, Women's Studies Newsletter, Canadian Resources for Feminist Research, Atlantis,* and *Canadian Women Studies* presented feminist research on the role and status of women. Federally funded research institutes began to support the cause. Whole publishing companies such as *Press Gang Publishers, Women's Press, Eden Press, Feminist Press, Quadrangle,* and *Pergamon Press* were founded to promote feminist monographs. University presses — Alabama, Chicago, Illinois, Wisconsin, Indiana, Arizona, Maryland, and Johns Hopkins — followed suit. Feminist magazines such as *Ms.* (founded in 1971 by Gloria Steinem) and *Chatelaine* (published in Canada, edited by Doris Anderson) gained circulation.

Although women's studies programs began on university campuses, efforts of feminist organizations such as the National Women's Studies Association led to the introduction of feminist theories into all areas of education. Educators modified grade-school curricula, continuing education courses, and courses at technical schools. Eventually the values and beliefs of feminism were found in newspapers, periodicals, newscasts and television programming. By the end of the 1970s, it was difficult to find any medium of communication not influenced by the trend.

PHILOSOPHY OF WOMEN'S STUDIES

The basic philosophy of women's studies is that meaning is arbitrary. History is a legacy of arbitrary male-defined meaning: *hisstory*. From economics to politics, psychology to linguistics, relationships to religion, men had forced their own definition of existence and truth upon women. According to feminists, women needed to challenge and change that which had been construed for male benefit. Adoption of a feminist perspective allowed women to dictate their *own* truth. Gloria Bowles, in *Theories of Women's Studies*, reasoned:

> . . . everything I know is open to challenge, there are no absolutes, meaning is socially constructed. . . . Accepting the arbitrary nature of [everything] has necessitated a reconceptualization of right and wrong. If everything I know is "wrong," that is, if there are no absolutes, no truths, only transitory meanings imposed by human beings in the attempt to make sense of the world, then "wrong" becomes a meaningless category. Instead of being frightened that something I am arguing for as truth, as right, as logic, may in fact be wrong, I am starting from the other end and arguing that I know it is temporary and inadequate. I am then searching for the "errors," the "flaws" that will help me to refine [that meaning].[6]

Feminists accused men of distorting reality by neglecting or intentionally quelling the female perspective. Feminists therefore viewed all morals, beliefs, attitudes and actions of society with suspicion; they believed these attitudes were inadequate, erroneous because of their androcentricity. *Andro* (male) *centric* (centered) referred to the male habit of defining reality according to his own perspective and for his own interest. Sheila Ruth Houghton, in an introductory women's studies text, explained:

> Androcentrism or masculism is . . . the mistaking of male perspectives, beliefs, attitudes, standards, values, and perceptions for all human perceptions. Both the cause and result of women's social and intellectual disfranchisement, masculism is pervasive in our culture except for feminist challenge, and it is most frequently unconscious.[7]

According to feminists, the task of women's studies was to expose the androcentric nature of society's beliefs and mores, and then to explore the female perspective for the redefinition of truth, values, standards and knowledge. But although feminists heralded the contribution of women's experience for the formulation of a new awareness and worldview, they believed that the majority of women were incapable of contributing to that awareness. According to feminists, women needed to be "de-programmed" and freed from traditional (male) patterns of thought. Women first needed their consciousness *raised* to a feminist perspective, which they regarded as the only one capable of drawing an accurate picture of truth and reality.

GOAL OF WOMEN'S STUDIES

The first goal of women's studies courses was to convince the participant that her *own* experience — as viewed through feminist glasses — was the *only* legitimate source of truth and value. As recorded in Houghton's introductory women's studies text, feminists sought to create a "new reality" and to usher participants into a "new space."[8] She observed:

> For those of us who teach courses in [women's studies], [a] new reality is constantly being created in the students with whom we work. . . . The women . . . are daily engaging in the creation of a social reality that, for many of them goes far beyond simple role innovation. They face the historical and current facts of sexism with shock, and out of that shock an initial impetus to achieve equality emerges. But as this occurs, a more important transformation engages them in a new sense of self and a new feeling for future possibilities. . . .[9] [Women] find [themselves] living in a new space, centered in the lives of women — they reclaim the right to speak — to name the self, the world, the meaning of their own existence.[10]

Houghton promised a religious, mystical inner fulfillment to all who graced the doors of women's studies. She dangled the tantalization of a new space — of a new reality far superior to the old — before hungry eyes. Undoubtedly, many students were seeking truth and meaning, and others were longing for inner fulfillment and peace. Houghton claimed that women's studies possessed the answers. According to Houghton, truth and wholeness could be found by passing through the corridors of the feminist experience. She cited Mary Daly's description of that feminist mind-space:

> The new space has a kind of invisibility to those who have not entered it . . . it is experienced both as power of presence and power of absence . . . it is participation in the power of being . . . an experience of becoming whole.[11]

Houghton agreed with Daly that the feminist key to wholeness was the *"power of being"* found in the *"actualization of one's own vision and the pursuit of equality."*[12] Through women's studies, Houghton wanted to see students experience a new consciousness — a new vision for themselves and for humanity. Furthermore, she hoped that they would translate this vision into support and/or activism for the feminist movement. According to Marilyn Boxer, another author of a women's studies text, women's studies courses were "notoriously successful" in inducing students to embrace feminist philosophy.[13]

In essence, women's studies courses in educational settings were strategic battalions for the feminist cause. Taly Rutenberg noted that as the feminist force, women's studies translated and communicated the ideas of the movement through the channels of education.[14] Women's studies was therefore not a mere academic exercise, but an educational strategy, a tool, to disseminate the feminist vision and induce change in the world.[15] In sum, the goal of women's studies was to empower women to name and define themselves, and then to encourage them to use this new knowledge as a base to name, define, and ultimately transform society.

TECHNIQUE OF WOMEN'S STUDIES

Feminists used consciousness raising, which was highly effective in the feminist community at large, as a teaching device for use in the classroom setting.[16] They viewed consciousness raising as the function of the formal feminist educational process. Rutenberg explained:

Although some lecture courses are held within Women's Studies, usually as introductory classes, most Women's Studies courses are conducted in the small discussion-group format. This format creates an intimate setting where students can feel comfortable reacting personally as well as intellectually to the ideas being discussed. The deconstruction of sexist myths which women often internalize on a deep personal level can only occur in a setting which facilitates the expression of both the intellectual and emotional realms.

The Women's Studies classroom is a place to identify feelings of oppression, ventilate these feelings and constructively redirect them towards change. Although Women's Studies delves intellectually into conflicts once they are identified, the identification process is inherently linked to a visceral experience. Contrary to the traditional disciplines, Woman's Studies has a firm commitment to subjective knowledge and learning.[17]

The "intimate setting" described by Rutenberg was an artificially induced environment designed to coerce students into the feminist space. The power of group dynamics exerted strong pressure on students to change. Furthermore, Houghton observed that "in a feminist classroom, one is apt to find group projects, small group discussions, self-directed or student-directed study, credit for social change activities or for life experience, contracts or self-grading, diaries and journals, even meditation or ritual."[18] According to Houghton's account, women's studies students received marks for personal and social feminist activism, and the instructor — as authority figure — often guided them in feminist ritual and meditation. In addition, the teacher monitored each student's progress of conversion to a feminist mind-set by reading the participant's diary and/or journal.

Therefore, the grade the student received for the course was often a reflection of the extent of transformation of her psyche.

Women's studies courses were effective because teachers told participants they were entering a higher realm of reasoning. Houghton told students:

> You will discover as you . . . pursue Women's Studies [that it] is anything but soft. You will find that consciousness-raising occurs as a result of new insights and innovative ideas, an event that should occur in any high-quality course. Rather than brain-*washing*, raised consciousness comes as a result of brain-*opening*.[19]

In Hans Christian Andersen's tale of *The Emperor's New Clothes*, the Emperor paraded down the street naked, believing he was dressed in the finest clothes. The people lining the streets nodded and commented with approval on the fine fabric with which his suit was woven. They would not admit that they did not see his clothing, for they had been told that it was constructed with "magic" thread, invisible only to those who were extremely stupid or unfit for their jobs. Pride prevented the Emperor, his aides, and all the people from admitting that they saw nothing at all. Women's studies courses used the same principle. Leaders told participants that their experience in the feminist classroom would "open" their brains to a higher realm of knowledge that was formerly inaccessible to their minds. It would have been extremely difficult for a young student to stand against the tide of students who were "getting" the higher knowledge. It would have been humiliating for anyone to admit that *her* brain was *closed*!

Feminists claimed that women's studies departed from traditional (male) authoritative impartation of knowledge in that it allowed students to direct their own learning. The feminist women's studies model did depart from standard academic practice, but the philosophy presented within women's studies courses was *not* directed by the students. Therein resided the power of the technique. Students believed they were discovering new knowledge for themselves, when, in fact, the knowledge they were deriving was strictly manipulated by the presentation of selective feminist "facts" and instructor-guided discussion.

A systematic process of conversion occurred. First the participant was convinced of the facts of patriarchy. Teachers presented selective statistics and case studies to establish the presence of patriarchy as the prevailing world religion. Teachers taught their students this premise was *unquestionable*. The emotions of anger and bitterness evoked by this revelation helped the instructor guide participants to question all their previously accepted beliefs. In the second step of conversion, teachers guided their students to "see" that all concepts of God, of right and wrong, of morality and justice had been arbitrarily formulated by males. Teachers encouraged students to question, and then to totally discard the influence of a Judeo-

Christian worldview. Third, teachers convinced their students that they had the right to define truth and reality based on their new feminist, conscious-ness-raised experience. Finally, teachers challenged participants to spread the gospel of feminist enlightenment to the rest of their world. Students were commissioned to apply a feminist perspective in their relationships, in their professions, and through political and social involvements.

INTRODUCTORY FEMINIST TEXT

The systematic process for converting students to the feminist cause can be traced in introductory women's studies course textbooks. In Houghton's text, for instance, a student would complete the journey in nine succinct chapters.

Chapter One: An Introduction to Women's Studies

The introductory chapter introduced the concept of bias in the academy. Houghton established the need for women's studies. She then presented some altruistic goals that women's studies would help achieve:

- to change women's aspirations, based on an increased sense of self-confidence and self-love, to allow women to create for ourselves new options in our own personal goals as well as in our commitments and/or contributions to society.
- to alter the relations between women and men, to create true friend-ship and respect between the sexes in place of "the war between the sexes."
- to give all people, women and men, a renewed sense of human worth, to restore to the center of human endeavors a love for beauty, kindness, justice, and quality in living.
- to reaffirm in society the quest for harmony, peace, and humane compassion.[20]

Houghton's text informed students that these goals were attainable through the raising of one's consciousness, a process she said would occur during the course. After explaining and defending consciousness raising, Houghton sought to prepare students for the emotional turmoil they were about to experience:

You will discover that consciousness-raising can be painful. Yet pain is not in itself something always to be avoided, for there are two kinds of pain — destructive pain and constructive pain. Destructive pain is suf-fered in a no-win situation. Embedded in the status quo, it leads to no benefits, no improvements. It just hurts. Such pain is better avoided. Constructive pain is very different. It is like the physical distress we feel when we decide to get our bodies in shape after some disuse. . . . Much the same thing happens when we grow emotionally or spiritually. Our insights, memories, and feelings, not accustomed to such use may cause us pain. Our new sense of autonomy and freedom, its attendant responsibility, may make us anxious. We hurt, but we grow stronger. Just as physical strength and health are necessary to well-being, so is emotional and spiritual strength.[21]

Next, in order to convince students of the emotional and spiritual benefits of consciousness raising, Houghton included personal testimonies of women who had been transformed through women's studies experience:

I feel like a ton of bricks has been lifted off my shoulders. I finally found me. For the first time in my life I really looked at myself and said "I like you!" I decided that there is only one companion that you can count on all through your life — yourself. If I don't like me, who will? I took a full survey of myself and decided what I liked and what I would like to change, not because I wanted to look good in someone else's eyes, but because I wanted to look good in my own eyes. I feel so free, happy; like I could lick the world. This is the way I want to stay — this is the way I always want to feel. And I will because I like me.[22]

Houghton concluded her introduction by telling students that preconceived ideas of male/female roles were stereotypical "ideals" and generally resistant to change. She challenged the participants to risk and reach out in order to "grow."

Chapter Two: The Dynamics of Patriarchy

In Chapter Two, Houghton contended that students lived in a male-identified, male-governed, masculist society which had created a male-directed definition of the role of women. She maintained that men had *forced* women to be weak, emotional, dependent, imprudent, incompetent, fearful, and undependable. According to Houghton, women were objectified by men as vessels of love and hate, fascination and horror. She argued that women were held and tolerated by men only so long as they served men and were controlled by them. According to Houghton, the entire traditional role of women was dictated by masculist values and needs.

Chapter Three: Images of Woman in Patriarchy:
The Male-identified Woman

In Chapter Three, Houghton augmented her argument by reviewing "basic female stereotypes" of wife, mother, playmate/lover. She argued that these stereotypes unquestionably established that women had been wrongly defined. Furthermore, Houghton claimed that her study of images of women presented in entertainment, the media and literature *proved* that it was man who had wrongly defined women. Throughout this chapter, Houghton assumed that each person had an immutable right to define truth, and that no absolute standard of truth and definition existed. According to

Houghton, men had sinned — they had "stolen" woman's right to define themselves.

It is necessary to grasp the fundamental fact that women have had the power of naming stolen from us. We have not been free to use our own power to name ourselves, the world, or God. The old naming was not the product of dialogue — a fact inadvertently admitted in the Genesis story of Adam's naming the animals and the women. Women are now realizing that the universal imposing of names by men has been false because it has been partial. That is, inadequate words have been taken as adequate. . . .[23]

As Mary Daly put it, "To exist humanly is to name the self, the world, and God."[24]

Chapter Four: Counter-Images: A Feminist Response

By Chapter Four, students should have been convinced that the patterns of the past were inadequate. They would have "come to see for themselves" the need for a higher, superior level of awareness. Houghton explained that "the process of coming to understand sexism fully, at the highest (sic) level of awareness, is called consciousness-raising. It functions both to intensify awareness with regard to the implications of sexism and to stimulate the search for alternatives."[25] Houghton offered feminism as the alternative. She encouraged students to accept the feminist paradigm which, she claimed, built a "desirable" reality. According to Houghton, "feminists are building new visions. . . we are *redefining what is desirable for us.* . . . What we shall be, what we should and can be, is still an open question."[26]

Chapter Five: Origins and Explanations

In the fifth chapter, Houghton explored some of the theories for the existence of patriarchy. She reviewed biological approaches as well as sociological and cultural theories. In her analysis, Houghton assumed that the prevalence of patriarchy in society was undeniable and also that feminism had the answers.

Chapter Six: Women's Private Space

In Chapter Six, Houghton bombarded the reader with feminist rhetoric. According to Houghton, marriage was a set-up; wives and homemakers existed solely to cater to men's pleasure; wives were merely "chattels"; and disillusionment, divorce, and poverty were the immanent culmination of the marital experience. In sum, she argued that private relations with men served only to quench women's character, integrity and spirit. She proposed that only feminism offered women hope, for feminism allowed the mystical triumph involved in reclaiming and rebuilding one's soul. Houghton explained:

Because the oppression of women has been in large part an oppression of
our souls . . . feminist activism is as much as anything else an attempt to
reclaim our souls, to rebuild them.[27]

Again, she urged students to "break from the familiar" and to embrace
the hazy rumor of a feminist utopia. Houghton acknowledged that this
quest would be difficult but promised students that feminism offered "something better" than that which they had known.

It is extremely difficult to break from the familiar, which is comfortable
even in its inadequacy. It is difficult to alter behaviors, relationships, and
values that hold at least some good and some attraction for us in order
to move toward something that we can only dimly see at times, but something that we know must be better. May Sarton has said, "It is only when
we can believe that we are creating the soul that life has any meaning, but
when we can believe it — and I do and always have — then there is nothing we do that is without meaning and nothing that we suffer that does
not hold the seed of creation in it."[28]

Chapter Seven: Discrimination

In the first six chapters, Houghton presented the premise of patriarchy and
the oppression of women as indisputable facts. In the seventh chapter, she
cited selective statistics which substantiated her claim. Houghton reviewed
studies that proved statistically that women were enslaved in oppressive
marital and mothering roles through economics (wage gap, poverty, social
assistance); male positions of power/influence (proportions of male vs.
female executives); law (abortion, sex discrimination); politics and religion.
In conclusion, she once more offered spiritual fulfillment as the pinnacle of
the feminist alternative.

I perceive feminism to be at base a spiritual movement. Feminists seek
increased opportunity for participation and gain, not as ends in themselves, not simply for the power they entail, but for the growth in the
quality of life they represent, and that is a spiritual matter.[29]

Chapter Eight: Distortions in Perspective and Understanding

After two or three months in an introductory women's studies course, the
students were ready for the concepts that Houghton presented in Chapter
Eight. In this chapter, she asserted that culture and environment, school curricula, media, art and films, social science, and religion — *especially* religion — were all used as instruments to brainwash women. Furthermore,
Houghton argued that anyone who did not accept the feminist analysis of
life had come under the "mind control" of patriarchy. According to
Houghton they were *unwittingly* being *controlled* by men.

For the most part, without counterbalancing ideas and perspectives, most women are unaware that their behavior, opportunities, and life possibilities are controlled by masculism and masculists, and that women did not freely come to choose [their role].[30]

One feminist quoted by Houghton suggested that the most effective form of slavery was one in which the oppressed group was socialized to love its slavery.[31] Houghton countered that an "even more perfect form of slavery was one in which the slaves were unaware of their condition, unaware that they were controlled, believing that they freely chose their life and situation."[32] The control of women by patriarchy, she concluded, was effected in just such a way. According to Houghton, patriarchy implied a mastery of beliefs and attitudes through the "management of all the institutions and agencies of thought formation and dissemination."[33]

Therefore, when all the feminist arguments and emotional pleas and selective statistics had been presented, if a student *still* did not agree with the feminist perspective, then she was regarded to be functioning in an inferior mind-set. According to Houghton, such a person had not yet had her eyes opened to a *higher knowledge* and *superior awareness*.

Chapter Nine: Feminist Activism
In the final chapter of the women's studies text, Houghton politicized what had been discussed to date. She surveyed the history of women's political activism and encouraged students to support and pursue feminist strategies to legislate the feminist agenda.

THE RIGHT TO NAME

The process of conversion to feminism which took place within women's studies courses in academic institutions was the same as that of the consciousness-raising groups within the larger feminist community. This process was based upon the precept of woman's right to name. First, leaders guided the participants, through discussion and personal experience, to believe that *men* had named reality and had used women for their own self-centered interest. Women characteristically responded to this revelation with bitterness, resentment, and anger towards men; that anger caused them to wrench the right to name away from men in order to claim it for themselves. Feminist conversion gave women the right to define and name not only themselves, but also the world. Leaders taught participants to be suspicious of all men, of male-female relationships, and of all traditional standards of morality and behavior. The right to name therefore gave a woman the right to change values and morals. It allowed her to transfer her faith from her formerly *male* standards to the new standards of feminism.

TOWARDS INTEGRATION

Women's studies were tremendously effective in advancing feminist change. However, it reached only those with a specific interest in women's issues — students who had enrolled in women's studies courses. Because of the limits of this audience, feminist academics directed their attention toward teaching women's studies courses within traditional departments, thereby reaching more students.

> Incorporation of insights from feminist scholarship and teaching into courses outside of women's studies has until very recently been carried out primarily by women's studies faculty teaching standard courses within their disciplines.
>
> The goal to which many women's studies faculty and scholars are hence now turning, in more systematic ways than in the past, is the transformation of the "main" curriculum. Individual campuses, through a variety of approaches and strategies, and often with the added impetus of new priorities from funding agencies sensitive to equity concerns, are developing programs with the explicit goal of expanding the impact of women's studies throughout the institution.[34]

The 1980 National Women's Studies Association Conference in Bloomington, Indiana featured five sessions on incorporating feminist scholarship into the curriculum. It provided impetus for two national conferences in 1981 that served to formalize the curricular change movement.[35] Large grants from federal and private sources expedited the revision of educational materials. The goal of curriculum change through the revision of textbooks further expanded to include the instruction of faculty in women's studies. In order to change faculty attitudes and behavior, some administrators agreed to reward staff doing feminist work, to appoint feminists to key committees and task forces, and to give public recognition to feminist project functions.[36] Schools awarded professors and teachers who went through consciousness raising with merit or salary points. At some colleges faculty CR courses were mandatory. Furthermore, anyone showing interest in feminist theory was quickly provided with the resources and technical assistance necessary for course revision. Books, materials, and speakers were furnished free of charge.

The integration of feminist theory into the mainstream was not confined to the academy. Women's studies courses and seminars within professions — the legal profession in particular — also became commonplace. Judges, law enforcers, medical professionals, politicians, social workers, and others began to have their consciousness raised to the feminist mindset. In this way, feminist theory became integrated into every level and sphere of academic and professional thought.

SUMMARY

Women's studies as an academic discipline was established in the early 1970s as the development of feminist theory entered into its second phase. Women's differences were no longer viewed as a source of weakness; rather, they began to be viewed as *a source of pride and confidence.* The phenomena of women's studies both culminated and mediated this change. Women had progressed from naming themselves to naming the world around them. They had used their unique experience as women to give new meaning to the knowledge, values, and mores of society.

Feminism spread into society at large as graduates of women's studies classes entered the work force. Eventually, women's studies was integrated into all levels of education — kindergarten to college — via the revision of textbook and other core teaching materials. The availability of an unprecedented number of feminist resources and the constant presentation of feminist philosophy in the media further buoyed the trend toward public awareness. Consciousness raising and woman-centered analysis thus moved out from the university and the small group to society as a whole.

Feminists often refer to the 1970s as the "Golden Age" of feminism. At the opening of the decade, their theory was being espoused by a small handful of radicals; but at the close, it had disseminated to the point where it had — to some extent — influenced and affected almost every member of society. Many women had claimed the feminist right to name themselves and their world. And a few, both in secular and religious circles, had started to claim another right — the right to name God.

PART THREE

Naming God

12

The Feminization of God

To exist humanly is to name the self, the world, and God.
The "method" of the evolving spiritual consciousness of
women is nothing less than this beginning to speak humanly
— a reclaiming of the right to name. The liberation of lan-
guage is rooted in the liberation of ourselves.

Mary Daly[1]

I'd like to thank God because *She* made everything possible," Helen
Reddy said when she accepted the Grammy Award for her 1972 song, "I
Am Strong, I Am Invincible, I Am Woman." Betty Friedan, earlier that year,
had predicted that the great debate of the decade would be "Is God *He*?"
To the ordinary Christian, these remarks seemed odd, and perhaps even
blasphemous. The thought that God could be referred to as female was
totally alien to the Christian psyche. Eccentric, pagan philosophers might
discuss it, but not committed believers. However, a decade later, the question was brought to the level of the common religious community. A New
York church forced the issue by erecting a statue of a female Christ on the
cross — complete with breasts, hips and vagina. Through this symbolic act,
feminists directed the attention of even the most uninvolved to the question
of inclusive language and the sex of God.

Christian theologians had, unbeknown to most, been drawn into discussion regarding the Church's use of language. This was not surprising, for
the question had been posed by the feminist linguistic debate in secular circles. Furthermore, Mary Daly had identified the "maleness of God" as a
major problem for the liberation of women in the Church. The secular discussion, initiated by Robin Lakoff, and continued by Casey Miller and Kate
Swift, supported Daly's claim. As Miller and Swift argued,

Nowhere are the semantic roadblocks to sexual equality more apparent
— or significant — than in the language of the dominant organized reli-

gions. . . . Since the major Western religions all originated in patriarchal societies and continue to defend a patriarchal worldview, the metaphors used to express their insights are by tradition and habit overwhelmingly male-oriented.[2]

In the mid-1970s, the National Council of Churches U.S.A. established a task force on sexism in the Bible. The task force was to recommend to the Division of Education and Ministry ways to use Biblical material that would "compensate for its sexism."[3] In 1976, the task force published *The Liberating Word: A Guide to Nonsexist Interpretation of the Bible*.[4] The book was an effort to draw church leaders and members into "finding ways for making worship and study more inclusive of all participants."[5] Letty Russell, whose feminist liberation theology we examined earlier, edited the volume. Sharon Ringe, Elisabeth Schüssler Fiorenza, and Joanna Dewey also contributed chapters.

These women were not alone in their concern over the interpretation of the Bible and the use of language in the Church. The United Presbyterians had embarked on a study concerning language about God, and the Lutheran Church in America had also commenced an investigation regarding the use of inclusive language. In addition, the World Council of Churches had initiated an international study on *The Community of Women and Men in the Church*.[6] The question uttered by Betty Friedan, "Is God He?," was prophetic. It *was* destined to become the debate of the decade.

NEW CONSCIOUSNESS — NEW IMAGES

Our consciousness has come alive in recent years to the sexist language and sex stereotypes in the literature that we read and other resources that we hear and see. . . . At a time when we are discovering clearly the reciprocal nature of language, social structure, and social behavior, we are forced to examine everything from literature to history for its reference, or lack of reference, to women. We are also forced to face the question, What of the Bible? How do we help those who study, teach, and interpret the Bible now to deal with sexism in the Bible? (Letty Russell)[7]

Christian feminists had rejected much of the Bible as "male-biased." Although the Bible "contained" God's words for humanity, they believed that it contained, to a greater extent, the words of men for the self-perpetuation of patriarchy. According to Christian feminists, the Bible itself needed liberation from the human fetters of misogyny that had shackled it. Letty Russell pointed out that:

The Bible was written in a patriarchal culture in which the father was supreme in clan, family, and nation, and wives and children were legally dependent. The interpretation and translation of the Bible through the centuries has been carried out in societies and Christian communities that are male-centered, or androcentric. Just as non-Western cultures must seek to liberate the white, Western interpretations of Scripture and theology so that they are heard anew in different cultures and sub-cultures, women must seek to liberate the interpretation of God's Word from male bias.[8]

As in secular society, Christian feminists identified the reciprocal relationship between language and practical reality. According to feminist theory, linguistic symbols gave shape to the way people acted. But, they noted, if people's behavior changed, then the traditional linguistic symbols were challenged. According to feminists, changing the linguistic symbols would then reciprocally reinforce and initiate further changes in behavior. Russell proposed that this was the case with the language used by the Church.

. . . language and social structures are reciprocal in relationship. Language not only shapes given concepts of reality and ways of acting, it is also shaped by changes in concepts and social behavior. . . . The type of Biblical and theological language used in church services of worship, discussion groups, educational institutions, and publications still tends to exclude women from the Christian community. More and more, women are becoming conscious of their social exclusion reflected in that language and are resisting these subtle and not so subtle forms of discrimination.[9]

Language is a human symbol. It describes a reality outside of itself. Gestures, pictures, images, rhythms, metaphor, myth, rituals — these too, are symbols. Traditional symbols of the Church had presented God as "He," and as King, Lord and Judge. Feminists maintained that these religious symbols excluded women. They argued that the symbols needed to be updated to accommodate the new feminist consciousness. According to feminists, linguistic symbols of the Bible and Church, as well as of God, needed to be altered in order to bring them into line with the inclusive equality of women. Russell argued:

All of us need to assist one another to find our way, not only through more inclusive forms of liturgy, hymns, and theology but also through more inclusive ways of interpreting Scripture. We cannot wait for a new generation of female and male scholars to publish new Bible translations and commentaries that eliminate the hitherto unconscious sexist bias of writers, most of whom are male. Right now, women sit with men in the pews of the church.[10]

THE PROBLEM WITH TRADITIONAL LANGUAGE

In *The Liberating Word*, Russell identified three problems with the use of traditional language in the Church. She declared that this language reinforced inferiority and superiority stereotypes, alienated women, and restricted a full concept of the person and character of God.[11]

Reinforced Inferiority and Superiority Stereotypes

Russell claimed that the language of the Church served to reinforce inferiority and superiority stereotypes. She argued that use of male language, namely, use of the generic *man* and male pronouns to refer to God, excluded women from full participation in the Christian experience, thereby reinforcing male supremacy and relegating the female to the position of "other." According to Russell, everyone was included by these words, "but only in the sense that man is the norm for human and woman is simply a less-than-human appendage of man."[12] Russell argued that the words used in worship were important because of the images they formed in participants' minds.

> The words we use in worship are important also because of the *images* they form in our minds. When we hear the word "man" or "brother" or "son," the image in our mind is most often a masculine image rather than a feminine one. Because these same words are used in reference to the male specific as well as the generic, the masculine becomes much more closely associated with it in our minds. Therefore, the tendency is to form a masculine image when hearing a statement such as "If any *man* is in Christ, *he* is a new creature." The image most of us form is likely to be of a male "man" rather than a female "man." Because the masculine is the image we carry in relation to that word, "man," we subconsciously receive a different message than the one actually intended, a message much more closely tied to the male than to the female human being. When a male or female is constantly bombarded with masculine terminology and masculine imagery, the result is to form the conclusion, unconsciously, that all life is lived in the masculine gender, by the male sex, thus placing the female outside the boundaries of *human* life, in a world of her own.[13] (emphasis added)

Russell, and other feminist theologians, agreed that using the generic "man" to refer to men and women assigned to women an inferior status. Moreover, they contended that the use of masculine pronouns for God contributed to the "fundamental namelessness" of women.[14] Miller and Swift argued that within the Church's use of traditional language, "women have no existence and no essence . . . no share in ontological reality, no relation to the thing-in-itself, which, in the deepest interpretation, is the absolute, is God."[15] They maintained that the language of the Church cast women as inferior and "other."

Inevitably, when words like father and king are used to evoke the image of a personal God, at some level of consciousness it is a male image that takes hold. And since the same symbols are used of male human beings — from whom, out of the need for analogy, the image of God has been drawn — female human beings become less God-like, less perfect, different, "the other."[16]

Alienated Women

Second, Russell argued that the use of traditional language in the Church alienated women. She pointed out that women whose consciousness had been raised found male language to be particularly abrasive. According to Russell, many feminist women were leaving the Church because "[their] consciousness . . . no longer allowed them to accept exclusive language."[17] Judith Weidman echoed Russell's sentiment. She observed that "the more one becomes a feminist, the more difficult it becomes to go to church."[18] Sharon Neufer Emswiler, coauthor of *Women & Worship: A Guide to Nonsexist Hymns, Prayers, and Liturgies*, described her own frustration:

> As I sing I try to imagine that these songs are speaking to me, but I am not accustomed to thinking of myself as a "man" or a "brother"; the identification is difficult, and most often impossible. The only way I can find to identify with these masculine words is to attempt either to deny or set aside my femininity. But I do not want to deny that part of my personhood; I want rather to affirm it. I want my femaleness recognized and affirmed by the Church also. As the worship progresses through the prayers, creeds, and sermon, the same language form keeps recurring — always the masculine when referring to people; always the masculine when referring to God. While I sing and during prayer I change the word "men" to "people," "mankind" to "humankind," "sons" to "children," "Father" to "Parent," but I feel as though I am outshouted by the rest of the congregation. My words are swallowed up by theirs.[19]

Women who had had their consciousness raised through feminism believed that generic language and traditional God-language excluded them. They blamed the language for making them feel hurt, unimportant, unaffirmed, and alienated.

Limited God

According to Russell, the third problem with the use of traditional language was that the Church ran "the risk of making God too small."[20] In conceptualizing God primarily as "Father," she argued that many rich, inclusive Biblical metaphors were neglected. Russell believed that this limited the believer's concept of the person and character of God, for God was thus reduced to male metaphors and masculine imagery. In sum, she reasoned that male language about God restricted people to thinking of God as male.

Virginia Mollenkott, in *The Divine Feminine: The Biblical Imagery of*

God as Female, drew attention to the "feminine" aspect of the character of God. Mollenkott noted that God was pictured in the Bible as a woman giving birth, as nursing mother, *Shekinah* (female presence of Holy Spirit), female homemaker, bakerwoman, mother eagle, mother hen, and Sophia, the Dame Wisdom.[21] She argued that the feminine imagery of God present in the Bible allowed feminists to refer to God as "Mother" as well as "Father." Mollenkott used Psalm 123:2, for example, "as the eyes of a maid look to the hand of her mistress, so our eyes look to the LORD our God . . ." to conclude that "Yahweh is, then, not only our Father and Master who is in heaven, but also our Mother and Mistress who is in heaven."[22] She argued that "If anyone needs any scriptural authorization to address the Lord's prayer to both Father and Mother, Psalm 123:1-2, with its male-female parallelism concerning the divine, would seem to provide that sanction."[23]

Feminists believed that in referring to God as Mother and Father, the concept of God would be "broadened." Russell argued that inclusive language restored wholeness to people's concept of God and also to their self-image.

> In order to relate to God personally in worship and faith, we may ascribe to God both feminine and masculine cultural metaphors as descriptions of our own changing human experience. When we use both feminine and masculine metaphors for God, we are not trying to reinforce stereotyped sex roles of a particular culture. Instead, we are trying to reflect a spectrum of those metaphors, *so that our images of ourselves and of God can be expanded and become more whole.*[24]

Ruether also argued that the male had no special right to image God. According to Ruether, those who imaged God as male were guilty of idolatry.

> If we are to seek an image of God beyond patriarchy, certain basic principles have to be acknowledged. First, we have to acknowledge the principle that the male has no special priority in imaging God. Christian theology has always recognized, theoretically, that all language for God is analogical or metaphorical, not literal. No particular image can be regarded as the exclusive image for God. Images for God must be drawn from the whole range of human experience, from both genders, and all social classes and cultures. To take one image drawn from one gender and in one sociological context (that of the ruling class) as normative for God is to legitimate this gender and social group as the normative possessors of the image of God and representatives of God on earth. *This is idolatry.*[25] (emphasis added)

According to Krister Stendal, dean of Harvard Divinity School, the maleness of God was a "cultural and linguistic accident." He regarded the choice of God-pronouns as having little or no significance. Stendal agreed with Ruether that those who believed that God was, in some way or another, male, were guilty of idolatry.

> The masculinity of God, and of God-language is a cultural and linguistic accident, and I think one should also argue that the masculinity of the Christ is of the same order. To be sure, Jesus Christ was a male, but that may be no more significant to his being than the fact that presumably his eyes were brown. Incarnation is a great thing. But it strikes me as odd to argue that when the Word became flesh, it was to re-enforce male superiority. . . . One started with the idea of "Father" and blew it up into divine proportions. The old process was reversed: Instead of saying that the One who created the world and nurtured the galaxies could even be called "Father" by the mystery of faith, anthropomorphism won out and the Father image became supreme. . . . The time has come to liberate our thoughts of God from such sexism; and a richer trinitarian speculation with the Spirit may be one way toward that goal. *It is obvious that those who say "God" and mean it, cannot accept a male God without falling into idolatry.*[26] (emphasis added)

Feminists argued that male language for God communicated to people that God was male. This was unacceptable to the feminist psyche. According to feminists, traditional language about God neglected the feminine aspect of the divine which was present in Scripture and thereby limited and distorted the picture of who God was.

SEARCH FOR A USABLE LANGUAGE

Feminists argued that traditional language was problematic for the Church. Fiorenza noted its "detrimental effects" on "women's self-understanding and role. . . ."[27] Feminists therefore formulated changes for Church and God-language they believed would enlarge the concept of God and would equalize the role and status of women. According to Russell, women needed a "usable language."[28] She maintained that linguistic changes in the Church were necessary in order to "implement the gospel mandate of full equality for all human beings."[29]

Russell suggested that women were allowed to alter language about God because they were "*theomorphic,* made in God's image."[30] The indwelling "image of God-in-woman" allowed women to experience God themselves and allowed them to express that experience in an appropriate, inclusively linguistic manner. Russell suggested the following changes to make church language inclusive:[31]

1. Do not use Man or Brotherhood in the generic sense, substitute inclusive language such as persons, people, everyone.

2. Avoid masculine pronouns to refer to men and women together by using "he and she," or by shifting to the plural form.

3. Avoid use of male-dominant phrases where all the people of God are to be included. Sons of God to children of God; "faith of our fathers" to "faith of our forbears, ancestors, or forerunners."

4. Call both women and men by their full names. Not John Brown and his wife, but John and Sally Brown, or Ms. when preferred by women.

5. Alternate references to women and men in speech and writing, he and she, she and he, etc.

6. Refer to the clergy as clergy persons rather than clergymen; clergy and spouses, not clergy and wives.

7. Avoid referring to people and the Church with female pronouns.

As Russell put it:

The regular use of feminine metaphors and pronouns for the church tends to reflect a cultural stereotype that the feminine is inferior to the masculine, as in the metaphor of a feminine church and a masculine God. It reflects a setting in which God and husband were identified as Lord, and Israel, church, and wife were identified as servant.[32]

Russell also suggested changes in the way Christians referred to God:

1. "Names for God should avoid excessive use of male imagery and pronouns and those which model the social relationships of patriarchal culture, such as 'Father,' 'King,' 'master.' . . . It is also helpful to include references of both masculine and feminine pairs (Mother and Father, he and she)."[33]

2. Avoid the overuse of the words "Our Father," substitute "Our parent" or "Our God."

3. Emphasize non-sex specific words for God, such as Spirit, Wisdom, Glory, Holy One, Rock, Fire, First and Last, Sustainer, Liberator, Creator, Advocate, Maker, Defender, Friend, Nurturer. In addition, it is suggested that the trinitarian formula of "Father, Son and Holy Spirit," be changed to "Creator, Redeemer, Sustainer," or "Source, Servant, Guide."[34]

4. Speak about Jesus as male only when the designation refers to his earthly life as a male.

5. Speak of the Holy Spirit as "she" or "it."

THE LORD'S PRAYER

Following is an example of an inclusive modification of The Lord's Prayer as proposed in *Women & Worship*.[35]

Traditional Reading	Modified Reading
Our Father, who art in heaven,	Our Mother/Father, who is everywhere,
Hallowed be Thy name.	Holy be your names.
Thy kingdom come,	May your new age come
Thy will be done,	May your will be done
On earth, as it is in heaven.	In this and in every time and place.
Give us this day our daily bread,	Meet our needs each day and
And forgive us our debts,	Forgive our failure to love
As we forgive our debtors.	As we forgive this same failure in others.
And lead us not into temptation,	Save us in hard times, and
But deliver us from evil.	Lead us into the ways of love.
For Thine is the kingdom, and the power,	For yours is the wholeness, and the power,
And the glory, forever. Amen.	And the loving, forever. Amen.

THE POWER OF IMAGERY AND SYMBOL

> ... [feminist] attempts at rethinking and re-experiencing call for a critique and renewal of the traditional language of theology and liturgy and everyday life. For that reason I take the matter of pronouns seriously. To many, such concerns seem trivial or ridiculous. They are not. Language is powerful.[36]

Russell pointed out that language, symbols, and metaphors are powerful. She believed they affected our view of God and of ourselves.[37] Therefore, she believed it was essential to alter the language used to refer to God in order to reflect a feminist understanding of God. But by changing the Biblical symbols, Russell altered and renamed God. This is a serious matter. For if feminism's altered view of God is out of synchronization with who God really *is*, as He has revealed Himself, then it is not really God whom they are imaging and worshiping; and *this* is the idolatry which the Bible condemns.

THE ALTERED IMAGES OF INCLUSIVE LANGUAGE

> A child who has been taught to pray to a Mother in Heaven would have a religious life radically different from that of a Christian child. (C. S. Lewis)[38]

God is not a man, but for the most part He chose to relate Himself to us as masculine. The inclusive language proposed by feminist theology alters the traditional masculine pronouns for God. It renames Him. Feminists argue that this is necessary in order to equalize the position of women in the Church. But is feminist inclusive language justified, or are the symbols themselves too important to be tampered with? In other words, do the pronouns and descriptors used in the Bible give real knowledge about who God is and what He is like, or do they merely evoke feelings of reverence toward a God who is basically ineffable and undefinable, and who will always remain hidden from human sight and understanding?[39] Can women *know* God, as He has revealed Himself, or are they left on their own to intuitively imagine who God is?

Feminist theologians reminded Christians that much of Scripture's language is symbolic and pictorial. But, rather than believing that the words give real knowledge about God, they viewed the Biblical words of faith as "ciphers of transcendence,"[40] alterable symbols pointing to a God who was an impersonal or suprapersonal force, or the "ground of all being." Essentially, feminist theologians regarded the language of faith as standing in the way of knowledge of God rather than the indispensable means for knowing God. They argued that the use of masculine pronouns for God limited the believer's concept of who God is. Because the Bible symbolizes God as possessing "feminine" characteristics, feminists felt that they could take the liberty of calling God "She" or "Mother." This, they argued, would more accurately communicate the true character of God. Feminists took a quantum leap, however, when they moved from observing the feminine characteristics of God to the practice of addressing God with feminine pronouns. When feminists changed Biblical language about God, they changed the Biblical image of God. Furthermore, in altering the Biblical image of God, feminists altered the image they held of themselves as humans. Although a detailed discussion is beyond this book's parameters, it is important to notice the effect that feminist inclusive language has had upon their image and definition of God and humanity.

Sexualized God

Feminists claimed that using female as well as male pronouns to address God would de-sexualize Him. In effect, the opposite occurred. When feminists switched from the masculine to the feminine in their description of God, they reduced God to sexuality. They presented an image of a deity who is bisexual or androgynous rather than one who transcends the polarity of the sexes.[41]

Depersonalized God

In renaming God as She/He, feminists stripped God of independent, personalized existence. God is an individual, personalized entity who chose to relate to us primarily as "male." God is not merely a "force." When feminists transformed the Biblical feminine metaphor for the Divine into a name for God, they needed to extend that practice to other metaphors as well. God became "rock," "eagle," "door," etc. His personality was thus further diffused to encompass all natural phenomena. Renaming God in a way other than He had named Himself logically led to an erosion of God's independent personality. God became a "force." This was transparently evident in feminist theology. By 1988, for example, "evangelical" feminist Virginia Mollenkott had extended God's name from He/She to "He/She/It."[42]

Attacked God's Character

Feminists insisted that God should not be addressed as *Father, Ruler, Judge, Master,* and *King.* They argued that these words bore patriarchal, male-associated overtones. However, disregarding these names for God reduced and castrated His character, for the words are not merely figurative, but reflect true aspects of God's character. The same could not be said of Jesus as the "door," or the true "vine." These were metaphors drawn from cultural experience that illumined and at the same time veiled the mystery of the divinity of Christ.[43] But such words as Father and Lord, when applied to God, although they too were analogies, were analogies *sui generis.*[44] That is, they were not derived from the experience of human fatherhood or lordship, but from God's act of revealing Himself as Father and Lord. Donald Bloesch, author of *The Battle for the Trinity: The Debate over Inclusive God Language,* maintained that "[t]hey are therefore more accurately described as *catalogies* than analogies insofar as they come from above."[45] He reasoned that they should be considered as "transformational images" in that they drastically alter the ordinary or cultural understanding of the terms. Bloesch explained that "it is not that God resembles a Father, but in calling him Father the Bible challenges the human view of what a father should be. The same is true for depictions of God as Judge, Lord, Savior, and Son."[46]

Lord, King, Judge, and *Father* are not symbols corresponding to inner feelings or experiences, but to ontological realities of *who God is.* Their frame of reference is objective rather than subjective. Bloesch pointed out that they are "hierarchical and organic symbols, not male images."[47] Therefore, in changing these symbols, feminists attacked the very essence of God's character.

Denied the Trinitarian Relationship

Feminist theologians suggested a number of alternatives to the traditional trinitarian formula of Father/Son/Holy Spirit. They proposed in its stead names such as Creator/Redeemer/Sustainer or Source/Servant/Guide. The difficulty with this practice is that it speaks to what God *does* rather than to who He *is.* Father/Son/Holy Spirit refers to a threefold self-relatedness within the Godhead and not to a human or societal relationship.[48] The trinitarian names are ontological symbols based on divine revelation rather than personal metaphors having their origin in cultural experience.

The feminist practice of inclusive Trinitarian language obscures the intra-trinitarian relation between the Son and the Father. The Son was obedient to the Father though He is equal to the Father. The Father, in love, sacrificed the Son. The Son, who had the right to refuse, submitted to the Father. Denial of the Trinitarian relationship denies the concept of equality and hierarchy that is evident in the Godhead and throughout Scripture. Furthermore, it would have been easy for a *Creator* to sacrifice a *Redeemer*, but it was not so easy for a *Father* to sacrifice his *Son*. Understanding God — Father/Son/Holy Spirit — as being in relationship within Himself is essential to understanding God. In denying this relationship, feminists deny who God is.[49]

Obscured the Person and Work of Christ

Inclusive language, in addition to obscuring Christ's relationship to the Father, obscured the person and work of Jesus. Feminists argued that the fact of Jesus' maleness is inconsequential. Emswiler reasoned, "if the society had been reversed and Palestine had been a matriarchy instead of a patriarchy, surely God would have sent her Daughter."[50] Feminists therefore urged believers to change their language about Christ. In the place of *Son of Man*, which was considered too masculine, they spoke of *the Human One*. Here again, an alteration in root symbols entailed a transformation in meaning. Bloesch observed that *Son of Man* is an honorific title indicating a supernatural being, whereas *the Human One* was merely a model of authentic selfhood.[51] Through feminist theologians' inclusive language, Christ is viewed as a model of the new humanity, the one sent by God to reveal to us what we could become, rather than God Almighty in the flesh, who took upon Himself the penalty for our sins.

Obscured Humanity's Relationship to God

Inclusive language obscured who God is, and it therefore obscured who we are. The Bible presents male and female imagery as being *fundamental* to understanding God's relationship to His chosen people, and for understanding who humans are in relationship to Him. The Church is presented as Christ's bride — all believers being "female" in this respect. In order to respond to God, all people, both male and female, need to be in touch with the feminine, intuitive, symbolic aspect of their character: "God is, after all, so masculine that we are all feminine in relation to Him."[52] The God of the Bible, unlike the gods and goddesses of pagan religions, had no consort. We, the Church, are His consort, and this means that the Church constitutes the feminine dimension of the sacred.[53] When feminists lost the God-imagery of masculinity and femininity taught in the Bible, they lost the ability to view themselves in the proper manner, and therefore lost the ability to interact properly with God.

Confused Personal Identity

Feminist theology and philosophy obscured, for many people, what it meant to be male or female. Many believers did not understand that masculine and feminine aspects of character coexist within the individual psyche of all humans, and also coexist in the character of God. Men and women who adopted feminist precepts lost touch with the feminine inter-relationship between themselves and God and correspondingly shunned masculine/feminine distinction in relationships between humans. They lost perspective of who God is and also perspective of who they — as male and female — are. An improper view of God led to an improper self-identity.

Renaming themselves and their world led feminist theologians to rename God. In this way, they claimed God's prerogative for themselves. They became the authority which named their destiny. For instance, feminist naming led Rita Nakashima Brock to deny the central role of Christ in Christianity:

> If Christology is to be reclaimed in feminist visions, the image of an exclusive divine presence in a "perfect" man called Jesus who came to be called the Christ is disallowed. The doctrine that only a perfect male form can incarnate God fully and be salvific makes our individual lives in female bodies a prison against God and denies our actual, sensual, changing selves as the locus of divine activity. . . . Jesus Christ need not be the authoritative center of a feminist Christian faith. . . . We reclaim the Christological symbol system when we see it as part of a *community self-naming process.*[54] (emphasis added)

Feminist naming led Rosemary Ruether to deny God's fatherhood and authority:

> . . . even parent language must be recognized as a limited image for God. It does not exhaust the way we should image our relationship to God. Overreliance on parental imagery for God suggests that we should relate to God primarily in the mode of childlike dependency. When this mode of relationship is made the primary language for God, it promotes spiritual infantilism and cuts off moral maturity and responsibility. God becomes the neurotic parent who wishes us to remain always dependent children and is angry with us when we want to grow up. . . . We need to see the *dynamic relationship between God as the source of our being* and God as the empowerer of *our aspiration* and growth toward new being, toward redeemed and fulfilled humanity.[55] (emphasis added)

NAMING GOD

The phenomena of inclusive language recognized and further served to reinforce the paradigm offered by feminist theology. It, more than the theological rhetoric, brought the feminist debate to the level of the ordinary believer, as women's studies had done. Feminist theology was thereby translated from an academic philosophy to the level of practical daily worship of the Christian community. Feminists had named themselves and their world, and now, through inclusive language, they and their Christian communities began to name God.

13

Changing of the Gods

God is going to change. We women are going to bring an end to God.

Naomi Goldenberg

The evening of April 23, 1976 was crisp. The fragrance of the crocus and the buds of spring laced the air in and around the old stone church in the heart of Boston. Women, who filled the church's antiquated wood benches and spilled over onto the floor and into the aisles, hardly noticed the aromatic bouquet. Their excited murmurs were hushed suddenly by the dimming of lights and the lone, still cry of a flute. A white-robed, almost luminous figure, followed by a small entourage, slowly approached the central rostrum to perform a ritual. The first national all-woman conference on women's spirituality had begun.

Through the Looking Glass: A Gynergenetic Experience — the title for the three-day conference was unusual, alluding to some sort of mystical personal discovery. It was, in fact, a conference that formally consummated the growing link between secular feminism and spirituality — between the women's movement and the immemorial Craft of Wicca (witchcraft).

Robin Morgan, feminist poet and priestess of a Dianic coven, led the ritual that best characterized the conference's tenor. Poised before the altar at the front of the church, her face illuminated by a flickering candle, Morgan spoke:

In the infinite moment before all Time began, the Goddess arose from Chaos and gave birth to Herself. . . before anything else had been born . . . not even Herself. And when She had separated the Skies from the Waters and had danced upon them, the Goddess in Her ecstasy created everything that is. Her movements made the wind, and the Element Air was born and did breathe.

A candle was lit in the east. Morgan spoke again.

> And the Goddess named Herself: Arianrhod — Carea — Astarte. And
> sparks were struck from Her dancing feet so that She shone forth as the
> Sun, and the stars were caught in Her hair, and comets raced about Her,
> and Element Fire was born.

A candle was lit in the south.

> And the Goddess named Herself: Sunna — Vesta — Pele. About her feet
> swirled the waters in tidal wave and river and streaming tide, and Element
> Water did flow.

A candle was lit in the west.

> And She named Herself: Binah — Mari Morgaine — Lakshmi. And She
> sought to rest Her feet from their dance, and She brought forth the Earth
> so that the shores were Her footstool, the fertile lands Her womb, the
> mountains Her full breasts, and Her streaming hair the growing things.

A candle was lit in the north.

> And the Goddess named Herself: Cerridwen — Demeter — the Corn
> Mother. She saw that which was and is and will be, born of Her sacred
> dance and cosmic delight and infinite joy. She laughed: and the Goddess
> created Woman in her own image . . . to be the Priestess of the Great
> Mother. The Goddess spoke to Her daughters, saying, "I am the Moon
> to light your path and to speak to your rhythms. I am the Sun who gives
> you warmth in which to stretch and grow. I am the Wind to blow at your
> call and the sparkling Air that offers joy. . . . I shall be called a million
> names. Call unto me, daughters. . . ."

A heavy iron cauldron was filled with fire, and soft chanting began.

> The Goddess Is Alive — Magic Is Afoot.
> The Goddess Is Alive — Magic Is Afoot.

The volume and intensity of the chant grew. Women began to jump,
stamp, clap, and yell. They stood on pews and waved their arms; some
danced bare-breasted on the pulpit. Women gave vent to uninhibited emotions as the rhythmic echo crescendoed.

> The Goddess Is Alive — Magic Is Afoot.

Morgan shouted:

We are Virgins, Mothers, Old Ones — All. We offer our created energy: to the Spirit of Women Past, to the Spirit of Women yet to come, to womanspirit present and growing. Behold, WE MOVE FORWARD TOGETHER!

"The goddess is alive — magic is afoot!" the crowd answered in unison. The cadence of the chant quickened, and the volume escalated to primeval proportions. The rafters of the church began to shake.

THE GODDESS IS ALIVE — MAGIC IS AFOOT![1]

Although the ultimate quest of the secular woman's movement had always been spiritual, the movement had, until this point, been focused primarily on political action. In the early seventies, woman-centered analysis of medicine had encouraged a return to the ancient art of witchcraft. Similarly, Elizabeth Gould Davis, in *The First Sex*, had hinted at the existence of a matriarchal goddess religion of the past. But it was Robin Morgan who, at a lesbian feminist conference in Los Angeles in 1973, initiated the merging of feminist politics with women's spirituality. In the keynote address of the conference, Morgan identified the need for personal empowerment in order to persevere with feminist corporate political activism. She cited her own source of strength as being drawn from the ancient art of Wicca. Morgan's closing words were drawn from *The Charge of the Goddess*:

Listen to the words of the Great Mother. She says: "whenever ye have need of anything, once in the month, and better it be when the moon is full, then shall ye assemble in some secret place . . . to these I will teach things that are yet unknown. *And ye shall be free from all slavery.* . . . Keep pure your highest ideal; strive ever toward it. Let naught stop you nor turn you aside. . . . Mine is the cup of the wine of life and the cauldron of Cerridwen. . . . I am the Mother of all living, and my love is poured out upon the Earth. . . . I am the beauty of the Green Earth, and the White Moon among the stars, and the Mystery of the Waters, *and the desire in the heart of woman.* . . . Before my face, let thine innermost divine self be enfolded in the raptures of the Infinite. . . . Know the Mystery, that if that which thou seekest thou findest not within thee, thou wilt never find it without thee. . . . For behold, I have been with thee from the beginning. And I await you now." [2]

Morgan's disclosure of herself as a witch popularized the pursuit of spirituality within the movement. Feminists such as Mary Daly in *Beyond God the Father*, Merlin Stone in *When God Was a Woman*, and Morgan herself in *Going Too Far* articulated their spiritual experiences and new religious concepts. Because feminism validated woman's experience, the neoteric propositions of these women gained rapid acceptance and were soon embraced *en masse* by others. One feminist, quoted by Margot Adler in *Drawing Down the Moon*, described the process:

> Feminism tells us to trust ourselves. So feminists began experiencing something. We began to believe that, yes indeed, we were discriminated against on the job; we began to see that motherhood was not all it was advertised to be. We began to trust our own feelings, we began to believe in our own orgasms. These were the first things. Now we are beginning to have spiritual experiences and, for the first time in thousands of years, we trust it. We say, "Oh this is an experience of mine, and feminism tells me there must be something to this, because it's all right to trust myself!" So women began to trust what they were experiencing.[3]

WOMEN'S LIBERATION AS SPIRITUAL REVOLUTION

Since its inception, the ultimate goal of women's liberation had been the attainment of personal meaning, value, and wholeness — an undeniably spiritual pursuit. Morgan, Daly, and Stone had come to recognize this fact. Daly observed:

> . . . the women's revolution, insofar as it is true to its own essential dynamics, is an ontological, spiritual revolution, pointing beyond the idolatries of sexist society and sparking creative action in and toward transcendence. The becoming of women implies universal human becoming. It has everything to do with the search for ultimate meaning and reality, which some would call God.[4]

Feminists believed that women would find themselves through the disintegration of sex roles and stereotypes. They would become transcendent when they discovered "God" as a personal experience of wholeness and meaning. Daly noted:

> The becoming of women may be not only the doorway to deliverance which secular humanism has passionately fought for — but also a doorway *to* something, that is, a new phase in the human spirit's quest for God.[5]

Secular feminists had named and defined themselves and the world around them in order to become whole. What remained to do — in order to fulfill the spiritual nature of their quest — was to name and define God.

THE CASE AGAINST GOD THE FATHER

To exist humanly is to name the self, the world, and God.[6]

The discourse surrounding women's spirituality first needed to deal with the question of who or what God is. Feminists first established that they could not accept the vision of the Yahweh Creator God presented by "traditional patriarchal religions." They rejected the Biblical God who delineated between right and wrong, who demanded complete worship and obedience, and who "lorded" it over people by judging those who did not conform to His will. Such a God, they charged, was dualistic and oppressive. Furthermore, the fact that this God was figured as a male legitimized male supremacy. "If God is male, then the male is God" was the feminist axiom.[7] Feminists reasoned that in rejecting men as "gods," they also needed to reject a God who was male. According to Daly, the male "God" functioned only to "legitimate the existing social, economic, and political status quo, in which women and other victimized groups [were] subordinate."[8] She reasoned that the patriarchy cast God as male in order to retain power for men over women. Morgan argued, "Not the least devastating gesture of patriarchal power has been to cast the cosmos itself — the life force, energy, matter, and miracle — into the form of a male god."[9] Daly concurred, maintaining that:

> The symbol of the Father God, spawned in the human imagination and sustained as plausible by patriarchy, has in turn rendered service to [patriarchal] society by making its mechanism for the oppression of women appear right and fitting. If God in "his" heaven is a father ruling "his" people, then it is in the "nature" of things and according to divine plan and the order of the universe that society be male-dominated.[10]

Not only had a male God functioned to oppress women, such a God had also denied women's inherent power and identity, feminists argued. According to Charlene Spretnak, a popular feminist author, He had prevented women "from achieving, or even supposing, their potential: that they are powerful in both mind and body and that the totality of those powers is potent force."[11] Naomi Goldenberg argued that a male God had further robbed women of "the experience of seeing *themselves* as divine beings"[12] (emphasis added).

The so-called "male-defined male" God of the Judeo-Christian religion was found to be unacceptable to a woman-centered analysis of reality and to the female quest for spirituality. Therefore, feminist women decided to discard Him. Daly observed:

> . . . the woman's movement . . . appears destined to play the key role in the overthrow of [God]. It presents a growing threat to the plausibility of the inadequate popular "God" not so much by attacking "him" as by leaving "him" behind. Few major feminists display great interest in institutional religion. Yet this disinterest can hardly be equated with lack of spiritual consciousness. Rather, in our present experience the woman-

consciousness is being wrenched free to find its own religious expression.[13]

Feminists left the Judeo-Christian concept of God behind in order to discover and name "God" for themselves. They used their own experience to judge the validity of the divine. As they had named themselves and their world, so they would name God. According to Daly:

> . . . [feminist] women will be forced in a dramatic way to confront the most haunting of human questions, the question of God. . . . There is a dynamism in the ontological affirmation of self that reaches out toward the nameless God. In hearing and naming ourselves out of the depths, women are naming toward God. . . .[14]

CHANGING OF THE GODS

> The new wave of feminism desperately needs to be not only many-faceted but cosmic and ultimately religious in its vision. This means reaching outward and inward toward the God beyond and beneath the gods who have stolen our identity.[15]

For feminists to move toward a new feminist God, they had to propose several new concepts. For instance, Daly suggested that God is a *verb* rather than a noun. She conceptualized "God" as the power of creative energy and the process of growth that constantly witnessed rebirth and renewal of the self in the process of self-actualization:

> When women take positive steps to move out of patriarchal space and time, there is a surge of new life. . . . I would analyze this as participation in God the Verb who cannot be broken down simply into past, present, and future time, since God is form-destroying, form-creating, transforming power that makes all things new.[16]

In contrast to Daly's obtuse description of God, Merlin Stone objectified Deity in a more concrete form by extensively researching ancient goddess cults. She explored Celtic, Greek, Egyptian, and other Eastern mythologies in order to present an overview of the actual practice of goddess worship. The religion of the goddess had focused on mythic female deities most often symbolized by stone idols or other art forms. Stone argued that patriarchal men had systematically replaced these female deities and the worship of the female with the Judeo-Christian mythology of a male God. While she did not advocate a revival of ancient goddess worship, she hoped that an awareness of the matriarchal religion would empower women to stand against and overcome Judeo-Christian patriarchal traditions and beliefs. Feminist poet Robin Morgan connected the ideas of Daly and Stone together and gave them pragmatic shape. According to Morgan, God could be understood as a process of being or discovering oneself, but could also be objectified and symbolized by a female deity. Belief in the power of the female, symbolized by the goddess, therefore became the religion that replaced patriarchal religions.

The feminist "right to name" allowed women to dictate the shape of religion based on their own experience. Feminists encouraged women to use their imagination in creating new visions of God and new forms of worship and ritual. Morgan chose to use the rituals and practices of Wicca; but, according to journalist Margot Adler, any and all forms of worship and religious expression were accepted as part of "The Goddess Experience."[17] This was evidenced throughout the three-day Boston conference on women's spirituality (1976) where many new forms of religious expression were explored. Some women led workshops on music, dance, and painting, while others taught rituals and incantations of witchcraft. Participants accepted all expressions of personal feelings as appropriate vehicles for communication of religious sentiments. Worship consisted of sharing skills useful in the nurture and representation of spiritual life. Leaders instructed participants to set aside a small corner of their homes as an altar to be used for meditation and focusing of their wills. They were to set up a mirror to represent the goddess. In that way, women would continually remind themselves that *"they* were the Goddess and that *they* had divine beauty, power and dignity."[18]

Feminist spirituality embodied the idea that each woman was her own judge of what constituted religious experience. Each woman could choose for herself how to symbolize and worship God, provided that she recognized God as being a female force. Feminists dethroned the Judeo-Christian male God and proudly set themselves up in His place. Lest this seem overly brash and presumptuous, they justified it by pointing to the ancient practice of goddess worship and witchcraft (which they claimed predated the Judeo-Christian religion) and which presumably exalted women and the female power.

THE SPIRITUAL/POLITICAL CONNECTION

Feminist theorists presented the spiritual aspect of feminism as being necessary for political action. Spiritualism was presented as the energy that would empower women to continue pursuing their feminist social and political agendas. Morgan, for example, taught that the separation of the spiritual from the political was a false idea born of patriarchy. According to Morgan, the spiritual aspect of feminism could not be separated from the political. Z. Budapest, a witch who established the Susan B. Anthony Coven, also saw an intimate connection between spirituality and day-to-day political action. Budapest called religion the "supreme politics."[19] Her coven's Manifesto stated:

We believe that in order to fight and win a revolution that will stretch for generations into the future, we must find reliable ways to replenish our energies. We believe that without a secure grounding in woman's spiritual strength there will be no victory for us. . . . We are equally committed to political, communal and personal solutions.[20]

In 1982, *The Politics of Women's Spirituality* was published. This massive volume, edited by Charlene Spretnak, presented dozens of essays on the rise of spiritual power within the feminist movement. The work was divided into three sections. The first, entitled "Discovering a History of Power," spoke of The Great Goddess, who she was and what she meant to women. It presented mythic Heras and Amazons as models of strength and wisdom. It also presented "phenomenological, psychological and political" reasons why women needed the goddess. The second section, "Manifesting Personal Power," explored feminist witchcraft, contemporary feminist rituals, meditations, communion with the goddess, hypnosis, Tarot, astrology, and the realization of personal power through self-discovery and knowledge. It spoke of women healers: psychics, herbalists, body therapists, energy healers, ritualists, midwives, dream-interpreters, deathguides, and of the healing power of women through the laying on of hands and imaging. The last section, "Transforming the Political," advocated the transformation of the political into a spiritual movement. It presented the women's movement as a "cosmic covenant" of sisterhood and as a communal journey into a religious space untouched by sexism, an "exodus community."[21] It argued that the personal and spiritual were indeed political and that every process of change had both a political and a spiritual dimension.[22] The book presented spirituality as the model for feminist revolution. In closing, Starhawk proposed a metaphysical feminist worldview; one centered on the "immanent divinity found within nature, oneself, and the world."[23] According to the feminist theorists who contributed to Spretnak's book, it was this worldview that was necessary in order to usher in a new era of existence for humanity. Spretnak agreed that a metaphysical mysticism would allow feminists to see their inner power and give them strength to push for the prevalence of the feminist vision:

The global feminist movement is bringing about the end of patriarchy, the eclipse of the politics of separation, and the beginning of a new era modeled on the dynamic, holistic paradigm. . . . The gains that we make in legal, economic, medical, and educational areas will be short-lived unless they are grounded in collective action that is continually fueled by a strong sense of our personal power and its elemental source. In fact, without that sense of inner power, without the sense that we are the source of change, our vision will not prevail.[24]

With the formal pursuit of spirituality, the impelling force of the feminist movement had finally bubbled up to the surface. Feminists held a vision far broader than the political and social goals initially pursued. Feminism had always been, in essence, a religious movement, and now it was openly recognized as such. Feminists had decided that they could not find wholeness and meaning within the traditional Judeo-Christian paradigm. However, their rejection of the traditional framework necessitated creation of an alternate source of spiritual fulfillment. For this, they looked to themselves. As Spretnak proclaimed:

> Ours is a working, activist philosophy of existence — on *our own terms*. At the center of our expanding spiral is a creative self-love and self-knowledge. We have barely tapped the power that is ours. *We are more than we know.*

> *Blessed Be*
> *It Is You Who Is a Hera*
> *It Is You Who Is Wise and Strong*
> *It Is You Who Are The Power*
> *and Flow of Change*
> *Blessed Be*[25]

14

Going Too Far: The Feminist Metaphysic

This Possibility: That you are God, and God is You.

Christine De Pisane[1]

The 1976 Boston conference ushered in the third phase of the development of feminist theory — the spiritual quest. Feminists had progressed from viewing their differences with pride and confidence, to viewing them as deitic in essence. This third phase, which emerged in the late 1970s and early 1980s, focused on esoteric metaphysics — an inner journey of self-discovery that supposedly provided the mystical answer to life's meaning by allowing the seeker to experience connectedness with the universe and with the reality of her own power. Secular feminist women had moved from defining themselves and their world towards defining and naming God.

The philosophy of feminism had convinced women that their own experience was the only valid source of meaning. As this philosophy developed, feminists naturally looked within to discover the "truth" about God. Since they had rejected an external "male god," they sought a new symbol that would affirm the legitimacy of their personal experience and self-definition: the goddess.

THE MEANING OF THE SYMBOL OF THE GODDESS

Initially, feminists reacted with scorn to the goddess and goddess worship. Why would intelligent, self-defining women want to bow down to ancient idols of stone? But feminists learned that goddess worship was not worship of an external deity; it was, in essence, worship of oneself. The goddess was merely a symbol that acknowledged the legitimacy of self-worship. As Carol

Christ, associate professor of women's studies and religious studies at San Jose State University, explained:

> The simplest and most basic meaning of the symbol of Goddess is the acknowledgement of the legitimacy of female power as a beneficent and independent power. A woman who echoes Ntozake Shange's dramatic statement, "I found God in myself and I loved her fiercely," is saying "Female power is strong and creative." She is saying that the divine principle, the saving and sustaining power, is in herself, that she will no longer look to men or male figures as saviors.[2]

According to Carol Christ, the symbol of goddess affirmed female power, the female body, the female will, and women's bonds and heritage.[3] She argued that the goddess symbol was of vital importance to women. Starhawk, a feminist priestess, agreed. She maintained that the importance of the goddess symbol for woman could not be overstressed. It was a symbol, she said, that energized and focused women's potential. Starhawk argued that through this symbol women could truly become whole.

> The image of the Goddess inspires women to see ourselves as divine, our bodies as sacred, the changing phases of our lives as holy, our aggression as healthy, our anger as purifying, and our power to nurture and create, but also to limit and destroy when necessary, as the very force that sustains all life. Through the Goddess, we can discover our strength, enlighten our minds, own our bodies, and celebrate our emotions. We can move beyond narrow, constricting roles and become whole.[4]

Most feminists identified the goddess as the power that flowed through the universe and could be tapped and realized in the individual female psyche. A few believed that the goddess was divine female — an actual "*personification* who could be invoked in prayer and ritual."[5] Although there existed some variance of opinion regarding the actual meaning of the goddess, feminists generally agreed that the goddess symbol was necessary. As Carol Christ pointed out, "Symbol systems cannot simply be rejected, they must be replaced. Where there is no replacement, the mind will revert to familiar structures at times of crisis, bafflement, or defeat."[6] The rejection of the Judeo-Christian God left a vacuum that needed to be filled. Feminists reached into themselves to fill the hole, and used the goddess as a symbol of their inherent right and power to do so. Margot Adler explained:

> Many of us had a real difficulty with the concept of a goddess. Who was this goddess and why was she created? We felt she represented different forms of energy and light to different people. Even though we had trouble with the words, we felt that the force of the goddess was inevitable, she was flowing through us all by whatever name, she was the feeling of

the presence of life. *Goddess was a new name for our spiritual journey, the experience of life.*[7] (emphasis added)

THEMES OF SECULAR FEMINIST SPIRITUALITY

Feminist spirituality did not begin as an organized religion with established doctrine; but by the end of the eighties, clear themes became apparent.

Monism: All Is One

Monism, the first theme of feminist spirituality, is the belief that everything exists as one, as unified parts of a whole.[8] All is interrelated, interdependent, and interpenetrating.[9] Ultimately, monism asserts there is no difference between God, a person, an apple, or a stone. They are part of a continuous reality that has no boundaries and no divisions. Feminist spirituality promotes monism. According to Starhawk:

> The Goddess is not separate from the world — She is the world, and all things in it: moon, sun, earth, star, stone, seed, flowing river, wind, wave, leaf and branch, bud and blossom, fang and claw, woman and man . . . flesh and spirit are one.[10]

Pantheism: All Is God

Pantheism, a closely related second theme within feminist spirituality, asserts that "all is God." All matter — plants, animals, objects — were said to partake of one divine essence. Pantheism stripped God of individual, independent existence. Feminists abandoned the idea of a personal God in favor of an impersonal female energy, force, or consciousness.[11] According to Spretnak:

> The revival of the Goddess has resonated with so many people because She symbolizes *the way things really are*: All forms of being are One, continually renewed in cyclic rhythms of birth, maturation, death. That is the meaning of Her triple aspect — the waxing, full, and waning moon; the maiden, mother, and wise crone. The Goddess honors *union and process*, the cosmic dance, the eternally vibrating flux of matter/energy: She expresses the dynamic, rather than static, model of the universe. She is *immanent* in our lives and our world. She contains both female and male, in Her womb, as a male deity cannot; all beings are *part of Her*, not distant creations. She also symbolizes the power of the female body/mind. There is no "party line" of Goddess worship; rather, each person's process of perceiving and living Her truth is a movement in the larger dance — hence the phrase "The Goddess Is All."[12]

Self Is God

The third theme in feminist spirituality logically followed the preceding two. For if all is one, and all is God, then God is in all, and God exists within the feminine psyche. Self is God. Starhawk believed that "the Goddess has infinite aspects and thousands of names." Furthermore, "she is the reality behind many metaphors. She is reality, the manifest deity, omnipresent in all of life, *in each of us.*"[13] Consequently, Starhawk argued that each woman needed to reveal her own truth. According to her analysis, "deity is seen in our own forms. . . . Religion is a matter of re-linking, with the divine within and with Her outer manifestations in all of the human and natural world."[14] Z. Budapest, founder of the Susan B. Anthony Coven, stated this precept quite succinctly when she observed:

> There was opposition within the feminist movement toward the spiritual movement. Those who didn't share the experiences wondered why intelligent women would want to "worship the Goddess." They missed the crucial meaning: *It is self-worship.* If the Goddess is seen as being "out there" (or "up there"), it is because all living things are a part of Her: trees, stars, moon, honeybees, rocks, and us. Just as She has thousands of different names, She can be worshipped in thousands of different ways. It will take time for women to get rid of patriarchal ways of worshipping. If some see Her as sitting up on a cloud with Her magic wand blessing them, maybe this is a step toward seeing Her inside themselves. In the Susan B. Coven, we teach that women are the Goddess every time we make a choice.[15]

Another feminist, Judith Antonelli, argued, "Women today who are trying to bring back Goddess worship are not worshipping idols, escaping through mysticism, or revering an external god-substitute. The Goddess represents nothing less than female power and woman's deification of her own essence. It is external only to the extent that this power is contained within the cycles of nature as well as within ourselves."[16]

A New Consciousness

In order for women to experience themselves as goddess, they needed a new framework. Women needed to purge themselves of the patriarchal (i.e., Judeo-Christian) system of thought that presented God as an external being. Starhawk argued that goddess worship unveiled an alternate form of consciousness. This consciousness, she explained, consisted of immanence — the theology of God pervading and being contained within the universe and self.

> . . . another form of consciousness is possible, indeed, has existed from earliest times. It underlies other cultures and has survived even in the West in hidden streams. This is the consciousness I call immanence — the awareness of the world and everything in it as alive, dynamic, interdependent, and interacting, infused with moving energies: a living being, a weaving dance.

The symbol, the "normative image," of immanence is the Goddess: the Divine embodied in nature, in human beings, in the flesh.[17]

A New Humanity

The fifth theme apparent in the new feminist spirituality is the creation of a new humanity. Through immanence, feminists believed they would usher in a new reality and context of meaning that would free humanity, nature, and even the whole universe from the fetters of patriarchy. According to Daly, "a new meaning context is coming into being as we re-create our lives in a new experiential context. The feminist experience is a coming out of nothing into a vocational/communal participation in being."[18]

The process of "being" and "immanence" consists of understanding one's own divinity and personal connectedness with all matter. Carol Christ presented this as the *essence* of humanity.[19] Metaphysics therefore became the new feminist vision for the realization of the equality of all peoples. Feminists believed that when all humanity is united in a new consciousness on a higher level of existence, women will be reinstated to their rightful position. Equality will be the mark of the new humanity and the new age.

The Experience of Personal Power

The final identifiable theme in feminist spirituality is the pursuit and experience of personal power. Starhawk argued that the goddess is the image of the "legitimacy and beneficence of female power."[20] She maintained that women had a *right* to power. They had the right to control their bodies, their life processes, and also to control and direct the shape of humanity's future. According to Starhawk, the symbol of the goddess is profoundly liberating for women, for it restores a sense of authority and power to the female body and all the life processes — birth, growth, lovemaking, aging, and death. She argued that the goddess as Mother represented women's authority over her life and her right to choose consciously how and when and what she will create.[21] In *The Politics of Women's Spirituality*, Baba Copper proposed that a woman should be viewed as holy because of the power she possesses. "The miracles of her body, her capacity for nurture and endurance, the magnitude of her powers, talents, and aptitudes — all are sacred."[22]

In order to unleash their power, feminists argued that women need to perceive it as residing in themselves. Then they will be able to channel and release it purposefully in order to change reality. An essay in *The Politics of Women's Spirituality* explained:

The power is in our minds. The reclamation of it is an act of mind, of the feeling mind, of intensity of purpose. This means, individually and together, we must focus our thoughts, specifically, on what we really want, what we really believe. We can recognize and direct our conscious intentions toward the purposeful release of positive energy. If we behave as if we perceive power to reside in ourselves, we will perceive that power, and so will others. Power attracts power; the latent power within all women will surface and ally itself with perceived power. Most importantly, power will go where we want it to go, do what we want it to do. If it takes saying to ourselves, several times daily, "I am powerful and I can change reality," then we must say that. Sooner or later, we will believe it, and then it will work for us.[23]

With all this talk of power, one may wonder whether feminists were merely seeking to invert the hierarchy in order to dominate men. Feminists did concede they sought a matriarchy, but claimed that a society in which women had power would be qualitatively different from the ones ruled by men. According to Adler, matriarchy is "a realm where female things are valued and where power is exerted in non-possessive, noncontrolling, and organic ways that are harmonious with nature."[24]

The sixth theme in feminist spirituality had practical application. Feminists desired to experience a new consciousness, and channeling their personal power was for the purpose of change. Feminists wanted to use power to accomplish change in personal relationships, in societal structure, and ultimately, in the whole of human existence.

NEW AGE TIES

The new feminist spirituality of the 1980s had much in common with the New Age philosophy that emerged at the same time. It was, in fact, merely a feminized, female-centered presentation of New Age beliefs. New Age philosophers shared the idea of releasing human potential by realizing the oneness of all things. They believed that God resides and exists in all. They believed in unlimited human potential because of human participation in the divine. Moreover, New Age proponents believed in the possibility of a new consciousness. They saw themselves on the vanguard of planetary transformation, as part of a new emerging culture. The similarities between these New Age beliefs and the beliefs of secular feminist spirituality are undeniable.

REBIRTH OF RITUAL

A dozen women sat naked in a circle in a darkened room. Small, bright flames from molded yellow candles cast a flickering pattern of light and shadow over their bodies. The pungent odor of incense and the muted aroma of flowers filled the room. The sounds of Brahms rhythmically entwined with a soft, chanted invocation: "Listen to the words of the Great Mother, who was of old also called Artemis, Astarte, Melusine, Aphrodite, Diana, Brigit . . . Listen to the words of the Great Mother. . . ."

The group rose and proceeded to the bathroom where a tub was filled with cool water, scented with musk and sprinkled with flower petals. A thin, blonde-haired girl piped a haunting tune on a silver flute while the women, one by one, entered the water, bathed, and were towel-dried by the others in the group. Mystical words were spoken to culminate the cleansing.

A brass goblet, filled to the brim with sparkling, crimson wine, was then passed sunwise around the circle. The energy was beginning to rise. Each woman took a small sip from the goblet, then dipped her finger into the wine and sprinkled a few drops into the air and onto the floor.

"Goddess Flora, I thank you for the coming of spring and summer."

"Laverna — Roman goddess of thieves — please find favor on your daughter to grant her acquittal in her court case."

"Demeter, Isis, Hecate, Diana —" — the names continue as the cup is passed from woman to woman.

"Aphrodite, bless my union with Gina."

"Artemis . . . deliver my body from pain . . . !"

The voices became defiant. The energy rose higher and higher.

"Hera, I am angered by the abuse I received from my Father. Empower me to take control of my life!"

The cup circled the room three times, and, with the final libation to a goddess of old, the women rose and danced to the pounding rhythm of timpani drums, tambourines and flute. The frenzy continued until the ebb of energy reached a crescendo. The women then joined hands and in one fluid thrust directed their hands toward the ceiling and released the energy towards the fulfillment of their requests.

Laughter and chatter broke out as a large fruit bowl — carved out of watermelon and filled to overflowing with blueberries, honeydew, cantaloupe, strawberries and grapes — was ushered in from the kitchen. The participants put their clothing back on and joined together in the feast. After many hours, the group joined hands in a final circle of unity. Finally, the crisp, night air enveloped them as they broke the circle and left for their homes, feeling refreshed, accepted, and empowered.

With the advent of spiritual consciousness, similar feminist rituals began to take place all over the country. Some feminists smeared menstrual blood on their faces by the light of the full moon, while others participated in dream circles, guided visualization, ritual theater, and collective meditation. Feminist rituals were based on but not restricted to goddess worship and witchcraft. They celebrated women's unique connection with the earth — her capacity to give birth, and the life phases of menstruation and estrus — by linking these capacities with the cycles of the moon and seasons of nature.

Feminist ritual followed no formula. But according to Barbara Starrett, it did contain a simple and reputedly essential structure, containing five basic elements: setting apart and purifying a special place; invoking the greater powers, whether these were viewed as the elemental forces, the goddess, or simply universal energy; raising the level of energy, through chanting, dancing, music, or such, until "a point of emotional catharsis is reached;"[25] celebrating, usually with food, drink, and merriment; and, finally, completing the process by "consciously opening the circle and sending the energy generated by it out to serve a purpose in the world."[26]

THE PURPOSE OF RITUAL

Feminist spiritualists claim that through ritual, "energy" is generated that empowers women to alter their state of consciousness. Participants become aware of their personal power and strength and are thereby energized to pursue fervent personal and political action for the creation of the feminist matriarchy.

Generation of Energy

In ritual, leaders encourage participants to do things out of the ordinary — perhaps things they have never done before, and certainly not in the full view of others. The risk of the unknown causes many participants to be expectant, excited, or perhaps even apprehensive before the ritual begins — their senses are primed for stimulation. The ritualistic environment involves all the senses: lighting is out of the ordinary, most often by candles; incense, music, chanting, massage, touching, drinking wine, and feasting are common aspects of ritual that arouse all five senses. The emotional tension, combined with escalating sensory stimulation, arouses strong feelings within participants. And, according to Starrett, this sensory bombardment escalates until "a point of emotional catharsis [is] reached."[27]

Feminists called the process of sensory bombardment contained in rituals *the generation of energy*. Feminists perceived the generation of energy as the prerequisite for a "successful" — that is, effective and/or satisfying — ritual. According to Adler, the generation of energy is necessary for providing an environment wherein the participants are able to experience a state of "ecstasy" and are able to connect with their eternal power.

> Ritual is a sacred drama in which you are both audience and participant. The purpose of it is to activate those parts of the mind that are not activated by everyday activity, the psychokinetic and telekinetic abilities, the connection between the eternal power and ourselves. . . . We need to re-create ecstatic states where generation of energy occurs.[28]

Altered Consciousness

The powerful, previously unexperienced emotional energy generated by rituals leaves participants seeking a framework within which to analyze and explain their experience. They are told, by feminist leaders, that their experience is an encounter with the source of eternal power hidden within. Leaders lead participants to believe that through ritual, a secret, superior knowledge has been revealed to them. Through ritual many feminists come to sense and believe in their connectedness with the universe — their consciousnesses are "altered." As Adler explained:

> Many have noted the interconnectedness of everything in the universe and also the fact that most people do not perceive these connections. Spiritual philosophers have often called this lack of perception "estrangement" or "lack of attunement"; materialists have often called it "alienation" or, in some cases, "false consciousness." Perhaps theory, analysis, and the changing of society can end our experience of alienation on the conscious level. Ritual and magical practice aim to end it on the unconscious level of the deep mind.[29]

> The purpose of ritual is to wake up the old mind in us, to put it to work. The old ones inside us, the collective consciousness, the many lives, the divine eternal parts, the senses and parts of the brain that have been ignored. Those parts do not speak English. They do not care about television. But they do understand candlelight and colors. They do understand nature.[30]

Personal Power and Strength

After a woman has experienced the generation of energy and has come to a higher consciousness (which interprets that experience as connecting with her own divinity), she will return to ritual again and again in order to psychologically empower herself. During the course of ritual, she is encouraged to visualize goddesses who will assist her, or to visualize herself as one of the deities. The purpose of this practice is to imbue her with a sense of personal power and strength in order that she might live as a "whole" being. The ultimate goal, however, is to give her the courage to demand her rights in day-to-day private relationships and to be involved in social and political feminist action. Adler pointed out that the ultimate goal of personal empowerment in ritual is practical, real-life change:

> In a society that has traditionally oppressed women there are few positive images of female power. Some of the most potent of these are the Witches, the ancient healers, and the powerful women of pre-classical Aegean civilizations and Celtic myth. Many women entering on an exploration of spirituality have begun to create experiences, through ritual and dreams, whereby they can become these women and act with that kind of power and strength, waiting to see what changes occur in their day-to-day lives.[31]

According to Adler, the goal of obtaining personal power is, in part, "to become what we potentially are, to become 'as the gods,' or, if we *are* God/dess, to recognize it, to make our God/dess-hood count for something."[32]

Create the Matriarchy

The final purpose of ritual is the creation of a matriarchy. Through ritual, feminist spiritualists hope to empower themselves to be change agents in the world. They hope that a society built on the feminine qualities of love, harmony, peace, equality, and wholeness will usher in the matriarchal New Age where all people will be one with each other and with all things. Adler explained:

> The idea of a matriarchy in the past, the possibility of matriarchy in the future, the matriarchal images in myths and in the psyche, perhaps in memories both collective and individual — these have led spiritual feminists to search for matriarchal lore. The road is not merely through study and research. It involves the creation of rituals, psychic experiments, elements of play, daydreams, and dreams. These experiences, women feel, will create the matriarchy, or re-create it.[33]

THE DEITY OF WOMEN RECOGNIZED

Feminist women had named themselves and their worlds, and now, in the third phase of the development of feminist philosophy, they named God. According to feminists, their differences were more than just a source of pride and confidence, they were deitic in essence. Feminist women concluded that they did not need an external, "male God," for they themselves were goddess. The feminist metaphysic taught that each woman contained divinity within her own being. As Z. Budapest admonished her feminist following: "let us never forget that we are *all* the Goddess."[34]

15

Household of Freedom

The scripture is the church's book. I think the church can do with its scripture what it wants to do with its scripture.[1]

Burton Throckmorton, Jr.,
Professor of New Testament
Member, NCC revision committee
for the RSV Bible

Secular feminists recognized woman's personal experience, not external authority, in the formulation of their philosophy. Feminist theologians also exalted the importance of women's experience in matters of Biblical study and theological interpretation. However, because they chose to remain in the Christian faith, they had to struggle with the question of Biblical authority. The Bible has traditionally been recognized as the authority in the life of the Christian believer; but feminists decided they were unwilling to accept as authentic truth any reading or interpretation of the Bible that did not align with their vision of equality. Letty Russell, in *Household of Freedom: Authority in Feminist Theology*, argued that "[t]he word of God is *not* identical with the biblical texts."[2] According to Russell, the Bible could not, therefore, be used as sole, authoritative canon in the formulation of a practical life theology. Katharine Doob Sakenfeld concurred with Russell. She reasoned that "to make the Bible worth using, some new conception of authority would need to be offered that could replace the old assumptions about the function of the Bible in the life of faith."[3]

Instead of locating authority in the Bible, feminist theologians decided to locate authority in the "community of believers." Russell noted that this new paradigm of authority allowed interpretations of the Bible to differ from traditional Christian theology.

Feminist theology is part of a revolution of consciousness that touches the issue of authority at every turn. In appealing to a paradigm of authority in community, it challenges both the content and the thought structure of Christian theology as we know it.[4]

Russell appealed to a model of authority that placed authority in the hands of the "individual in community." According to Russell, the truth of the Bible could only be discerned though a personal, experiential struggle for the corporate liberation of the oppressed (in this case, women). If a woman perceived that some of the Bible's words did not liberate and give wholeness to the oppressed — if they did not "ring true to her inner capacity for truth" — then she could legitimately judge those words as inauthentic or incongruent with the "Word of God." Margaret Farley maintained:

> The biblical witness, on the contrary, claims to present a truth that will heal us, make us whole; it will free us, not enslave us to what violates our very sense of truth and justice. . . . In its own terms, then, it cannot be believed unless it rings true to our deepest capacity for truth and goodness. If it contradict this, it is not to be believed. If it falsifies this, it cannot be accepted.[5]

A group of feminists in the American Academy of Religion (AAR) and the Society of Biblical Literature (SBL) began in 1980 to specifically address the question of Biblical authority and feminism. This came as a result of an SBL centennial session on "The Effects of Women's Studies on Biblical Studies," moderated by Phyllis Trible. Much dialogue regarding the woman-centered analysis of the Bible ensued, and feminist theologians subsequently decided to make use of these annual meetings to develop a project of feminist hermeneutics. In seeking to clarify for themselves and for others the distinctive character of feminist interpretation, the group then embarked on publishing *Feminist Interpretation of the Bible*, edited by Letty Russell (Westminster Press, 1985). A dozen feminist scholars contributed to the volume.

The contributing theologians agreed that feminism started from a radically different presupposition from that of historic Biblical scholarship. Russell pointed out that the feminist theory of interpretation began "with a different view of reality, asking what is appropriate in light of personally and politically reflected experience of oppression and liberation."[6] She noted that feminist interpretation did not begin with "dogmatic statements about the authority of scripture and canon but rather with feminist perspective and praxis."[7] Ruether argued that woman's *experience* — "that experience which arises when women become critically aware of [the] falsifying and alienating experiences imposed upon them as women by a male-dominated culture"[8] — is the key to hermeneutics. According to Ruether, women's experience implies "a conversion experience" through which women get in touch with, name, and judge their experiences of sexism in patriarchal society.[9] She believed that apart from such a conversion, women are unable to interpret the Bible properly.

The contributors further agreed that some minimal criteria were necessary for feminists to be able to determine which parts of the Bible were inspired words of God. Ruether proposed that the "critical principle" of feminist theology was "the affirmation and promotion of the full humanity of women."[10] Whatever denied, diminished, or distorted the full humanity of women was therefore to be appraised by feminists as "non-redemptive."[11] Fiorenza likewise argued that only the "nonsexist and nonandrocentric traditions" of the Bible and the "nonoppressive traditions" of Biblical interpretation had the "theological authority of revelation."[12] Ruether, Fiorenza and other feminist scholars therefore established feminism as the parameter which defined the limits of Biblical authority.

FREEDOM PERSPECTIVE ON AUTHORITY

. . . the systematic transformation of the whole theological pattern in light of the alternative norm of women's equivalent personhood, the translation of this into transformed preaching, ministry, and community — all seems to await a future that has only just begun. This might be daunting indeed if it were not necessary and inevitable for women, once empowered to do theology, to *believe in their own equivalent personhood as the normative starting point of theology* more than they can believe in any past accumulation of tradition which has been carried on without and against women's participation.[13]

As feminism in the Church developed, feminist theologians began to place more and more emphasis on the value of personal experience. Women's experience had been introduced as the norm for theological study in the early seventies, but as time progressed, experience increasingly became the focus, and theology the appendage of that study. As a result, feminist scholars began taking greater liberties with "freedom." Feminists first implemented inclusive language and changed the pronouns for God. Then they began to take greater liberties with interpretive hermeneutic methods, using women's experience as the norm.

In 1987, Letty Russell published *Household of Freedom: Authority in Feminist Theology.* She extensively explored the issue of authority, its definition and source in feminist theology. Russell concluded that experience equals authority.[14] She stated that "the Bible has authority in my life because it makes sense of my experience and speaks to me about the meaning and purpose of my humanity in Jesus Christ."[15] She viewed authority as a "partnership" whereby "the text only has authority as I agree with it and interpret it to my experience."[16] Russell concluded that any Scripture that did not compel or evoke her assent was not authoritative.[17]

TOWARD A NEW CANON

Feminists had introduced a hermeneutic of creative actualization to embellish and expand the usefulness of the Bible for women. They were seeking to establish a "usable future" for the liberation of women within the boundaries of the Christian faith. But it was not long before these theologians found that the search for a Judeo-Christian heritage that affirmed feminist theology yielded "meager fruit."[18] They therefore decided that a usable future could not rely on the canon of Scripture alone. According to feminist theologians, the search for meaningful script would need to be expanded beyond the boundaries of the traditionally accepted canon.

Feminists began to look to sources outside the Bible and placed them alongside the canon. Ruether noted that they expanded their search to include mystical and sectarian groups "who focused on the reconciliation of the masculine and feminine"; to groups such as the Montanists and Quakers "who touched on the connection between the liberation of the oppressed and the reconciliation of the feminine and the masculine"; and finally to "pre-Christian and non-Christian religions that affirmed the image of the divine as female as well as male."[19]

In *Womanguides: Readings Toward a Feminist Theology*, Ruether compiled a series of texts and essays chosen from both Biblical and non-Biblical texts. Her collection included writings from the ancient Near East, Hebrew and Greek mythology, Christian Science, paganism, goddess worship, and new "post-Christian consciousness."[20] According to Ruether, anything that legitimized and recognized the full value of the female could be viewed as canonical.

> We can read between the lines of patriarchal texts and find fragments of our own [i.e., woman's] experience that were not completely erased. We can also find, outside of canonized texts, remains of alternative communities that reflect either the greater awe and fear of female power denied in later patriarchy or questionings of male domination in groups where women did enter into critical dialogue. Whether anathematized and declared heretical or just overlooked, some of these texts are recoverable. We can resurrect them, gather them together, and begin to glimpse the larger story of our experience.
>
> In so doing, we read canonical, patriarchal texts in a new light. They lose their normative status and we read them critically in the light of that larger reality that they hide and deny. In the process, a new norm emerges on which to construct a new community, a new theology, *eventually a new canon.*[21]

Ruether claimed that stories became authoritative through community use in a historical movement of liberation. This was true, she said, for the patriarchal text of the Old Testament, compiled by the nation of Israel in its struggle for liberation. Like the Jewish nation, women — as an oppressed group — were free to choose their own authoritative stories, which were paradigms of redemptive experience for them, so that these new stories, through community use, could become a new authoritative canon. Ruether explained:

> So feminism . . . recognizing that patriarchal texts deform the liberating spirit for women, rejects a theology confined to commentary on past texts. We are not only free to reclaim rejected texts of the past and put them side by side with canonized texts as expressions of truth, in the light of which canonized texts may by criticized; but we are also free to generate new stories from our own experience that may, through community use, become more than personal or individual. They may become authoritative stories, for it is precisely through community use in a historical movement of liberation, which finds in them paradigms of redemptive experience, that stories become authoritative.[22]

REDEEMING THE REPRESSED

As feminism in the Church matured, women used their personal authority to add to the Bible; they added text from any source that addressed the "whole personhood" of women. Elaine Pagels, in *The Gnostic Gospels*, proposed an extensive argument for the inclusion of Gnostic texts alongside the Bible. Barbara MacHaffie, in *HerStory: Women in Christian Tradition*, surveyed church history to uncover examples of women's stories that had been "repressed" by patriarchy. Alongside the Biblical examples, she included a survey of women in Montanism, gnosticism, ascetics, witchcraft, and sectarianism. Ruether, as mentioned, had compiled texts from these various traditions as a book of readings proposed for inclusion in a new canon.[23] Earlier, Ruether had co-edited a book, *Women of Spirit*, with Eleanor McLaughlin which presented a survey of those women in the Jewish and Christian traditions who were shunned for heresy.[24] *Women of Spirit* reviewed church history in much the same manner as Barbara MacHaffie's *HerStory*. In addition, Joan Chamberlain Engelsman published *The Feminine Dimension of the Divine*, and Susan Cady, Marian Ronan and Hal Taussig published *Sophia: The Future of Feminist Spirituality*, two books which presented the "Wisdom" of the Bible — Sophia — as a personified goddess.[25] Fiorenza likewise, in *In Memory of Her — A Feminist Theological Reconstruction of Christian Origins*, explored the early Christian history of Montanism, gnosticism, goddess worship, as well as the mythology of Jewish *Sophia theology* to "reconstruct" Christian origins to include a feminist perspective.[26] In this manner, feminists reconstructed the basic foundations of theology itself. They moved away from the Bible as the sole source of authority and toward a theology built on a collection of texts that were credited with similar authority.

Following is a brief survey of some of the usable traditions and texts which feminist theologians introduced for development alongside the Bible.

Gnosticism

Gnosticism was a cult that drew upon a multitude of religious and philosophical ideas circulating at the end of the first century. The gnostics generally believed that God was not directly responsible for the creation of the
material world. Creation was the result of disobedience or malice toward
the supreme spirit God, and the material world that resulted was therefore
evil. In the mechanics of creation, however, small sparks of divinity from
the supreme God were captured in human beings. The gnostics believed that
a redeemer had been sent to release these captured sparks by giving people
special knowledge (*gnosis*) of the existence of God and the true origins of
the world.

Gnosticism had a profound impact upon the interpretation given to the
life and work of Jesus. The gnostics argued that Jesus was the redeemer who
had been sent to unleash the special knowledge necessary for salvation.
Gnostics backed up their ideas by appealing to certain parts of the New
Testament as well as to their own books, which, they claimed, had been
handed down by the apostles.[27]

In 1945, an Arab peasant discovered thirteen papyrus books, bound in
leather, sealed in an earthenware jar. The astonishing archaeological discovery of these ancient volumes included portions from some fifty-two texts
from the early centuries of the Christian era. Besides the *Gospel of Thomas*,
the *Gospel of Philip*, and the *Gospel of Mary*, the find included the *Gospel
of Truth* and the *Gospel to the Egyptians*, as well as the *Secret Book of
James*, the *Apocalypse of Paul*, the *Letter of Peter to Philip*, and the
Apocalypse of Peter.[28] These Coptic translations were dated at about A.D.
350-400. The texts were diverse, ranging from secret gospels, poems, and
quasi-philosophical descriptions of the origins of the universe, to myths,
magic, and instructions for mystical practice. They were, from all appear-
ances, translations of early Gnostic writings.

Elaine Pagels extensively researched and expounded on these Gnostic
texts. She claimed that gnostics were Christians who were shunned and
deliberately suppressed by the orthodox church for political, power reasons.
The orthodox teaching legitimized a hierarchy of authority of God over
mankind, of priest over person, and furthermore a social hierarchy of men
over women. In suppressing Gnostic teaching, the theologians were merely
seeking to secure power for themselves — as priests and as men. According
to Pagels, gnosticism was not heretical, but merely an interpretation of
Christian reality from a different point of view. As Pagels reasoned:

> . . . the majority of Christians, gnostic and orthodox, like religious peo-
> ple of every tradition, concerned themselves with ideas primarily as
> expressions or symbols of religious experience. Such experience remains
> the source and testing ground of all religious ideas (as, for example, a man
> and a woman are likely to experience differently the idea that God is mas-
> culine). Gnosticism and orthodoxy, then, articulated very different kinds

of human experience; I suspect that they appealed to different types of persons.[29]

Gnosticism came from the Greek word *gnosis*, usually translated as "knowledge." As the gnostics used the term, it could be translated as "insight," for *gnosis* involved an intuitive process of knowing oneself.[30] To know oneself, at the deepest level, was to simultaneously know God; this was said to be the secret of *gnosis*. As the gnostic teacher Monimus exhorted his followers,

> Abandon the search for God and the creation and other matters of a similar sort. Look for him by taking yourself as the starting point. Learn who it is within you who makes everything his own and says, "My God, my mind, my thought, my soul, my body." Learn the sources of sorrow, joy, love, hate. . . . If you carefully investigate these matters you will find him in yourself.[31]

The gnostics contradicted the events and the interpretation of events offered by the writers of the Biblical Gospels. Gnostics taught that self-knowledge was knowledge of God; the self and the divine were identical. Second, their interpretation of Jesus spoke of illusion and enlightenment, not of sin and repentance. Instead of coming to save us from sin, Jesus came as a guide who opened access to spiritual understanding. When the disciple attained enlightenment, Jesus no longer served as spiritual master; the two had become equal — even identical. Third, orthodox Christians believed that Jesus was Lord and Son of God in a unique way; He remained forever distinct from the rest of humanity whom he came to save. Yet, gnostics claimed that all humanity received their being from the same source and in the same way; humans were just as much part of God as Jesus.[32] Furthermore, gnosticism refuted the orthodox theology of Monotheism — that of one God. In Gnostic writings, the Creator was often castigated for his arrogance by a superior feminine power, Wisdom or Sophia.[33] Instead of a distinct, personal being, God was presented as more of a metaphysical dualism. Pagels cited one Gnostic text which quoted God as saying, "I am androgynous. I am both Mother and Father, since I copulate with myself . . . and with those who love me. . . . I am the Womb that gives shape to the All. . . . I am Me[iroth]ea, the glory of the Mother."[34] According to gnosticism, God was a diad: Mother *and* Father, the Parents of the divine being (Christ) and furthermore the "dweller in heaven and humanity," the ineffable source and depth of *all* being.[35]

The primary attraction of gnosticism to feminist theologians was the value that gnosticism placed upon personal experience. Gnostic literature was diverse, taken from a variety of Christian, Jewish, pagan, and Greek sources. Furthermore, it was often contradictory. Diversity of teaching was the very mark of the gnostics. The gnostics allowed virtually any belief on the basis of one's own experiential *gnosis*. The early Church Father Tertullian found this outrageous:

> ... every one of them, just as it suits his own temperament, modifies the traditions he has received, just as the one who handed them down modified them, when he shaped them according to his own will.[36]

Tertullian and Bishop Irenaeus, in addressing the Gnostic heresy, also noted that many women had been enticed into joining the cult. They observed that *gnosis* had deceived these women into believing in a female God. Furthermore, it had encouraged them to teach and prophesy in the Church and had allowed them to be appointed on an equal basis with men as priests and bishops. Irenaeus and Tertullian were doctrinally opposed to this. But Pagels rejoiced in the freedom that *gnosis* offered women. She agreed with the Gnostic argument that "only one's own experience offers the ultimate criterion of truth, taking precedence over all secondhand testimony and all tradition."[37]

Montanism

Montanus and two women, Priscilla and Maxima, led another religious movement that emerged at the end of the second century. The Montanists, as their disciples came to be called, enthusiastically proclaimed their message, believing themselves to be channels for divine truth. They preached that the end of the world was near and therefore encouraged Christians to actively seek persecution, and even martyrdom. Opponents of the movement recorded that leaders often committed suicide and that participants used the blood of children in sacrificial rituals.[38]

Montanists believed that since Eve was the first to eat of the tree of knowledge, women were more likely than men to receive divine wisdom and revelation. Hence Priscilla and Maxima were not just Montanus' companions and followers, but also enjoyed exercising spiritual gifts and authoritative leadership. The pronouncements of these first three prophets were written down and gathered as the movement's sacred documents. The two best-known oracles of Priscilla and Maxima were significant. When Priscilla was asleep, "Christ, in the form of a female figure, appeared to her saying that this was a holy place and here would Jerusalem descend out of heaven."[39] After the death of Montanus, Maxima became the leader of the movement. Once, when she was persecuted and tested at the hands of her opponents, she bitterly complained, "I am pursued like a wolf out of the sheep fold; I am no wolf: *I am word and spirit and power.*"[40]

Fiorenza claimed that Montanism was not a heretical movement and that its doctrine was essentially orthodox. She argued that opponents could not refute the movement on doctrinal grounds, so they attacked it by slandering its leading prophets with accusations of immorality, the abandonment of their husbands, and charges of suicide and murder. According to Fiorenza, the opponents did this in order to discredit a movement that valued women's equal participation in religious leadership. Fiorenza concluded: "Thus, despite their basic doctrinal orthodoxy, the Montanists were reviled and finally driven out of the mainstream church."[41] MacHaffie concurred that "we must at least consider the possibility that orthodox Christianity, which had already succumbed to its male-dominated cultural environment, excluded and persecuted the gnostics and Montanists because of the varied roles they gave to women."[42]

Asceticism

Ruether and MacHaffie examined the ascetic movement that dominated Christianity in the fourth century. The ascetics emphasized a body-soul dualism in which the soul was viewed as spiritual and holy, and the flesh as carnal and evil.[43] Ascetics denied themselves physical pleasures such as eating and warmth, doing only what was necessary to survive. They practiced voluntary poverty and complete abstinence from sexual relations. They viewed asceticism as both a good preparation for martyrdom and a way to a more holy or perfect life in the eyes of God. Some ascetics also believed that the Kingdom of God and the end of time would be brought nearer if the followers of Jesus practiced self-denial.[44]

Ruether pointed out the negative side of asceticism. She argued that women were in double jeopardy because men regarded them as inferior, and ascetics feared them as the symbol of the carnal. Nevertheless, she suggested paradoxically that asceticism liberated women from the roles of marriage and motherhood. Ruether reported that as ascetics, women were freed from the curse that limited their fate to bearing children in sorrow and being subject to their husbands. She noted that women dedicated to this way of life had the support of the Church in making decisions against their family's demands that they marry and bear children for the patriarchal clan.[45] In this one aspect of asceticism, feminists found value.

Sectarianism

Sectarians were defined by feminists as "those groups which consciously set themselves apart from the culturally dominant beliefs and practices of a particular time and place."[46] In America, sectarians were identified as those who were doctrinally outside and against mainstream Christianity. Feminists found that sectarian groups such as the Shakers, Christian Scientists, Mormons, and the Perfectionists contained traces of theology that were usable for the formation of a uniquely woman-centered theology.

The United Society of Believers in Christ's Second Appearing, commonly called the Shakers, were founded as a variation of English Quakerism in the mid-eighteenth century. The key person in Shaker development in colonial America was a woman, Ann Lee. Not only was Ann Lee the founder and leader of the sect, but her followers eventually identified her as the female Messiah. In an 1806 publication expounding Shaker doctrine, Elder Benjamin S. Youngs argued that true spiritual life, based upon the practice of celibacy and abstinence from all sins of the flesh, was revealed by Jesus and Mother Ann.[47] Shakers proclaimed the idea of a dual deity and dual Messiahship, through Jesus and Ann Lee. Furthermore, Shakers defined the Godhead in four persons — Father, Son, Holy Mother Wisdom, and Daughter.[48]

The Shakers dramatically altered the traditional picture of the ideal woman as wife, mother, and keeper of the hearth. The family was seen, rather, as a stumbling block, for it diverted the attention and efforts of women and men away from the good of the community. Ann Lee claimed that she had received a vision from Jesus revealing to her that the original sin of Adam and Eve was sexual intercourse to satisfy their animal lusts. Shakers therefore strictly enforced celibacy in the self-sufficient Shaker communes. Men and women ate at different tables, worked separately, used separate stairs to their living quarters, and sat on opposite sides of the room. Men and women, however, shared responsibility for child-rearing. Groups of adults cared for orphans and the children of new converts; both men and women shared equally in the work of the community. The presiding Shaker Ministry was also divided equally between men and women, and an equal number of Elders and Eldresses supervised the spiritual life of the Shaker communes.

Feminists pointed out that the Shakers stood against the status quo to offer a truly egalitarian theology of God and human life. This sect appealed to feminists because of the Shakers' strong emphasis on the female principle and their androgynous mother-father understanding of God. Barbara Brown Zikmund approved of these Shaker teachings.

> All life and activity animated by Christian Love is Worship. Shakers adore God as the Almighty Creator, Fountain of all Good, Life, Light, Truth and Love, — the One Eternal Father-Mother. They recognized the Christ Spirit, the expression of Deity, manifested in fulness in Jesus of Nazareth, also in feminine manifestation through the personality of Ann Lee. Both, they regard as Divine Saviors, anointed Leaders in the New Creation. All in whom the Christ consciousness awakens are Sons and Daughters of God.[49]

Christian Science was another sectarian movement that brought female images into its theology. Founded almost a century after the Shakers by Mary Baker Eddy, Christian Science also emphasized the idea of an androgynous God. In 1875 Eddy published *Science and Health: With Key to the Scriptures*. She argued that reality was contained in the spiritual mind, and that the spiritual mind could overcome physical limitations and sicknesses: the material world, including pain and disease, was merely illusory. According to Eddy, God (and the human reflection of the divine image) is the only reality; and to be in touch with God, a person needed to live on that level of reality alone.[50] Furthermore, she preached that God is Mother and Father, a dual expression of the masculine and feminine. Although she used men to fill administrative positions, she sent women throughout the country to preach her message. Eddy also employed women as the prime practitioners of healing within the movement.[51]

A third sectarian group, the Mormons (Church of Jesus Christ of the Latter-Day Saints), did not reject patriarchal theology, but feminists noted that they had expanded their view of deity to include a divine family. God the Father had a wife, the eternal mother.[52] In 1915 a Mormon authority iterated the theological belief that people were "literally sons and daughters of Divine Parents, the spiritual progeny of God, our Eternal Father and of our God Mother."[53] Feminists extracted this theological morsel of an androgynous God from amidst the less palatable aspects of Mormonism. Moreover, feminists even approved the Mormon practice of polygamy — although it reinforced a patriarchal style of marriage — because each Mormon household thus became a small commune of shared responsibilities and freedoms.

Finally, feminists found value in the Oneida Perfectionists, founded and led by John Humphrey Noyes. Noyes believed that monogamy and unchecked childbearing had unduly limited women. He argued for "complex marriages" in which a group of men and women were able to freely relate to each other at all levels, including sexually.[54] Unlike the Shakers, Noyes did not reject sex as evil; rather he argued that both sexes should enjoy it. Noyes claimed that sexual relations were a gift from God that would not disappear in the Kingdom but rather would be extended to include all the saints. This, he believed, was the meaning of the phrase, "They shall neither marry nor be given in marriage."[55]

To reduce the chances of pregnancy, Noyes taught a method of birth control in which the male partner could, through discipline, eliminate the ejaculation of sperm during sexual intercourse. In addition, the leaders of the community regulated the sexual liaisons between men and women so as to ensure that no permanent attachments developed. The formation of bonds between mothers and children was also discouraged, and child care was relegated to men and women of the community in a special wing of the house. Feminists pointed out the egalitarian aspect of Oneida communes. They valued the perfectionist theology that freed women from the shackles of monogamous marriage, husband, childbearing, and the traditional role of homemaker.

Sophia — The Goddess of the Bible

Joan Chamberlain Engelsman, in *The Feminine Dimension of the Divine*, introduced the concept of a female divine persona in the Bible, Sophia. According to Engelsman, Sophia had traditionally been presented in the Bible as an allegoric figure named "Wisdom." *Sophia*, the Greek word for wisdom (or rather a transliteration of that word), immediately suggested a person rather than a concept, but Engelsman argued that this was precisely what the Bible had originally intended. She argued that the translators' use of the title *Wisdom* rather than the name *Sophia* was a male ploy to avoid and repress this unique, female, divine person. Engelsman, and Susan Cady, Marian Ronan and Hal Taussig, authors of *Wisdom's Feast*, wanted to see Sophia recognized as a real Biblical deity.[56]

> Sophia is a real biblical person, then, a real part of the Jewish and Christian traditions, yet we have never learned to call her by her name and have never really acknowledged her dignity and worth. Many of us, of course, have come across various references to Wisdom in the Bible. Yet for some of the same reasons that women have been ignored and repressed within the biblical traditions. . . . Sophia has never had the impact on us that she could have. The struggle to formulate a feminist spirituality, and our enormous need to find symbols of connectedness require that we now reconsider Sophia, in all her splendor and mystery.[57]

Feminists presented Sophia as a female goddess-like figure who appeared clearly in the Scriptures of the Old Testament, and less directly in the New Testament Gospels and epistles. Cady, Ronan and Taussig claimed she was related to the goddesses of the Hellenistic era, particularly Demeter, Persephone, Hecate and Isis.[58] According to these feminists, Sophia was the one at the heart of God's creative process. Cady, Ronan and Taussig quoted Proverbs 8:27-31: "When God set the heaven in place, I was present. . . . I was by God's side, a master craftswoman, delighting God day after day. . . ."[59] They argued that this verse highlighted Sophia's role in the creation of the universe. But they did not merely see Sophia as creator at the beginning. According to these feminist authors, she was a part of the "ongoing creative process."[60] Furthermore, because she was at the heart of all things coming into being, they proposed that she pervaded and permeated *all* things.[61]

Cady, Ronan and Taussig presented Sophia as teacher, lover, law, tree, and plant. "She is a co-creator with the Hebrew God, she is a heavenly queen, she is a messenger from God, and she is God's lover."[62] Furthermore, they argued that Jesus Christ was Sophia, a female divinity which presented herself, for the sake of the culture, as a human male.[63] Engelsman maintained that although Sophia began as a personified hypostasis of God — one of the aspects or essences of God's character — and continued as a creation of God contained within monotheistic Judaism, her importance was such that her power was similar to that of any Hellenistic goddess.[64] Cady, Ronan and Taussig noted that Sophia even rivaled Yahweh's power in her demands for people to follow her and her promise of salvation to those who did so. "She is to all intents and purposes divine, creating, judging, and ruling just as God is."[65]

Feminists argued that Sophia's power as a divine female figure was repressed by patriarchy. According to Engelsman, this repression began with Philo, who substituted a personified, masculine *Logos* for the feminine Sophia. Philo at first equated *Logos* with Sophia, then substituted *Logos* for Sophia, until the masculine person of *Logos* "had taken over most of

Sophia's divine roles, including the firstborn image of God, the principle of order, and the intermediary between God and humanity."[66] Furthermore, the process of repression was continued with Christ replacing Sophia as personified Wisdom. Cady, Ronan and Taussig argued that New Testament writers Paul and John chauvinistically transformed "Sophialogy to Christology by transferring Sophia's power and attributes to the Logos, then identifying Christ as Logos incarnate."[67] Finally, the Church Fathers in the third and fourth centuries ensured Sophia's continued censorship by their Christology, at which point "Sophia disappeared from western theological consideration."[68] According to Engelsman, Sophia never developed fully as a divine person co-equal with Yahweh, due to the limitations imposed on her by Judaism's strict monotheism.[69]

Cady, Ronan and Taussig argued that the Bible texts referring to Sophia were "fragmentary and unfinished."[70] They stated that there was "a definite incompleteness about Sophia in the Hebrew tradition."[71] According to them, Sophia was patriarchally "truncated and suppressed at a number of different times in her history."[72] These feminists found in Sophia "a female figure of considerable promise, rooted in the Biblical traditions, yet requiring extensive development if that promise is to be fulfilled."[73] Other feminists agreed. They regarded it as their task to complete and fulfill the image of Sophia that had been repressed and neglected by the Biblical authors.

According to Cady, Ronan and Taussig, Sophia offered possibilities "for connection and transformation" that would prove invaluable for women.[74] They noted that the power of this female image of deity was precisely one of "connectedness and shared power."[75] They reasoned that the image of Sophia was critical for the internal transformation of Christianity and Judaism, for it established a link between Judeo-Christianity and all other spiritual traditions. Sophia allowed Christians "to develop a new consciousness which realized the connectedness of all that was and is."[76] The image of Sophia allowed for a connection between God and a female goddess within the Bible, and therefore a connection between the God of the Bible and all the other goddesses which existed outside of Biblical tradition. Therefore, through this image of Sophia, God could be linked to the goddess of witchcraft, of sectarian cults, and of Greco-Roman mythologies. According to Cady, Ronan and Taussig, Sophia was valuable because she could be developed into a powerful integrating figure for feminist spirituality, mainstreaming individuals from diverse, separate religious heritages into "a new consciousness of connectedness."[77]

Goddess Worship and Neo-paganism

In searching for usable texts for women, feminists in the Church also embarked on the exploration of ancient goddess worship. Ruether, in *Womanguides*, included many goddess texts extracted from Babylonian and Greco-Roman poetry, novel, and myth. She recorded a "Psalm to Ishtar, — Shepherdess of the People," an initiation rite for "Isis, Queen of Heaven,"

Sumerian and Babylonian creation and paradise stories, as well as texts containing Platonic, Gnostic, and sectarian references to the divine female.[78] Ruether believed that literature from any source which, in her opinion, valued and esteemed the female, was permissible for religious use. Following is an example, extracted from the "Psalm to Ishtar, Shepherdess of the People":

I pray to thee, O Lady of ladies, goddess of goddesses.
  O Ishtar, queen of all peoples, who guides mankind aright,
O Irnini, ever exalted, greatest of the Igigi,
  O most mighty of princesses, exalted is thy name.
Thou indeed art the light of heaven and earth, O valiant daughter of Sin
  [the Moon]. . . .
  At the thought of thy name heaven and earth tremble.
The gods tremble; the Anunnaki stand in awe.
  To thine awesome name mankind must pay heed.
For thou art great and thou art exalted. . . .
  See me O my Lady; accept my prayers.
Faithfully look upon me and hear my supplication.
  Promise my forgiveness and let thy spirit be appeased. . . .
To thee have I prayed; forgive my debt.
  Forgive my sin, my iniquity, my shameful deeds, and my offence. . . .
Let thy great mercy be upon me.
  Let those who see me in the street magnify thy name.
As for me, let me glorify thy divinity and thy might before the [people],
  [saying],
  Ishtar indeed is exalted; Ishtar indeed is queen;
The Lady indeed is exalted; the Lady indeed is queen.
Irnini, the valorous daughter of Sin, has no rival.

The feminist quest for a usable future transcended the boundaries of Christianity and extracted from all traditions that which contained value for women. Feminists deemed that religious practices borrowed from witchcraft, neo-paganism, and the New Age were legitimate (at least in part), as were ancient heresies and sectarian philosophies of the Biblical and patristic era. They claimed that men, in the interest of retaining power for themselves, had labeled these valid philosophies heretical. Religious feminists argued that the men who wrote the Bible did so with their personal interests in mind, as did the men who chose which books were to be included in the canon. Fiorenza argued that historical studies "demonstrated that the early Christian writers did not include all the extant materials in their writings, but selected and rewrote early Christian traditions that were important for their theological argument."[79] Feminists therefore believed that they needed to redeem rejected texts and include them alongside the patriarchal texts of the Bible in order to achieve balance for the whole personhood of women.

NON-JUDGMENTAL FEMINIST PLURALISM

Not all feminists within Christendom were comfortable with including goddess and neo-pagan worship alongside Christianity. But just as secular feminists were forced to tolerate lesbianism, likewise, religious feminists found that they could not justifiably condemn those who advocated pagan worship practices. For example, Zikmund reasoned that ". . . even for those who want to stay within the Jewish and Christian legacy, the work of neo-pagan or nonbiblical feminist spirituality is important. Goddess religions have powerful symbols that stretch our understanding of religious practice and human experience."[80] In 1982, Virginia Mollenkott wrote an article for *The Christian Century*, "An Evangelical Feminist Confronts the Goddess." She admitted that she had initially rejected the goddess because "goddess worship excluded men" and therefore she felt that "we would trample on God's image (and therefore ourselves) if men were excluded from our concerns, our worship and our language."[81] But although she rejected indiscriminately changing Christian terminology from "God" to "Goddess," she noted that goddess worship was valuable as a source of reference for the evangelical Christian. Through her years of feminist study, Mollenkott had come to the conclusion that the word *God* was non-sex-specific, it was merely a "job description for the all encompassing Being/Becoming" who created and empowered the universe.[82] When confronted with goddess worship, Mollenkott reasoned that the evangelical Christian should be stirred to "articulate more intelligently the difference between self-worship and worship of God within the authentic self, between superficial, ego-centered activity and activity emerging from our profound center of being."[83] In essence, she agreed with Fiorenza that the goddess of radical feminist spirituality was not so very different from the God whom Jesus preached and whom he called "Father."[84]

Mollenkott advocated a "non-judgmental pluralism" between feminists in secular and religious spheres.[85] Ruether, likewise, proposed that none of the various forms of feminism could be judged wrong.[86] These women, together with other religious feminists, therefore joined hands with their secular sisters. In doing so, religious feminists hoped to realize the *ekklesia (church)of women*. *All* women bore the image of God, and *all* were regarded as members of God's Church. As Fiorenza pointed out:

> The *ekklesia* of women as the new model of church can only be sustained if we overcome the structural-patriarchal dualisms between Jewish and Christian women, laywomen and non-women, homemakers and career women, between active and contemplative, between Protestant and Roman Catholic women, between married and single women, between physical and spiritual mothers, between heterosexual and lesbian women, between the church and the world, the sacral and the secular . . . we will overcome these dualisms only through and in solidarity with all women . . . in a sisterhood that transcends all patriarchal ecclesiastical divisions.

These patriarchal divisions and competitions among women must be transformed into a movement of women as the people of God. Feminist biblical spirituality must be incarnated in a historical movement of women struggling for liberation.[87]

ESOTERIC METAPHYSICS

In 1985, the *Journal of Feminist Studies in Religion* commenced publication. This periodical was edited by Judith Plaskow and Elisabeth Schussler Fiorenza, and included, on its editorial board, persons such as Carol P. Christ, Naomi Goldenberg, Carter Heyward, and the Dianic Witch high priestess, Starhawk. Its publication was significant because it underscored a fundamental truth of the feminist movement that had been obscured until now: religious and secular feminism were of the same essence. They were based on the same presuppositions, and were therefore destined to intersect and merge. In the third phase of the development of religious and secular feminist philosophy this intersection occurred. The alteration of God-language and the increasing hermeneutic liberty employed by feminist theologians had catapulted the religious movement forward onto the same path as that of secular feminism. In both, the third phase of philosophical development centered on esoteric metaphysics. Esoterism was similar to *gnosis* as it referred to a private or secret knowledge, understood only by those who had reached a higher level of consciousness. Metaphysics referred to that branch of philosophy which related all as being interconnected — all matter and non-matter were a part of the web of nature, the web of being. Esoteric metaphysics therefore referred to a special, inner knowledge of one's own connectedness with the universe and the source and origin thereof, God. It claimed that inner wholeness and meaning would be found through the realization of this new consciousness. The religious feminists called it salvation. And although the secular feminists did not attach the same label, they were in pursuit of the same goal and, more importantly, were pursuing it in the same manner. As a result, the religious feminists on the editorial committee of the *Journal of Feminist Studies in Religion* were entirely comfortable with the inclusion of secular, neo-pagan radical feminists, as were the pagan feminists with the presence of their religious counterparts. Together they began to work toward the realization of a new consciousness and a new humanity. Together they wanted to usher in "God-with-Us" through the liberation of the oppressed and the dawning of the new age, the coming of the Kingdom.

16

Godding

Human responsibility, in its deepest and fullest dimension, entails godding, an embodiment or incarnation of God's love in human flesh, with the goal of co-creating with God a just and loving human society.

Virginia Mollenkott[1]

In the third phase of the development of feminist philosophy, the secular and religious merged. Religious feminists retained some personal distinction and identity, and yet were simultaneously united with secular feminists in vision and purpose. Therefore the two were joined, as it were, in wedlock.

Religious feminists distinguished themselves from secular feminists by working within traditional religious spheres. Whereas secular feminists viewed Christianity as an oppressive institution of patriarchy that would best be abolished, Christian feminists saw organized religion as a powerful, usable agent for feminist transformation. Religious feminists were not willing to break ties with their religious heritage; instead, they systematically transformed religion to align with their own feminist worldview. The major vehicle for this transformation was the alteration of the Christian language and symbol system. Religious feminists used the Bible and Christian terminology and were found within the Church, but they redefined the language and altered images to the extent that the message they were proclaiming was no longer part of that tradition.

SLIPPERY LANGUAGE

The themes of religious feminism were, in essence, identical to the themes of secular feminism. However, these themes were shrouded by remnants of Christian imagery and language. Religious feminists used language loosely, subtly blurring the distinction between the Christian and pagan. Their use of Biblical terminology often obscured the fact that their definitions and visions were *identical* to that of their secular counterparts; they masked their common vision by semantics. Secular feminists, for example, spoke of "creating the matriarchy." Religious feminists, on the other hand, were working toward "Women-Church." Secular feminists wanted to alter consciousness and generate energy, while their religious sisters desired repentance, redemption, and the empowerment of the Spirit. Secular feminists longed for a new humanity and a new age, while religious feminists longed for the time when all would be children of God in the Kingdom of God. Secular feminists strove to be "truly human," while their counterparts strove to be "Christ-like." Both agreed that evil and sin consisted of "alienation from self" and the oppressive systems of racism, sexism, classism, heterosexism, and militarism.[2] Religious feminists were "saved" from this, while secular feminists found their reprise in the experience of a higher consciousness.

Virginia Mollenkott provides a prime example of the feminist use of slippery language. As a Christian feminist, she refused to "surrender" her "Christian terminology," choosing rather to "utilize specifically Christian terms" for the benefit of those in her own family of faith.[3] However, even Mollenkott was careful to point out that "when we use [Christian language] we must learn to make clear that although we use Christian terms out of our own life experience, we understand that other religions may have their own terms for similar visions. *Our primary interest is not in insisting on our own terms, but rather in bringing about the New Creation purged of racism, sexism, and classism. Our common goal is the New Humanity in the New Creation.*"[4] Furthermore, she argued that

> . . . we err whenever we unconsciously assume that the terms of one religion exclude from the experience being described all people who would not use the same terminology. The experience of godding, which is a spiritual matter of the attitudes that are expressed in human relationships, is open to people of every religion. Across the face of the earth are people of various religions who would use different terms for those who love their neighbors as they love themselves and whose faith is alive because it leads to practical and structural acts of mercy. They, too, are members of the New Humanity.[5]

Mollenkott did not believe that acknowledgment of Jesus meant that only Christians were acceptable to God.[6] Furthermore, although she recognized the terminology of Paul and Peter in the Bible as specifically Christian, she was "convinced" that their vision included "any person who wants to live significantly."[7] Mollenkott defined sin as a "dualistically defined self-understanding of separateness from God."[8] She believed that people became Christians as they recognized their oneness with God, whom she regarded as the all-inclusive, all-encompassing ground of being. She argued that true Christianity consisted of "remembering" one's union with

God and of emulating Jesus in seeking to free others from oppressive situations.

> To be "in Christ" is to remember our union with the One who sent us, as Jesus did, and to seek to do God's will as Jesus did. The point here is not cognitive agreement with a set of doctrines and terms, but the embodiment of Jesus' vision in our lifestyles.[9]

When Virginia Mollenkott and other feminist theologians speak of becoming Christians and living in a Christ-like manner, when they speak of redemption, salvation, Christ, and God, they do so with language that is often the same as Biblical Christianity, but which, when analyzed, is radically different, and even antithetical to it.

THEMES OF RELIGIOUS FEMINISM

Because religious feminists do not use the same terminology as secular feminists, it may not be obvious that their beliefs are the same. But upon close examination of their definitions, it becomes apparent that the themes of feminist theology are, in fact, one with those of secular feminist philosophy. The themes of religious and secular feminism align completely.

Monism: All is One

Christian feminists share their secular sisters' belief in monism; but they are reticent to equate God with material objects such as stones. Instead, they speak of "connectedness" and "union" with God, the Creator of all that is. They view God as the source and depth of *all being*. Moreover, they argue that all that was created was joined in a mystical organic union with him (her). As Mollenkott reasoned:

> When Jesus says, "Nobody comes to the Father and Mother but by me," might he not be referring to an abiding sense of oneness with his divine Source, a sense of organic union that Jesus never forgot? No one comes to God except by remembering that organic oneness with the Source of us all![10]

According to Mollenkott, God is the "all encompassing reality"[11] that connects humans to each other, to organic and non-organic matter, to nature, to the universe, and ultimately to the Divine. God is the reality that unites all things — including him/herself — as one. She reasoned:

> For many centuries people believed that the four basic elements of the universe were earth, air, fire, and water. So the biblical images of God as rock and ground (earth), wind (air), fire, and water encompass the whole universe and therefore affirmed the holiness of all things. . . . Humankind is holy, but so is the environment.[12]

Mollenkott does not distinguish how the holiness of nature differs from the holiness of humans, and how this, in turn, differs from the holiness of God. According to feminists, all of creation is holy in the same way — all is connected to the Source, the Ground of all being. All is One. Mollenkott argued that "the biblical images of God as natural phenomena will, if utilized, help us recognize our milieu as divine . . . the New Creation makes sisters and brothers out of all the birds, the beasts, the fish, the sun, the moon, the stars, and all of humankind."[13]

Although Christian feminists do not openly confess Monism, it is a philosophy that evidently shapes their theology. Monism, the belief that everything is connected through the source of being, blurs the traditional distinctions between the Divine, humanity and the rest of creation. It is an integral part of both secular and religious feminism. According to the secular feminist, *all is one*. And according to the Christian feminist theologian, *God is One*.[14] The words differ, but the meaning is the same.

Pantheism: All is God

Christian feminists are obviously pantheistic, as are their secular sisters. Mollenkott, for example, when speaking of the jealousy of God, insisted that God was "not jealous in the sense of one prideful Potentate who insists on having all attention focused on Himself, but *jealous instead that He/She/It be recognized everywhere in everyone and everything.*"[15] In a feminist litany written *in praise of God's presence in all things*, the leader reminded the participants "how wide our world is and *how God's mysterious presence penetrates all things and all people.*"[16] Furthermore, Cady, Ronan and Taussig presented Sophia as "the image of the God who revealed "herself or himself within the workings of the universe and who want[ed] to help people see God there. She(God/Sophia) *pervades and permeates all things.*"[17] They argued that "the divine is at work not only in human experience, but in *all things.*"[18]

Religious feminists suggest using names for God that recognize her/his material aspect. Alongside non-material names, such as *love, word, spirit, verb* and *light*, feminists call God *rock, door, water*, and *plant*. This practice goes beyond allegory in that God is not just *like* the created matter in some aspect of character, but that he/she is actually regarded as being *present* in the matter in a mysterious way. According to Mollenkott, the divine image resides in matter, yet is bigger than any matter, encompassing the being and becoming of all.[19] She maintained that all creation is pluralistically energized by the same divine spirit.

> Viewed from a more biblical perspective, the concept of one Source affirms rather than denies pluralism. If creation contains the infinite variety that it obviously does contain, and yet *stems from a single source and is energized by one single Spirit*, then we must conclude that the one Source and the one Energy [God or the Spirit of God] has a powerful preference for pluralism![20] (emphasis added)

Just as in secular feminism, religious feminism came to identify *God* as an impersonal force or energy. This was obvious in Mollenkott's reference to God as "He/She/It." Other religious feminists now suggest that believers forego gender pronouns altogether. They refer to God as *the womb of being, Primal Matrix, the divine Generatrix, Eternal Spirit, Growth in Qualitative Meaning, Cosmic Benefactor,* and *Ground of All Being.* All these feminist terms attest to the feminist concept of "God" as a force which permeates all things. Therefore, religious feminism is pantheistic, as is secular feminism.

Self Is God

Christian feminists do not openly identify themselves as God(s) — this would be intolerably blasphemous to their religious communities — but they do manage to carefully incorporate a Self-Is-God philosophy into their theology through slippery language. Consider the following quote by Mollenkott:

I really *am* one embodiment or manifestation or incarnation of God, but I am not God. I am part of the "all" that God is "above," and "in," and "through," but my infinitesimal parameters do not contain the whole of who God is, And yet they *do*, in the sense that God is completely present at every point.[21]

Mollenkott argued that although she did not encompass all that God is, she is, nevertheless, God, — or at least a "mini-god." Feminists reason that they can identify themselves in this manner because of the Biblical concept of God's indwelling Spirit. They argue that God is present in all, and that Christian conversion merely entails recognizing that fact. Mollenkott expressed the idea in typical religious feminist language:

Nor need we fear to acknowledge God's presence within ourselves, in one sense communicating with us in the depth of our spirit, and in another sense fully identified with us. God is both "other" and ourselves, more fully ourselves than our superficial body-identified personalities could ever be, and yet beyond us, more all-encompassing than we could imagine Her to be, more mysterious than any of His names![22]

While secular feminism brashly identifies self as being god, religious feminism "humbly" recognizes that the self is only one among many manifestations of God. But even though one's personal godhood is merely a part of a larger whole, the feminist theology of "self-as-God" is credited with "empowering" the psyche. Mollenkott explained:

Godding is a humbling experience because it makes me aware that I am only one manifestation among infinite millions of manifestations. Yet godding is also empowering because I am a manifestation of *God*. God Herself! God Himself! God Itself! Above all. Through all. And in us all.[23]

Christian feminists believed that self is God, or at least *one* manifestation of God. Many of them therefore see conversion as coming to the realization that God resides within the human psyche. According to Mollenkott, repentance is "a humbling and exhilarating identification with the One God."[24]

A New Consciousness

Religious feminists agree with secular feminists that a new consciousness is needed to abolish dualisms such as right and wrong and do away with the process of "splitting *Us* from *them*." According to religious feminist theology, people will be saved when they identify with Jesus Christ's inclusive acceptance of all people. Mollenkott argued that humans would be ushered into a higher level of consciousness with the "recognition of one's self with God" and a recognition that "all human beings were the children of one divine Parent."[25]

According to Mollenkott, it is important for humans to first recognize their connectedness to God, and second, to bring home to the heart of the Church all those who have been defined as "other."[26] Feminists believe that the essence of Christianity is a new consciousness whereby Christians recognize their connectedness and therefore cease to categorize. The religious feminist vision is one in which the dualisms of right/wrong, holy/sinful, and dark/light will be abolished and all will be embraced as one. Mollenkott pictured this scenario:

> White people will be able to acknowledge their own irresponsibilities and will not have to project them onto darker-skinned people; men will be free to acknowledge their own irrational fears and childishness and will not be forced to project them onto women; heterosexuals will be free to acknowledge their own lustful urges and will no longer have to project them onto homosexuals and bisexuals. And so forth.[27]

A New Humanity

The fifth theme which secular and religious feminists hold in common is that of a New Humanity. Both secular and religious feminists believe that feminist spirituality will usher in a new reality and context of meaning. They believe that as all become children of God — or, to use the secular term, "come to consciousness" — a new humanity will be ushered in. Christian feminists believe that this new humanity will actually *be* the Kingdom of God and the return of Christ.

Co-creating a just and loving, ecumenical, pluralistic human society is the goal of both secular and religious feminism. Mollenkott argued that Christians were to "co-create" a just and loving human society with God.[28]

She explained that in doing so, Christians accepted their union with Christ and became the New Humanity.

> . . . in accepting our union with the Christ-nature, that is, in affirming our willingness to do God's will, we become the New Humanity in which are dissolved all the barriers of racism, classism, sexism, heterosexism, and the militarism that grows out of them.[29]

According to Mollenkott, all who work toward the New Humanity are "God's righteous agents upon the earth." She maintained that all those who are involved in political and social activism to liberate the oppressed are children of God who acknowledge Jesus:

> . . . the acknowledgment of Jesus on earth does not mean that only Christians are capable of godding, of being God's righteous agents upon the earth. Acknowledging Jesus means living the life of Jesus as members of the New Humanity, as citizens of the New Creation, transformed by faith into new creatures who are empowered by God's grace to love our neighbors as we love ourselves. Acknowledging Jesus also means recognizing and acting out of our oneness with our Source, the Holy Spirit of the One God, just as Jesus recognized his oneness with the same Source and prayed that we also would be one as he was one with God (John 17:21). To be one with God means to recognize our oneness with all those who also have derived their being from the same Source: Muslims; Jews; post-Christian or post-Jewish feminists; gay people or heterosexual people; liberal or fundamentalist people; communist or capitalist people; black, white, red, or yellow people.[30]

Religious feminism advocates an ecumenism that dissolves boundaries between categories. According to feminists, the New Creation prophesied in the Bible is to be a peaceful, worldwide society in which there are no oppressed peoples and no distinctions, merely a global "us." According to Mollenkott, this is ecumenism's goal.

> The goal of ecumenism is not dogmatic, doctrinal, or even liturgical agreement. The goal of ecumenism is mutual cooperation and respect as the affirmation of a single faith-experience, a shared membership in the New Creation. According to Saint Paul, this New Creation is a just and fair world in which the barriers of racism, classism, and sexism are melted, in which there is no longer any of them but only a global us.[31]

The primary interest of religious feminism is, in Mollenkott's words, "bringing about the New Creation purged of racism, sexism, and classism."[32] She explained that the primary goal is "the New Humanity in the New Creation."[33] Ruether agreed that feminist Christianity anticipates the new age and expects it soon to dawn upon the earth. She too argued that God's new age will be patterned after "the social order of redemption."[34]

The Experience of Personal Power

The experience of personal power is the final theme shared by religious and secular feminists. But it is another one which, for the religious feminist, is somewhat awkward to express. After all, personal power is not a quality that the Bible values. Again, the difficulty is overcome through carefully worded explanations such as the one made by Cady, Ronan and Taussig:

> One of the most important connections embodied by Sophia is that of the creator and the created. As we have seen in Proverbs 8, Sophia was there at the beginning, a master craftswoman, and an ongoing part of the creative process. No sharp division exists between Sophia as creator, and Sophia herself created by God.
>
> By bridging the supposed gap between creator and creation, Sophia provides exactly the image needed to make us aware of our own collective power, not as God's puppets, but as co-creators of this planet.... As we touch down again and again into the creative process, in parenting, in gardening, in politics and resistance, in the arts, in sport, in prayer and ritual, we fill out Sophia's image as creator and created in our own lives.[35]
> ... Sophia brings power. She has power to share, and this power is especially available to women. Women who incorporate Sophia's symbolism within themselves can experience an extraordinary affirmation of every aspect of their being. Through Sophia women can claim power as their right, exercise it creatively, share it, and be sustained by it. They can be strong and independent.[36]

Religious feminists agree that the divine is known and encountered through human experience.[37] They claim to be empowered (by the Spirit) in order to be true to their own feelings and experiences. Being in touch with their true selves puts them in touch with God and further empowers them to work for fulfillment of the feminist vision — both personally and in society. Mollenkott argues that being in touch with her inner self allows God to be embodied within her.[38] She views the end goal of this embodiment as action on behalf of others who are oppressed. Therefore, just like secular feminists, religious feminists seek to experience power for the ultimate purpose of pursuing change.

GODDING

Religious feminist theology developed along the same lines as secular feminist theory. Both secular and religious feminists concluded that "God" is not an external, independent, knowable entity, but rather regarded Him/Her/It as an intuitively perceived, internal "force." Furthermore, they both maintain that the higher consciousness of esoteric metaphysics —

knowledge of the connectedness of all that exists — allows for the liberation of all oppressed people and matter, beginning with women themselves. Mollenkott called this "godding." According to her, feminist women "godded" when they used their knowledge of their connectedness with God to act for the equality and liberation of others. Secular feminists had outrightly named themselves as gods, and, although it took somewhat longer, and was couched in traditional Christian terms, religious feminists began to do the same.

17

Women-Church

She, who's been involved in creating the entire universe, who's helped make the stars and planets, the solar systems, the black holes, the atoms and the quasars — this same One in and through whom rivers and trees and mountains and deserts and oceans came into being. . . . She, who orders the affairs of the universe, has come to the city to live, she has come to the city to rest, and she has settled in and put down roots. The Divine One has come to live among humanity.[1]

The participants assembled in a semicircle around a lone bowed figure. Sunlight trickled through the window and joined in dance with the light of a candle. A hush of expectancy settled upon the kneeling group as the initiate revealed her chosen name and its meaning. Emotions were touched by the recounting of her story. Suddenly the initiate and community stood. Together they recited a litany of exorcism from the powers and principalities of patriarchy. Each phrase of disaffiliation was heightened by the ringing of a bell. Their voices rose to a crescendo.

"Powers of corruption of our humanity, which turn males into instruments of domination and shape women to be tools of submission, BEGONE!"

The denouncements echoed before fading into silence. The initiate's tongue was touched with salt, and the group then proceeded in single file to a garden pool at the rear of the building.

The initiate shed her clothing piece by piece until she was draped only by the light of the sun. Naked she descended into the water. Three times she was submerged.

"Through the power of the Source, the liberating Spirit, and the forerunners of our hope, be freed from the power of evil. May the forces of violence, of militarism, of sexism, of racism, of injustice, and of all that diminishes human life lose their power over your life. May all the influences of these powers be washed away in these purifying waters. May you enter the promised land of milk and honey and grow in virtue, strength, and truthfulness of mind. And may the oil of gladness always anoint your head."

The initiate rose from the waters and was clothed in a white garment. Her forehead was anointed with oil and a candle put into her hands. A brightly embroidered stole was placed around her shoulders. She was then led in procession back to the celebration circle.

The new community shared sweetbread and a cup of milk mingled with honey.

". . . this is the cup of salvation, the taste of the good land flowing with milk and honey, which is our true and promised home."

Each member sealed the covenant of the new constituent with a kiss of peace. The community then stood with linked hands to join together in a final song.

A ritual performed by an obscure feminist cult? No. The narration depicts a rite of baptism and sharing of Eucharist Rosemary Ruether proposed be used within a mainstream feminist women-church group in America.[2]

Feminists had discovered that they could not always freely recognize and celebrate the themes of religious feminism within the boundaries of their traditional patriarchal religious structures. In the most recent development in religious feminism, therefore, feminist women have begun to establish independent worship groups that allow for the development of the religious feminist vision. Fiorenza calls this the "Ekklesia of Women."[3] Ruether calls it "Women-Church."[4]

The *Ekklesia (church) of Women*, or *Women-Church*, is a feminist counterculture movement that interacts with, but is not controlled by traditional religion. Feminist theologians suggest that women separate themselves somewhat from the Church — collectively, as women — in order to initiate the formation of a true Christian redemptive community. According to Ruether, this separation could take on many forms: from small Bible-study groups and women's groups associated with a traditional church, to large, independent women's churches; from women's courses at traditional Bible schools and seminaries, to feminist exodus training and retreat centers. According to Ruether and Fiorenza, the purpose of these groups is to form a *critical culture* or *exodus community* that rejects patriarchy — both in the Church and in the world. The goal, as described by Ruether, is to "create real transformation" and, in effect, "redefine the boundaries and the content of what it meant to be Church."[5] Ruether explained:

> Women-Church represents the first time that women collectively have claimed to be church and have claimed the tradition of the exodus community as a community of liberation from patriarchy. . . .
> Women-Church is the Christian theological expression of this stage of feminist collectivization of women's experience and the formation of crit-

ical culture. It means that women delegitimize the theological myths that justify the *ecclesia* of patriarchy and begin to form liturgies to midwife their liberation from it. They begin to experience the gathering of liberated women as a redemptive community rooted in a new being. They empower themselves and are empowered by this liberated Spirit upon which they are grounded (the two are not contradictory, since one empowers oneself authentically only by being empowered by the Spirit that grounds one) to celebrate this new community, to commune with it, and to nurture themselves and be nurtured in the community of liberated sisterhood.[6]

Feminists viewed Women-Church as the true Church of God(dess). They regarded themselves as the exodus community from the bondage of patriarchy, leading the Church to its new home. According to feminist theologians, women are the Church. As Ruether argued:

I would contend today that we as women can indeed speak as Church, do speak as Church, not in exile from the Church, but rather that the Church is in exile with us, awaiting with us a wholeness that we are in process of revealing. . . . We are not in exile, but the Church is in exodus with us. God's Shekinah, Holy Wisdom, the Mother-face of God has fled from the high thrones of patriarchy and has gone into exodus with us. . . .

We are Women-Church, not in exile, but in exodus. We flee the thundering armies of Pharaoh. . . .[7]

According to Ruether, the strength of Women-Church is its "transformational dialectic." By establishing an independent counterculture movement, and yet refusing to totally disengage themselves from traditional religion, feminists hope that they can create pressure that will dialectically transform the Church from both within and without. In Ruether's words, "the feminist option will be able to develop much more powerfully at the present time if it secures footholds in existing Christian churches and uses them to communicate its option to far larger groups of people than it could possibly do if it had to manufacture these institutional resources on its own."[8] Women-Church therefore seeks to gain a stronghold within the existing Church while it concurrently dialogues with traditions outside of the Church. Ruether explained:

Feminists who have opted to remain in dialogue with the historic traditions of Judaism and Christianity, although not necessarily accepting their limits, thus engage in a double dialogue. On the one hand, they are in dialogue with the historic culture of parent institutions and are able to appropriate its best insights into their new option. But they are not limited to this dialogue. They also engage in dialogue outside this tradition and never before allowed by it, dialogue with heresies and rejected options of earlier Christianity that can now be read with new eyes, dialogue with pre-Christian and pre-Biblical religion. They also engage in a contemporary dialogue with other religious feminists who opt to work in other traditions, Jewish feminists and Goddess feminists who themselves interpret their roots in the past in a variety of ways. Perhaps feminists of other religions, such as Islam, will also join the dialogue.[9]

Feminists hope that men will eventually join Women-Church so that all of humanity can be liberated. At that time, Ruether projects, the feminist community will simply be known as "church." But for the time being, she argues that it is necessary for women to worship on their own, free from the influence of men. She therefore views Women-Church as an ongoing movement that will exist right up until the dawning of the new age.

Women-Church must form an ongoing commitment to establishing autonomous bases of community and cultural formation that are both in dialogue with the people of the churches, but outside their institutional control. This commitment must last for as long as it takes to defeat patriarchal power totally and transform all of its social and cultural expression; in short, we might say, until the coming of the reign of God/ess.[10]

WOMEN-CHURCH FUNCTION

Ruether explained that Women-Church differs from traditional church communities in a number of ways. She points out that Women-Church seeks to dismantle clericalism, establishing all women as ministers. It radically reappropriates ministry "as the articulation of the community whereby the community symbolizes its common life, communicates it to one another, and engages in mutual empowerment."[11] According to Ruether, dismantling clericalism does not do away with authentic leadership. It simply means that expressions of liturgy, learning, and service are delegated to a number of women, based on their function and skills, rather than being assigned to an elite clerical caste. The second aspect of church life that Ruether extensively developed for Women-Church is liturgy — "collective prayer and celebration."[12] Third, she believed that the community should engage in some social praxis that would make it "a community witnessing to a new option for human life."[13] Counseling at a rape crisis center, or being involved in women's political lobby groups, is considered social praxis. Finally, Ruether encouraged the community to collectivize its life together at some level. She explained that this could take the form of a regular meal together, sharing financial resources, collective work projects, or even collective living.[14]

WOMEN-CHURCH WORSHIP

Ruether's development of liturgy and worship are by far her most important contributions to Women-Church. Liturgy empowers women to transform the traditional sacraments of the patriarchal Church and to introduce new traditions that express and celebrate women's journey of liberation. Ruether explained that she had constructed Women-Church liturgical rituals from many layers of Mediterranean and Western religious traditions: non-Biblical ancient New Eastern tradition, Jewish tradition, and usable Christian tradition. Rituals and observances include the natural (celebration of the cycles of nature and the "reharmonization of humanity with nonhuman nature"[15]; the historical (celebrating the passover, or remembering tragic historic events); and the eschatological (expressing the messianic hope for final deliverance from the sin of patriarchy and the coming of the new age).

Ruether compiled an extensive collection of liturgies in *Women-Church: Theology and Practice*. In this volume, she presented four types of liturgy that were to be practiced by Women-Church. The first sequence of liturgies focused on the formation of the Church as a community of liberation from patriarchy and all oppression. Ruether included, for example, rites of conversion and baptism into the exodus community; rites of "Mind Cleansing from the Pollution of Sexism"; rites to exorcise patriarchy from Biblical texts; a litany of disaffiliation from patriarchal theology; litanies of remembrance of oppressed foremothers; and blessings for communion in the traditional Christian bread and wine:

Blessing of the Bread: "As these grains were once scattered on the hillsides and plains and now are brought together into one loaf, so gather your people, O Wisdom-Spirit, into the community of justice and peace. May the world of patriarchy vanish away and the new age of love and joy between sisters and brothers arise.

Blessing of the Cup: "We are the new wine of life that flows in the branches of the vine tree. We remember our brother Jesus, who poured out his blood to water the roots of this vine. We also remember the many brothers and sisters who have died that a new world might be born: Oscar Arnulfo Romero, Martin Luther King, Ita Ford, Dorothy Kazal, Maura Clark, and Jean Donovan, whose blood fertilized and gave new growth to this vine tree. In sharing this blest cup, we share our lives with one another for the sake of the beloved community. We pledge to continue their struggle until all humankind can sit down together in peace and joy at the table of life.

The bread and wine are shared with the salutation, "The bread of life": "The cup of salvation."

In addition to the bread and wine, Ruether added a Eucharist of blessing and sharing the apple "since," she argued, "this innocent and good fruit has been absurdly turned into a symbol of evil and an assault against women as the source of evil."

Blessing the Apple: This is the apple of consciousness raising. Let the scales of false consciousness fall from our eyes, so that we can rightly name truth and falsehood, good and evil.[16]

Ruether's second sequence of liturgies dealt with rites of healing from particular occasions of violence and crisis. Ruether included rites meant to heal women from distress of mind or body, to heal from violence, from incest, wife-battering, rape, abortion, miscarriage, and divorce. She included a rite of naming wherein a divorced woman empowers herself by discarding her husband's name and claiming a new, personally chosen name. Also included was a self-blessing ritual and a coming-out celebratory rite for lesbians.

Third, Ruether outlined liturgies that celebrate the life cycle and its rites of passage. She included in this collection a naming celebration for a new child; birthday blessings and invocations to the Mother-Spirit; a puberty rite (performed with symbolic dolls and eggs) in which the young girl is instructed in sexuality, contraception, and menstruation; a ritual for a person "coming of age" and leaving home; "covenanting celebrations" for creating new families (for couples, both hetero- and homosexual, who wished to enter into a committed relationship, but not marriage); a marriage rite; a covenant celebration for a lesbian couple; a liturgy in preparation for childbirth; a menopausal liturgy; a croning (retirement) liturgy; a dying vigil; and a liturgy for a funeral.

Ruether's fourth and final collection included liturgies for celebrating seasonal and annual rites and for expressing eschatological hope. Ruether entitled this section: "Encircling Our Transformation: Seasonal Celebrations."[17] She suggested rituals for celebrating the cycle of day and night and of the week. She also included rituals to celebrate the cycle of the month: menstrual rituals and rituals of the moon. Her fall ritual of "Hallowmas" remembered "the holocaust of women throughout history." It included a litany of remembrance and a symbolic memorial offering of fruit and flowers. Rituals for celebrating the summer and winter solstices and autumnal and vernal equinoxes (witchcraft practices) were also included by Ruether. A proposed Ash Wednesday liturgy sought repentance for the sins of the Church, and a walk for justice was suggested for Good Friday. The Good Friday ritual reenacted the passion of Christ as applied to human liberation, and the suggested Easter liturgies were celebrated with an eye to women's deliverance. Ruether also outlined other rites celebrating nature, such as an earth day celebration.

All liturgies and rites that Ruether outlined for Women-Church groups included sensory stimulation. She incorporated symbolic items such as stones, plants, flowers, and foods into the ceremonies and used candles, incense, scented body oil, and music to contribute to the atmosphere. Some rituals required singing, repetitive chants, incantations, touch, dance and rhythmic movement. Some rites required women to bathe together, and some were to be performed without clothing. Ruether even conceptualized a building for an independent Women-Church congregation that contained hot and cool tubs, gardens, crypts, and personal retreat cabins to facilitate performing these rituals.

THE GODDESS AND THE BRIDE

The feminist Christian commitment is not to a saviour who redeems us by bringing God to us. Our commitment is to love ourselves and others into wholeness. Our commitment is to a divine presence with us here and now, a presence that works through the mystery of our deepest selves and our relationships, constantly healing us and nudging us toward a wholeness of existence we only fitfully know. That healed wholeness is not Christ; it is ourselves.[18]

Except for the occasional Biblical reference and the sprinkling of selected Christian terminology, the rituals that Ruether suggested for Women-Church are indistinguishable from those practiced by secular feminism. Indeed, she is proud of the fact that she pluralistically included many other traditions alongside Christianity. However, it is important to note that in the process of doing so, she totally turned away from the God and Christ of the Bible. As the above quote points out, the feminist Christian commitment is not to a Savior. The feminist Christian commitment, like the secular feminist commitment, is to self. Feminists, including religious feminists, have named themselves, their world, and their God. In doing so, they have exalted the creation rather than the Creator. They have refused to submit to an external God, but have insisted rather that God submit to being who they want Him to be.

He who created the entire universe, who made the stars and planets, the solar systems, the black holes, the atoms and the quasars — this same One by whose hand the rivers and trees and mountains and deserts and oceans were created . . . He who formed the dust and clay, breathed life, and spilled His own blood for our redemption . . . He has been forsaken. The Bridegroom has been betrayed for another.

She has come to the Church to live, she has come to the Church to rest, and she has settled in and put down roots. The female one has come to live among God's people, and the chosen ones remain blind to the subrogation. The spirits of darkness dance in celebration of the union, for the betrothed has forsaken her first love. The Christian community has opened its arms to feminism. The goddess has joined the Bride.

PART FOUR

Assessing the Right to Name

18

Biblical Feminism

For Christian women, liberation may be a long and difficult process. Many women have not even begun to understand what the movement means to others or to themselves.

Letha Scanzoni and Nancy Hardesty

All the various forms of feminism developed in an overarching pattern that systematically progressed from feminists claiming the right to name self towards feminists claiming the right to name God. Radical feminists were responsible for introducing and furthering feminist theory, but the precepts they presented, softened with the passing of time, were eventually accepted by those who espoused a less radical feminist stance. Many feminist women claimed that their philosophy differed from that of the radical feminists. However, they failed to note that the philosophy they accepted was merely a time-worn version of the radical feminist theory of years gone by.

In the first three sections of this book, I trace the development of feminist theory which was, most often, proposed by those at the radical, cutting edge of the movement. In the development of religious feminism, the theology was forwarded by those whom many would classify as "liberal" theologians. But conservative evangelical Christians are not unaffected by feminism. Many of them view the philosophy of feminism as a valid adjunct to their faith. They believe that the basic tenets of feminism are supported by the Bible and that feminism can naturally, easily and homogeneously be combined with Christianity. These evangelicals do not always go to the extremes of changing doctrine as did feminist theologians Ruether and Russell. They are much more conservative in their approach to the Bible, merely challenging traditional Biblical interpretation in the area of hierarchical gender roles in Church and marriage. They call themselves "Biblical feminists," for they believe in the Bible, but also believe in feminism.

THE ADVENT OF BIBLICAL FEMINISM

At the historical moment when secular society is just beginning to wake up concerning centuries of injustice to women, it is unwise and unjust for evangelical publications to stress biblical passages concerning ancient inequalities between the sexes. By continuing on such a course, evangelicals will only add fuel to the widespread secular concept that the Christian church is an outmoded institution dedicated to the maintenance of the status quo no matter how unjust and inhuman. (Virginia Mollenkott)[1]

Conservative evangelical Christians began to incorporate a feminist perspective into their theology in the early to mid-1970s. Not quite willing to change Scriptural interpretation to the extent of feminist theology, but feeling societal pressure to update the Church's stance on the role of women, Biblical feminists reinterpreted the Bible to align with the definition of equality that had gained widespread acceptance in the secular world. To this end, they reexamined Scriptural texts and altered traditional hermeneutics to present the thesis that equality between men and women was to be reflected by the obliteration of sex roles in Church and marriage. Four works were instrumental in introducing a Biblical feminist position to evangelical Christianity: *Women, Men & the Bible* by Virginia Ramey Mollenkott; *All We're Meant to Be: A Biblical Approach to Women's Liberation* by Letha Scanzoni and Nancy Hardesty; *In Search of God's Ideal Woman*, by Dorothy Pape; and *Man as Male and Female*, by Paul Jewett. These books presented a view on the role of women that has come to be known as the *egalitarian position*. Egalitarians prided themselves in being both feminist *and* Biblical.

THE EGALITARIAN POSITION

The basic definition of an egalitarian is "one who believes in the equality of all people." Historically, most theologians believed in human equality, and would have thus fit this description. But Biblical feminists argued that hierarchically structured relationships, by their nature, served a condition of *in*equality. Different meant unequal. They argued that those who believed that the two sexes were equal, and yet assigned different roles, were nonegalitarian hierarchists. In the past, equality and hierarchy were viewed as mutually inclusive and harmonious; for instance, Karl Barth argued for the full equality of woman and yet upheld female subordination in the institution of marriage and governance of the Church.[2] Biblical feminists, however, rejected the traditional view of equality and claimed the right to name and define for themselves what equality meant and what it needed to look like. In doing so, they adopted the basic precept of secular feminism. Ground-level feminists had, at that time, sought to overcome women's differences in order to become *just like men*. Not only did they reject stereotypical male/female roles, but they also totally rejected the possibility of a "different-yet-equal" framework. Biblical feminists followed suit. They rejected those stereotyped male and female roles in the Church that they believed oppressed women and also rejected the notion that equality could exist within a structure of hierarchy.

Dorothy Pape maintained that hierarchical roles indicated superiority and inferiority.[3] Scanzoni and Hardesty agreed.[4] They vehemently stated that "Equality and subordination are contradictions!"[5] They felt that "true egalitarianism (equality) *must* be characterized by what sociologists call *role-interchangeability.*"[6] Mollenkott, in turn, argued that the hierarchical model was "psychologically unhealthy" and "carnal."[7] She asked, "Since egalitarianism is healthy, can a church be justified in denying equality to its women?"[8] Jewett concurred that a hierarchical structure could not be taught "without supposing that the half of the human race which exercises authority is superior in some way to the half which submits."[9]

These Biblical feminists were reacting against a real problem in the Church. Many men *were* authoritarian, domineering, proud, and abusive of power. Women, on the other hand, were often passive and insecure, having been denied recognition of their full capacity for ministry. Furthermore, men and women were cast into stereotyped roles of service and behavior. The abuse and distortion of the hierarchical model which Biblical feminists observed led them to reject the model altogether and to deny that it could be compatible with the equality that the Bible taught. Biblical feminists therefore dealt with the problems in the Church in essentially the same manner as secular feminists had dealt with the problems in society. Both sought to obliterate sex roles and express equality through role-interchangeability. Biblical feminists adopted the secular definition of equality and then confidently proclaimed that the Bible was *"properly interpreted as supporting the central tenets of feminism."*[10]

BIBLICAL FEMINIST HERMENEUTICS

In order to "properly" interpret the Bible so that it supported the central tenets of feminism, Biblical feminists needed to adjust the traditionally accepted methods of Biblical interpretation. To begin, they identified their *"crux interpretum."* They then modified some hermeneutic presuppositions and methods, and culturalized Biblical directives, in order to harmonize their crux and their predetermined definition of equality.

Crux Interpretum

Rosemary Radford Ruether and Letty Russell chose liberation as their *crux interpretum* when developing feminist liberation theology. They reasoned that since women were a class of people oppressed by men, the Bible should be interpreted to support their vision for the liberation of women. Many foundational Biblical doctrines were revised in order to align with their chosen theme.

Biblical feminists approached Scripture in a similar manner. Whereas Ruether and Russell chose "liberation," Biblical feminists chose "equality" as their *crux interpretum*. They interpreted all questionable texts to align with their own understanding of sexual equality, which they defined as monolithic, undifferentiated role-interchangeability. Although these Christian feminists did not revise Bible doctrine to the extent of the liberation theologians, the trend towards such revision was initiated. In demanding that all Bible interpretation and doctrine align itself with their particular definition of equality, Biblical feminists adopted the same posture as their radical feminist sisters.

Biblical feminists chose Galatians 3:28, "In Christ there is neither male nor female . . . ," as the crux around which to interpret Scripture. Notwithstanding that the context of this verse dealt with who could become a Christian and on what basis — and not with male/female roles — they dubbed this "the Magna Carta" of humanity.[11] They claimed that the phrase "neither male nor female" indicated God's desire to see sex roles obliterated in a social context. Equality, they reasoned, meant getting rid of role distinctions. Moreover, they judged the validity of New Testament directives pointing towards *distinctive* male/female roles in light of this definition.

For example, Jewett proposed that any interpretation of Scripture that did not align with "*Paul's fundamental statement of Christian liberty*" was "incongruous" with the Bible, for it "breaks the analogy of faith."[12] Scanzoni and Hardesty proposed that "we must immediately suspect any reading [of Scripture] which contradicts the *thrust of the whole Bible* toward human justice and oneness in Christ."[13] "Any teaching in regard to women," they said, "must square with the *basic theological thrust* of the Bible."[14] Mollenkott reasoned that "the Bible was not in error to record Paul's thought-processes. But we are in error to absolutize anything that denies the *thrust of the entire Bible* toward individual wholeness and harmonious community, toward oneness in Christ."[15]

For Biblical feminists, the *crux interpretum* of equality, and the feminist definition thereof, became the measuring stick by which Scripture was appraised. Scanzoni and Hardesty argued,

> Interpretations of Scripture relative to women must not conflict with either the unequivocal, universal, and identical sinfulness of both sexes, or the grace bestowed on both sexes through Jesus Christ. Likewise, any interpretation that does not stress equal responsibility of both sexes in the kingdom of God must be rejected. An interpretation that absolutizes a given historical social order is unacceptable, as is one that is based on only isolated texts.[16]

Biblical feminists decided that *equality* meant monolithic, undifferentiated role-interchangeability. Rather than gleaning their definition of equality from the Bible, Biblical feminists adopted the feminist definition of equality that was current in contemporary North American society. They chose "equality" as their *crux interpretum* and then demanded that all Biblical interpretation support their predetermined, feminist definition. In doing so, they claimed the right to name for themselves.

Hermeneutic Presuppositions and Methods

While I do not wish to extensively explore the hermeneutics (rules and guidelines for interpreting the Bible) of Biblical feminism, a brief overview is necessary in order to see how Biblical feminism related to secular feminism and to the more radical aspects of feminist theology. I have dealt with Biblical feminist theology in more detail in a previous work, *Women, Creation and the Fall* (Crossway, 1990). This summary is extracted from that analysis.

Traditionally, Christians have believed that the Bible presents an absolute standard for right and wrong. They have stood against the premise that truth is relative and that the truth of the Bible is subject to alteration. Biblical feminists did not overtly subscribe to a synthetic system of logic — one that sees truth as dynamic and evolutionary — but in the matter of male/female roles, they began to lean towards that stance. These Christians acknowledged that directives for the role of women were set in place in the epistles, but they countered that the directives were not meant for all time. The teachings were meant to *evolve* and change with culture. Scanzoni and Hardesty argued,

> None of the apostles advocated the *immediate* overthrow of cultural custom — Christianity was controversial enough without that! Yet they did not shy away from the radical cutting edge of the gospel which would *gradually* undermine society's oppressive policies and restore God's intended harmony. . . . Social distinctions are meant to be transcended — not perpetuated — within the body of Christ.[17]

Scanzoni and Hardesty believed in the progressive nature of Biblical interpretation with regards to male and female roles. So much so that they argued that Ephesians 5 allowed for an *evolution* or *development* of the ideal of marriage as God intended it.[18] Mollenkott agreed that some Biblical directives were evolutionary in nature. She maintained that

> The apostle Paul knew that the sinful social order could not be changed overnight. But he apparently glimpsed two truths concerning human society: that *eventually* the principles of the gospel would bring about a more egalitarian society, and that *ultimately* God's plan for a redeemed social order was an egalitarian one.[19]

Jewett also reflected this opinion:

If revelation is historical — as the Christian church teaches — then it does not wholly transcend history and culture; rather it redeems history and culture. And *redemption is a process*, sometimes a slow and gradual process.[20]

The Biblical feminist's belief in the evolving, developing nature of revelation with regards to male and female roles poses some difficulty for the interpretation of other Scripture. For if this particular teaching is meant to evolve, it logically follows that other teachings that are now socially unacceptable are likewise changing. Evangelicals could therefore justifiably update Christian doctrine to approve of homosexuality, adultery, divorce, euthanasia, and abortion. Furthermore, Biblical revelation might eventually evolve to support the total annihilation of marriage, family, and biological sexual differentiation. The presupposition is the same. It is merely a matter of degree of application.

Biblical feminists also altered traditional presuppositions regarding the inspiration of Scripture. Whereas Christians have traditionally believed that the *whole* Bible is inspired by God, Biblical feminists maintained that only *some* Scripture is so inspired. The rest is so male-biased, so influenced by the writers' own culture and prejudices, that it is inapplicable to the contemporary Church. Mollenkott argued,

At this point we must begin to face a serious problem in our interpretation of the Bible. Although the Bible is a divine book, it has come to us through human channels. And it seems apparent that some of the apostle Paul's arguments reflect his personal struggles over female subordination and show vestiges both of Greek philosophy (particularly Stoicism) and of the rabbinical training he had received from his own socialization and especially from Rabbi Gamaliel.[21]

Mollenkott accused the Apostle Paul of transmitting the "prejudice, superstition, and bias of his own time" in his writings. In spite of his shortsightedness, she graciously excused his limitations and did not "denounce him for not anticipating and addressing concerns that have only recently been raised to a *high level of consciousness.*"[22] With regards to the inspiration of the Bible, she maintained that Scripture must not be forced into parameters which were arbitrarily drawn. She maintained that the *facts* of Scripture — that is, Paul's confusion, conflict, and contradiction regarding male/female roles — should indicate the "limits and manner" of Biblical inspiration.[23]

The presupposition of the inerrancy of Scripture was also altered by Biblical feminists. When they encountered disagreeable passages, they merely labeled them as unauthentic and/or incorrect. For example, Scanzoni and Hardesty stated that Paul, in his letter to Timothy, was *wrong* in his interpretation of Genesis 2.[24] The Biblical feminist position on inerrancy threatened the concept of the *unity* of Scripture. Scripture is commonly regarded by evangelicals as being unified in its message. Therefore, when two apparently contradictory ideas are found, it is assumed that they are both authentic parts of a whole — complementing one another in presenting various aspects of a complete, unified picture. Biblical feminists, however, argued that Bible passages contradict each other. They quoted Scripture *against* Scripture to support their arguments.

Scanzoni and Hardesty, for example, maintained that Paul's teaching in the epistles led to a subordination of women that was *incompatible* with the gospel he expounded in Galatians 3:28.[25] They identified "tension" and "inconsistency" between the two texts.[26] Jewett also believed that Paul's view of the male/female relationship "was *not altogether congruous* with the gospel he preached."[27] He saw a "*disparity or incongruity* within Scripture itself."[28] Mollenkott argued that Paul's interpretation of the creation narrative "could not be substantiated by the Genesis story."[29] She asked, "Are we to insist on the *literalness* of Genesis 2? [As Paul did] . . . Or are we going to recognize that Genesis 2 is poetic narrative?"[30] (And thus come to a better understanding of this Scripture and male/female roles than Paul had.)

Not only did Biblical feminists feel justified in altering basic hermeneutic presuppositions regarding the nature of revelation, as well as the inspiration, inerrancy, and unity of Scripture, but in order to harmonize Biblical texts with their definition of equality they also tampered with traditional hermeneutic methodology. Interpretive rules such as "context determines meaning," "unclear passages yield to clear," "incidental passages yield to didactic," and "Scripture interprets Scripture" were violated.[31] Furthermore, feminists dealt with unpalatable Scripture by searching for alternate meanings of Greek words and then arguing that these "newly discovered" definitions altered the meaning of the text. The discussion regarding the definition of *kephale*, the Greek word for head(ship), is a prime example of this.[32]

Finally, passages that could not be discounted in any of these ways were handled by labeling them "cultural" and hence inapplicable to the contemporary Church.[33] Pape maintained that Paul *accommodated* himself to local thinking for the sake of making the gospel palatable to *his society*.[34] Mollenkott stated that the Church's higher (*sic*) understanding of human equality *forced* it to recognize that the famous sections on women in the Church were simply *descriptions of first-century customs* applied to specific situations in local churches.[35] Scanzoni and Hardesty likewise argued that Paul's teachings were merely presented to support cultural custom and that "all social distinctions between men and women should have [by now] been erased in the church."[36]

BIBLICAL FEMINISTS AND THE FEMINIST MIND-SET

Biblical feminists formulated a definition of equality for Christian women that concurred with the definition put forth by secular society. Equality meant role-interchangeability. With this definition in hand, Biblical feminists turned to the Bible. They found that while the Bible did teach the essential equality of women and men, it also taught role differentiation. In order to harmonize the Bible's teachings with their view of equality, these feminists found it necessary to determine which Scriptural texts were dynamic and which were static, which were inspired and which were the author's bias, which were true and which were in error. In doing so, Biblical feminists adopted a feminist mind-set. Secular feminist philosophy had taught women to name themselves and their world. The experiences and perceptions of women were regarded as a valid source for redefining truth and reality. Christian feminists adopted this mentality when they used their own definition of equality to judge the validity and applicability of the Bible. In this way, feminist experience overruled commonly accepted hermeneutic principles. Even for conservative evangelical feminists, women's experience became the new norm for Biblical study and theological interpretation.

THE "NEW" CHRISTIAN PSYCHOLOGY OF GENDER

The conservative Christian feminist argument for monolithic equality was similar to that of secular feminism and the same as that used by the early liberal religious feminists. All first pointed out how men had wrongly defined women, then encouraged women to exercise their right to name and define themselves. Secular feminists justified this by exalting the importance of women's experience. Liberal and conservative Christian feminists justified it by choosing a "theme" of the Bible that supported their predetermined point of view. They were then able to argue for equality while citing the Bible as their base. The Biblical feminist monograph *Gender & Grace*, by Mary Stewart VanLeeuwen (InterVarsity Press, 1990), is a representative sample of this.

VanLeeuwen, a psychologist and professor of interdisciplinary studies at Calvin College, sought to present a "new" model for insight into sexual identity and the relationship between male and female. She wanted to define new Christian parameters for "love, work and parenting in a changing world."[37] Essentially VanLeeuwen attempted to use psychology to harmonize the feminist view with conservative evangelical Christianity. Because she was formerly an editor for *The Reformed Journal* and a senior editor for *Christianity Today*, VanLeeuwen's book received a great deal of attention. VanLeeuwen began her discussion on male and female by referring to the "acts" of the "Biblical Drama": creation, Fall, redemption, Pentecost and renewal.[38] Rather than beginning at creation, she chose to start with Pentecost and renewal. In this way — before any discussion or Biblical interpretation took place — VanLeeuwen defined her *crux interpretum*.

I am going to start with act four — one that many people ignore completely — and flash back to acts one through three from there. Act four,

Pentecost, is a *very significant event for our basic understanding of sex and gender.*[39]

VanLeeuwen stated that at Pentecost, God "*seemed* to be saying that the era of obedience under the Law was over, to be replaced by an era of freedom and empowerment in the Spirit."[40] She pointed out that:

Pentecost has sometimes been called "women's emancipation day," because of women's inclusion with men in the outpouring of the Spirit. . . . "You are all one in Christ Jesus" is how Paul summarized it in Galatians 3:28.[41]

VanLeeuwen noted that whenever the Church is in a state of revival, arguments about which sex does what seem to recede into the background. At other times, she argued, men and women alike seemed to "regress to a *pre-Pentecost anxiety about gender roles and become preoccupied with details concerning headship and submission*"[42] (emphasis added).

The suppositions underlying VanLeeuwen's study are evident in the first three pages of her discussion. She saw the role of women as equal, that is, undifferentiated from men. She believes that women's role is to be a contemporary pentecostal expression of "an era of freedom" rather than an "era of obedience to the law." VanLeeuwen implies that equality could not mean role differentiation, for those who are "preoccupied with details concerning headship and submission" are reverting to a "pre-Pentecost anxiety." VanLeeuwen thereby defined her *crux* for interpreting the Bible as her own definition of equality. Following the delineation of this *crux*, VanLeeuwen proceeds to interpret the other three "acts" she had cited.

According to VanLeeuwen, a Christian feminist is a person of either sex who sees women and men as "*equally* saved, *equally* Spirit-filled and *equally* sent."[43] She does not take this to imply, however, that there are no differences between the sexes. To understand what the differences between the sexes are, VanLeeuwen turned her attention to the acts of creation and the Fall. From the act of creation, she extrapolated first that the image of God is intrinsically *social*.[44] Man and woman, created in the image of God are social beings. Second, she noted that both man and woman were given *dominion* over the rest of creation. She viewed these two traits of *sociability* and *dominion* as the essence of the pre-Fall male/female condition of equality.

According to VanLeeuwen, in the act of the Fall, the balance of equality was distorted. The woman abused her *dominion* by eating of the forbidden fruit; the man, in turn, abused his *sociability* by accepting some of the fruit "even though he knew that their unity as man and woman was not to supersede their obedience to God."[45] VanLeeuwen argued that woman's abuse of *dominion* and man's abuse of *sociability* were used by God as the basis for the judgment against the sexes. She argued that, from the Fall on, man would be tempted to disregard his *sociability* and turn his natural *dominion* of the earth into *domination* of women. Women, on the other hand, would be tempted to focus on *sociability* and "use the preservation of those relationships as an excuse not to exercise accountable *dominion*."[46] In essence, VanLeeuwen reasoned that man's sin would be to dominate woman, woman's sin would be to let him do it.[47] She noted that the act of redemption through Jesus was the reversal of the effects of the Fall. Therefore, through Jesus, and through the coming of the Holy Spirit at Pentecost, she reasoned that men and women were enabled to revert to their created condition of equal dominion and equal sociability. Furthermore, she argued that the sinful behavioral tendencies of men to dominate and of women to accept that domination could be overcome through the liberating gospel.

In ordering and interpreting the Biblical "acts" in this way, VanLeeuwen laid the theological basis for her argument. From this point on, she interacted almost exclusively with history and the social sciences in order to "prove" her thesis — namely, that sex-related behavioral tendencies are the consequence of the Fall, that these tendencies are magnified and reinforced by conditioning, and finally, that as redeemed people Christians should seek to restore role androgyny and minimize (if not do away with) role differences between the sexes. First, VanLeeuwen provided selected research on hormones, brain lateralization and cultural conditioning which supported the argument that sex roles were learned rather than innate. Second, she showered readers with statistical rhetoric about the "facts" of patriarchy and the abusive nature of the traditional family structure:

- Although eighty per cent of sexual abuse and family violence occurs in alcoholic families, the next highest incidence of both incest and physical abuse takes place in intact, highly religious homes.[48]

- Next to alcohol and drug abuse the most reliable predictor of wife battering is zealous, conservative religiosity.[49]

- Traditional homemakers, despite their self-reports of happiness, show increasing signs of psychological distress as the marriage progresses.[50]

- The pre-Civil War American South, Nazi Germany, present-day white South Africa — all these societies have supported, even glorified, women's role as keeper of the home and transmitter of values to the next generation.[51]

VanLeeuwen argued that patriarchy began at the time of the Fall, but traced the same steps as her secular feminist sisters when she attributed the perpetuation of patriarchy to the physical and biological differences of women, to the dualistic split between public and domestic spheres, and finally to the process of social conditioning that occurred in the formation of gender identity. According to VanLeeuwen, men are taught to "fear and devalue women."[52] Christian men are not exempt, she argued, for "the problem that has no name . . . affected Christians almost as much as non-Christians."[53]

VanLeeuwen's work is a recent conservative Christian exercise in feminist consciousness raising. The difficulty for most readers is to separate the valid observations she makes from the invalid conclusions she draws. VanLeeuwen noted many valid problems in society and the Church. While she concedes that the origin of these problems is sin, she incorrectly assumes that the problems are perpetuated by a view that differentiates between male and female roles. VanLeeuwen equates hierarchical structure with abuse and/or stereotyping. Hierarchy, according to VanLeeuwen, is correctly modeled by the stereotyped 1950s model of the wife washing the floor and cooking the meal and the husband sitting in the easy chair watching T.V. Although some people did apply hierarchy in this way, VanLeeuwen uses this stereotype to dismiss the hierarchical structure altogether and to dismiss the contemporary applicability of the Bible's male/female role directives for Christians. But there are *two* issues here, and we must distinguish between them. On the one hand, we must agree with VanLeeuwen that the expression of Biblical hierarchy has often been distorted and abused. On the other hand, we cannot accept her proposed feminist solution of claiming the right to name and define our own boundaries. VanLeeuwen confuses the issues when she rejects Biblical structure along with the abusive expression of that structure.

Biblical feminists have been beguiled into defining women's role in the home and Church for themselves. They accept the feminist precept that individuals have the authority to name. This precept is dangerous because the right to name self leads to the right to name the world, and eventually to the right to name "God." Christian women who begin to name themselves often move into the second phase of feminism, which allows them to name theology and alter other Bible doctrines to bring them into harmony with a feminist worldview. Ultimately, many move toward renaming and redefining God.

THE DEVELOPMENT OF BIBLICAL FEMINISM

In 1974 a group of Biblical feminists founded the Evangelical Women's Caucus (EWC). The opening declaration of this group heralded their purpose as presenting "God's teachings on male-female equality to the whole body of Christ's church." According to their brochure, they believed "that the Bible which bears witness to Christ is the Word of God, inspired by the Holy Spirit, and is the infallible guide and final authority for Christian faith and life."[54] But they also believed that the Bible, "when properly understood, supports the basic equality of the sexes."[55] To this end, their goal was "to share the good news of Biblical feminism with the oppressed as well as the oppressors with the hope of bringing about both individual and institutional change."[56] The organization was originally conservative in belief. The only recognizable area in which they differed from traditional Christianity was in the matter of Biblical interpretation regarding the ordination of women and the role of women in marriage. By 1987, however, a number of women found it necessary to withdraw from this organization in disagreement with its apparent endorsement of lesbianism.[57] Subsequently, the remaining members renamed the group the Evangelical *& Ecumenical* Women's Caucus (1990 — emphasis added), a change that accurately reflected its departure from the boundaries of evangelical Christian doctrine.

The dissenting members of the Evangelical Women's Caucus formed another group whose philosophy reflected that of the original caucus: Christians for Biblical Equality (CBE). This organization is a national chapter of Men, Women and God, International, and is associated with John Stott's London Institute for Contemporary Christianity.[58] In July of 1989, the leaders of CBE unveiled a position paper entitled "Men, Women and Equality," in which they affirmed a belief in the Bible as the inspired Word of God. This was precisely the position of their EWC forerunners. Furthermore, their document also presented the belief that the Bible taught the full equality of men and women (that is, monolithic equality — role-interchangeability). This was also EWC's stance.

It should be noticed that conservative Biblical feminism is no longer advanced by those who initiated it. Writers such as Scanzoni, Hardesty, and Mollenkott have left evangelicalism to join liberal religious feminism. Their original theme, carried on by authors such as Margaret Howe, Elaine Storkey, and Charles Trombley, is now being proclaimed by others, such as Patricia and Stanley Gundry, Gilbert Bilezikian, W. Ward Gasque, Gretchen Gaebelein-Hull, Roger Nicole, Alvera Mickelsen, Catherine Kroeger, Walter Liefeld, and Mary Stewart VanLeeuwen.

It appears that many evangelical believers who adopted a conservative feminist position regarding the role of women at one point gravitated towards a more radical one as time wore on. EWC began by being evangelical, but is now far from it. Given this trend, it is entirely possible that the most recent evangelical and feminist leaders and CBE may be destined to follow suit.

FUNCTIONAL EVALUATION — THE STARTING POINT

The primary concern of Biblical feminists is the question of the ordination of women — whether or not women should be allowed to occupy the office of elder (pastor, presbyter, bishop, priest). A second related concern is the mutual sharing of authority and responsibility in the marital relationship — "mutual submission."[59] Biblical feminism does not directly challenge theological doctrines such as sin and redemption, and thus seems far removed from the more radical forms of feminism that have infiltrated the Church. However, the presuppositions and methods of interpretation that Biblical feminists employ have implications that directly and logically support the theological developments executed by radical feminists. In many ways, these conservative evangelicals are placing themselves at the same starting point as the more liberal theologians of the early 1960s.

In the flow chart depicting the development of feminist theology in the Appendix, I have depicted Biblical feminism as developing separately from the more radical forms of religious feminism. But Biblical feminism also feeds back into the point at which the more radical forms originated. The first diagram illustrates that although Biblical feminists are distinguishable as a group, they too are part of the feminist continuum. Their presuppositional beliefs are the same as the radicals, but they have not followed them to their logical conclusion. Biblical feminists have stepped over the line delineating the Christian worldview from the feminist one by accepting the feminist logic that allows them to place themselves above the Bible in respect to male and female roles. This step, in comparison to radical feminism, may seem small; indeed, most Biblical feminists are true evangelical believers. Although small, the step is significant; if left unchecked, it is dangerous, for it places Biblical feminists on the same slippery slope as their predecessors.

Biblical feminists seek to retain an evangelical base while at the same time modifying Biblical interpretation to be sympathetic to the concerns of the women's movement. However, in order to embrace both, Biblical feminists need to compromise the Bible. Biblical feminism therefore has become a theological crossing point between traditional conservative evangelical theology and liberalism. The examples of the early Biblical feminists bear witness to this fact. Many have crossed over to liberalism and have adopted radical feminist theology. New leaders of Biblical feminism have constantly arisen as their predecessors have drifted further into the liberal and secular streams.

Biblical feminists have tried to join feminism and conservative Biblical Christianity in a harmonious stream. But even though the two were forced, as it were, to flow out of the same tap, they remain inapposite. Feminism and Christianity are like thick oil and water: their very natures dictate that they cannot be mixed.

19

The Inevitable Intersection

Feminists and pagans are both coming from the same source without realizing it, and heading toward the same goal without realizing it, and the two are now beginning to interlace.[1]

Feminist philosophy in society and feminist theology in the Church have followed the same path of development. It is readily apparent that the leading edge of these streams of feminism are beginning to flow together. Pagan witch Margot Adler (quoted above) notes the intersection of pagan witchcraft and feminism. While this quote refers specifically to secular feminism, it could easily be expanded to include religious feminism. Witches, paganists, secular feminists, and religious feminists are all coming from the same source without realizing it, and heading toward the same goal without realizing it, and *all* are now beginning to interlace. All forms of feminism are based upon the same presupposition, and all are therefore destined to gravitate towards the same end.

Feminists are often categorized in groups according to their political theories or historical mentors. Josephine Donovan has drawn distinctions between enlightenment liberal feminists, cultural feminists, Marxist feminists, Freudian feminists, existential feminists, and radical feminists.[2] Religious feminists have likewise been categorized according to theology. One religious woman-studies text delineates them as Biblical (evangelical), mainstream (reformist), and radical (revolutionary).[3] I am certain that a major criticism of this book will be that I have neglected to point out the nuances of these various feminist categorizations, choosing rather to place all forms of feminism together onto one philosophical continuum. While I do not deny that feminists vary in political theory and theology, I maintain that all are part of a larger continuum which supersedes and encompasses those variations. A feminist, at any given point in time, may not see her or himself at the radical end of the movement, and I am certain that some individuals will never change their personal views to that extent. But the dissociation of one's own brand of feminism from the remainder of the feminist movement is a naive denial of reality. The philosophical progression of feminism is both coherent and logically immanent. Furthermore, it is the radical end of the movement that provides impetus and direction for all the others: what seems radical in 1960 is mainstream in 1980. Nonetheless, even though some brands of feminism may exhibit behaviors that distinguish them from others, all adhere to a common presupposition. Mary Daly stated it clearly: "To exist humanly is to name the self, the world, and God."[4]

INTERSECTION PREDICTED

There will of course be nothing to prevent people who practice new religions from calling themselves Christians or Jews. Undoubtedly, many followers of new faiths will still cling to old labels. But a merely semantic veneer of tradition ought not to hide the fact that very nontraditional faiths will be practiced. . . . The feminist movement in Western culture is engaged in the slow execution of Christ and Yahweh. Yet very few of the women and men now working for sexual equality within Christianity and Judaism realize the extent of their heresy.[5]

In 1979 Naomi R. Goldenberg, a feminist psychologist of religion, predicted the intersection of secular and religious feminism. Her book *Changing of the Gods: Feminism and the End of Traditional Religions* argued that the tenets of feminism and Christianity were totally incompatible. She predicted that the feminist presence in religion would force a redefinition that would alter the very essence of the Judeo-Christian religious belief system. According to Goldenberg, Christian feminists were destined, in their attempts to integrate feminism into theology, to "slowly execute" Christ and Yahweh.

Many scholars of religion disagreed with the radical direction Goldenberg predicted for the Church. They said that Christianity and Judaism could survive the very basic changes that were necessary to adapt to a feminist framework. The scholars insisted that a religion was whatever its followers defined it to be. Christianity and Judaism, therefore, could consist of whatever those who call themselves Christians and Jews understood to be religion. Theoretically then, Christianity could exist without Christ, and Judaism could exist without Yahweh's laws as long as Christians and Jews thought these departures from traditions were in basic harmony with their faiths.[6] Goldenberg disagreed. She argued that texts could not be altered, nor female imagery added to the concept of God, nor new rituals and doctrines invented without bringing about the end of Judaism and Christianity. The introduction of feminism into Christianity constituted nothing less than the invention of a *new religion*. Of course, Goldenberg conceded, many followers of the new feminist faith would still cling to old labels and call themselves Christians or Jews. But according to Goldenberg this was "merely semantic veneer." She argued that the introduction of feminism into traditional religion would violate the essence of that faith. Thus Goldenberg hypothesized that in accepting feminism the Judeo-Christian religion would die.

> The Jewish and Christian women who are reforming their traditions do not see such reforms as challenging the basic nature of Christianity and Judaism. Instead, they understand themselves to be improving the practice of their religions by encouraging women to share the responsibilities of worship equally with men.
>
> As a psychologist of religion, I do not agree that [this] is a minor alteration in Judeo-Christian doctrine. The reforms that Christian and Jewish women are proposing are major departures from tradition. When feminists succeed in changing the position of women in Christianity and Judaism, they will shake these religions at their roots.[7]

Goldenberg reviewed the writings of many mainline and evangelical Christian feminists. She scoffed at the naivete and self-deception of such women. For instance, Goldenberg said Sharon Neufer Emswiler's *Women and Worship — A Guide to Non-sexist Hymns, Prayers and Liturgies* typified the emotive, irrationality of religious feminism. As I noted in Chapter Twelve, this book suggested methods for revising the Bible and the liturgical service in order to alleviate the problem of sexism in Christianity. As I also noted, Sharon Emswiler perceived the masculine focus of her traditional church service as personally "painful, exclusive and demeaning." She informed readers that she tried to affirm herself in the service by changing the words in her own mind, but that this personal solution did not work well. She could not "out-shout" the rest of the congregation. Emswiler wanted to have her internal reality — her own experience and self-affirmation — confirmed by her surroundings. When the church service did not affirm her in the way she desired, she undertook to change it.

Goldenberg related Eimswiler's motivation for writing *Women and Worship* with sarcasm. She pointed out that Eimswiler naively changed the whole thesis of Christianity because she "didn't like" the service. Goldenberg was incredulous that Emswiler could propose such radical changes and yet remain totally oblivious to the colossal implications of her actions:

> It is important to note that the impetus to write the book and alter the images comes from her experience in sexist church services. In actual fact, she is treating her private experience as sufficient authority to change sacred scripture and tradition. This is a truly radical move, which Emswiler will not admit even to herself. . . . *Women and Worship* goes on to propose detailed reforms both in the church services and in the roles men and women play in such services. The assumption is that such

reforms in no way damage the Bible or the Church on any basic level, but rather work within these holy structures to make them more true to their intrinsic sanctity. This assumption is naive.[8]

... The issue of whether modifying a sacred text on the basis of personal experience does not somehow indicate a re-evaluation of the sacredness of both the text and the experience is not seriously confronted.[9]

Goldenberg could not believe that Christian feminists did not see and/or would not admit the extent of their heresy. She noted that religious feminists simply refused to acknowledge that conforming Biblical images to personal experience elevated their experience to the level of text.[10] According to Goldenberg, when the imagined change was incorporated into official text it was treated as equal to that text. Goldenberg pointed out that "one might even argue that it is being valued more than the text itself, since it is considered sufficient authority to alter the text, while the text is not being used as authority to question the imaginal experience."[11]

The point of Goldenberg's discussion was not to argue that religious feminists were wrong in what they were doing, but merely to point out *what* they were doing. She wanted Christian women to realize that they could not be feminists and at the same time maintain the integrity of the Christian faith. Her goal was to help religious feminists *see* their heresy and *admit* it. Through this process, Goldenberg hoped that Christian feminists would be encouraged to leap right out of the boundaries of patriarchal religion (which, in essence, they were doing anyway).

Goldenberg cited the example of Elizabeth Cady Stanton — an American suffragist who in 1895 wrote *The Women's Bible* — as a model for contemporary religious feminists to emulate. Goldenberg pointed out that Stanton did not pretend to adhere to Biblical authority, but attacked the very belief in the sacredness of Scripture. In order to question Biblical prescriptions for human behavior, Stanton had to take a stand against the authority of the Bible itself. "The time has come," she said, "to read the Bible as we do all other books, accepting the good and rejecting the evil it teaches."[12] She added, "the more I read, the more keenly I felt the importance of convincing women that the Hebrew mythology had no special claim to a higher origin than that of the Greeks, being far less attractive in style and less refined in sentiment. Its objectionable features would long ago have been apparent had they not been glossed over with a faith in their divine inspiration."[13] Goldenberg praised Stanton for her courageous analysis of the Bible. According to Goldenberg, Stanton exhibited insight that many of the new-breed religious feminists were lacking:

Many feminists recommend ignoring parts of the Bible, but still claim that the book as a whole is God-given. It is hard to deny that an eventual consequence of criticizing the correctness of any sacred text or tradition is to question why that text or tradition should be considered a divine authority at all. It is to Stanton's credit that she never hedged on this issue.[14]

Goldenberg wanted religious feminists to move outside of the restrictive confines of Judeo-Christianity in order to formulate new metaphors and images that would be useful to them. Feminism, she argued, would not find adequate answers in the external God of Christendom. Goldenberg noted that feminism demanded that patriarchal dualisms be overcome. She argued that the concepts of the "beyond," the "ultimate," the "transcendent," and the "universal" would therefore need to be redeemed with the female-associated concepts of "body," "material," and "temporal."[15] For this, she concluded, feminists would require an internal rather than external God. Goldenberg argued that religious feminists were moving toward an internal God — a god totally antithetical to the Judeo-Christian one. Their progress towards this goal was thwarted, however, by a naive effort to hold on to some semblance of submission to Scriptural authority. Goldenberg was trying to tell religious feminists: "Wake up and realize where you are headed — it will help you get there faster."

In 1979, when Naomi Goldenberg published *Changing of the Gods,* religious feminists had not yet incorporated goddess worship, witchcraft, and self-deification into their theology. At the time, her predictions regarding the inevitable intersection of the religious with the secular were not taken seriously. I cannot help but wonder if now — over twelve years later, having witnessed the unfolding of the feminist drama — Naomi Goldenberg is not breathing a quiet, satisfied, "I told you so!"

THE WATERSHED ISSUE

As Naomi Goldenberg perceived, feminism challenges the Church to its core. It also challenges the role of Scripture in the life of the believer. In Francis Schaeffer's last work, *The Great Evangelical Disaster*, he used an illustration to demonstrate what he called "the watershed issue": the nature of Biblical inspiration and authority. It is precisely the issue that is presented by feminism in the Church. I have found no better illustration, so I will take the liberty of quoting Dr. Schaeffer directly.

Not far from where we live in Switzerland is a high ridge of rock with a valley on both sides. One time I was there when there was snow on the ground along that ridge. The snow was lying there unbroken, a seeming unity. However, that unity was an illusion, for it lay along a great divide; it lay along a watershed. One portion of the snow when it melted would flow into one valley. The snow which lay close beside would flow into another valley when it melted.

Now it just so happens on that particular ridge that the melting snow which flows down one side of that ridge goes down into a valley, into a small river, and then down into the Rhine River. The Rhine then flows on through Germany and the water ends up in the cold waters of the North Sea. The water from the snow that started out so close along that watershed on the other side of the ridge, when this snow melts, drops off sharply down the ridge into the Rhone Valley. This water flows into Lac Leman — or as it is known in the English-speaking world, Lake Geneva — and then goes down below that into the Rhone River which flows though France and into the warm waters of the Mediterranean.

The snow lies along that watershed, unbroken, as a seeming unity. But when it melts, where it ends in its destinations is literally a thousand miles apart. That is a watershed. That is what a watershed is. A watershed divides. A clear line can be drawn between what seems at first to be the same or at least very close, but in reality ends in very different situations. In a watershed there is a line.

What does this illustration have to do with the evangelical world today? I would suggest that it is a very accurate description of what is happening. Evangelicals today are facing a watershed concerning the nature of biblical inspiration and authority. It is a watershed issue in very much the same sense as described in the illustration. Within evangelicalism there is a growing number who are modifying their views on the inerrancy of the Bible so that the full authority of Scripture is completely undercut. But it is happening in very subtle ways. Like the snow lying side-by-side on the ridge, the new views on biblical authority often seem at first glance not to be so very far from what evangelicals, until just recently, have always believed. But also, like the snow lying side-by-side on the ridge, the new views when followed consistently end up a thousand miles apart.[16]

Feminism is, to the evangelical Church, a watershed issue. In order to introduce feminist concepts into Christianity, basic beliefs regarding the inspiration and authority of Scripture need to be adjusted. Evangelical Christians who accept feminist precepts may appear very close in doctrine and theology to those who do not, but the process of time will see them end at a destination far from Evangelicalism. Just like the snow that lies side by side, these two current philosophies of Evangelicalism will melt and flow into separate valleys, rivers, and finally into distant oceans, thousands of miles apart.

20

The Slippery Slope

*Principles which one generation accepts provisionally, in the
context of other cultural commitments, soon harden into icy
dogmas for a generation brought up on nothing else.*[1]

One difficulty in discussing the relationship of Christianity to feminism
lies in one's definition of feminism. Many Christians view feminism as
an ideology that merely promotes the genuine dignity and worth of women.
If this were true, feminism would definitely be compatible with Christianity,
for the Bible does teach that women and men are of equal value in God's
sight, co-created as bearers of God's image. But the philosophy of feminism
adds a subtle, almost indiscernible twist to the basic Biblical truth of
woman's worth. Feminism asserts that woman's worth is of such a nature
that it gives *her* the right to discern, judge and govern that truth herself. It
infuses women with the idea that God's teaching about the role of women
must line up with their own perception and definition of equality and/or liberation. Feminism does not present itself as an outright affront to the Bible,
but it nevertheless contains an insidious distortion that erodes the authority of Scripture. Like the snow lying side by side on the watershed, acceptance of the feminist thesis may not drastically alter one's initial beliefs, but
if followed, it will naturally lead to an end miles away from the Christianity
of the Bible.

I want to be careful in discussing the relationship of Biblical feminism
to the more radical forms of feminism in the Church. I strongly believe the
two are of the same essence; however, I do not wish to accuse individual
believers of being "guilty by association." There are many genuine, sincere,
and wonderful Christian brothers and sisters who espouse Biblical feminist
theology. Although I believe they have unwittingly set themselves on the
wrong side of the watershed, and thus on a slippery slope, I do not wish in
any way to slander them, and I *do* empathize with their concerns. I myself
am deeply angered when I hear women maligned. In fact, up until a few

years ago, I called myself a feminist and would have unashamedly stood with others who did so. There *are* chauvinistic attitudes in the Church, and there *are* atrocities and crimes of abuse, degradation and shame to which the feminist movement justifiably calls attention. The difficulty for Christians is to deal with the very real problems and issues without being beguiled by the true impetus and philosophy of the feminist movement. Feminism heralds the value of women's experience and perspective. It urges women to pursue freedom by challenging the lines drawn by a male interpretation of reality. In response to the feminist call, Christians have questioned the traditional boundaries taught by the Church. While reevaluation of Biblical interpretation is commendable, feminism often entices Christian women to move or step over Scriptural lines simply because those lines were drawn and expressed through men. At stake is the authority of the Bible and our genuine obedience to God's revealed pattern for living. Sadly, many evangelical Christians are toeing the line, and others have already stepped over. Again, while I do not wish to imply guilt by association, I fear that many Biblical feminists, in zeal for realizing the true worth of women, have set themselves on a course that compromises the Word of God.

THE SLIPPERY SLOPE

I live in a part of the continent which experiences snow for a good part of the year. Sometimes, during a snowstorm, when the temperature drops to a very low level, a condition commonly referred to as "black ice" occurs. Black ice is an invisible sheet of ice-crystal that forms haphazardly on road surfaces. It cannot be seen — it blends inconspicuously with the blackness of the asphalt — but if you happen to encounter it, it can send your vehicle spinning recklessly out of control. Black ice is especially dangerous when it occurs on an inclined surface. This past winter I experienced the terror of sliding uncontrollably down a hilly road sheeted with it. The road had not appeared dangerous to the eye, nor was it slick for the first hundred feet, but when I hit the ice, the brakes of my front-wheel drive locked, and for a few agonizing moments I wrestled with the steering wheel to keep my vehicle from tipping over the embankment. The danger intensified as I steadily slid toward the intersection at the bottom of the hill sideways, still unable to curtail my descent. I closed my eyes and threw a prayer heavenward as I skidded through a red light and into the crossing. My vehicle finally came to rest in the middle, turned a full 180 degrees from its proper direction.

My black ice experience vividly illustrates the principle of the "slippery slope." *Slippery slope* is a term meaning that *provisional* acceptance of a faulty presupposition will — if not for a certain individual, then certainly for the next generation — lead to its *complete* acceptance. Biblical feminists have provisionally accepted the precept of feminism which exalts the importance of personal experience in defining one's worldview. In doing so, they have stepped over the watershed onto a slope that will certainly lead to total acceptance of radical feminism. The only difference between the conservatives and the radicals is that conservative Biblical feminists have not yet followed their presuppositions through to their logical end. Eventually, however, they may find themselves sliding uncontrollably down the hill, through the red light, and into the intersection, only to discover when they finally stop that their vehicles are pointing the wrong way.

Readers who call themselves feminists may dissociate themselves with the feminist philosophy that has been presented to this point. "I am a Christian, and I am a feminist, but I don't believe in THAT! . . . and I certainly will not slip into the beliefs of radical feminism!" The problem is that it is extremely difficult to separate truth from error once you have associated yourself with a particular philosophy. Even if you personally may be clear on the dangers of feminism, your association with the feminist label may lend validity to feminist philosophy for others possessing less discrimination. For this reason, I have totally rejected the feminist label, even though I completely believe in (and pursue) the dignity, worth, and value of women. I understand, empathize, and in some respects agree with those who feel it necessary to call themselves feminists, but the danger of the slippery slope frightens me. Slipping away from God by rejecting His pattern for my life is a risk I am not willing to take.

OBSERVING THE TRACKS

Feminism is a slippery slope that leads towards a total alteration or rejection of the Bible. I would like to review the histories of three feminist women which bear witness to this fact. Mary Daly's journey vividly demonstrates the natural progression which the process of "naming" follows. Although Rosemary Radford Ruether began with a liberal religious perspective, her story is noteworthy because it also illustrates the progressive nature of the feminist precept. Finally, I have included the story of Virginia Mollenkott, who began her journey as an evangelical Biblical feminist. Mollenkott exemplifies the danger of the slippery slope for conservative Christian feminists.

Mary Daly

Mary Daly was one of the first pioneers of religious feminism. It is interesting to study the path Daly has taken, for she has been on her "journey" for a longer period of time than many. Moreover, her ability to reason clearly has taken her further and at a faster pace than most feminists are able to go. For this reason, I will begin with Daly and will trace her tracks in more detail than the others.

Young Mary Daly was blessed with a brilliant mind. Furthermore, she had always been interested in spiritual things and had developed, through her growing years, a passion for studying theology. The privilege of obtaining the highest degree in theology was denied women in the Catholic colleges of the United States, but Daly would settle for nothing less than the "highest" religious education could offer. What she would do with a theological doctorate she had no idea, but her quest led her to study in Fribourg, Switzerland, where the theological faculty was state-controlled and therefore could not legally exclude women. Daly earned a dual doctorate at the University of Fribourg, first in theology and then in philosophy.

Over the course of time, Daly's zeal for knowing God became clouded by her constant struggle against the religious establishment. She had been hurt, reviled, and put down by men for her efforts to search out the knowledge of God. Daly received the message that women were not worthy of the spiritual knowledge which men claimed as their exclusive right. It was therefore with great expectation that Daly traveled to Rome in 1965 — to the Second Vatican Council — in hope of witnessing change in the attitudes and policies of the Church towards women. She was hoping, in her own words, for the "greatest breakthrough of nearly two thousand years." Again Daly was hurt and disappointed. She returned to Fribourg with a renewed sense of purpose to improve the status of women in the Church. Her resolve was based upon a hope in the God who loved women and was fueled by anger against men who didn't.

Earlier that same year, Daly had written her first article on sexism in religion. "A Built-In Bias" was published by *Commonweal* in January of 1965. Just a few months later, a British publisher in England, who had spotted the article, commissioned Daly to write *The Church and the Second Sex*. This was the event that launched Mary Daly full-force into her feminist journey. A contract was signed in May 1965, and by the time her book was published — in 1968 — Daly had returned to America to teach at a Jesuit-run college in Boston.

Daly's book aroused the fury of many Catholics. She presumed that Boston College served her a terminal contract as a direct result of its publication. The commotion caused by the book was outdone only by the massive demonstrations objecting to the College's action. Daly's "case" became a *cause célèbre* for thousands of students marching for freedom of speech. Even more significantly, it became a source of intense personal pain and anguish for Daly. The pressure and emotional turmoil following the publication of *The Church and the Second Sex* took its toll on Daly's psyche. Her hope in the Church, and her hope in God, were slowly being sapped from her heart. As Daly recalls,

> As a result of . . . *The Church and the Second Sex*, I had been hurled into instant fame as exposer of Christian misogyny and champion of women's equality within the church. . . . I lectured to academic audiences and women's groups across the country about the sexism of the Christian tradition. . . . Often in the late sixties I encountered hostility in women, not toward the patriarchs whose *misogynism* I exposed but toward me for exposing them. But by about 1970 this phenomenon of misplaced anger had almost disappeared. More and more people had caught up with *The Church and the Second Sex*, and the lines that formerly had elicited hostility brought forth cheers. But the "I" who was then standing before the

friendly audiences and tossing out the familiar phrases was already disconnected from the words, already moving through a new time/space. I often heard the old words as though a stranger were speaking them — some personage visiting from the past. My concern was no longer limited to "equality" in the church or anywhere else. I did not really care about unimaginative reform but instead began dreaming new dreams of a women's revolution. This was becoming a credible dream, because a community of sisterhood was coming into being, into be-ing. In the hearing/healing presence of these sisters I had grown ready to try writing/speaking New Words.[2]

Five years following the publication of *The Church and the Second Sex* Daly published *Beyond God the Father*. In the preface of that work she wrote,

The perceptive reader will notice that essentially the same anger and the same hope are the wellsprings of this book, but that the focus has shifted and the perspective has been greatly radicalized. The transition to a wider and deeper perspective within the author's own consciousness has been dramatic — as have been the five years between publication dates.[3]

In *Beyond God the Father*, Daly moved out of the boundaries of traditional religion. She was still seeking for God, but had come to the conclusion that the Judeo-Christian male God and His bastions of male religious establishment were in juxtaposition to the liberation of women.

Daly's initial thoughts about changing traditional perceptions of God and the Bible, as described in her first book, naturally and logically led to her doing just that. In *Beyond God the Father*, Daly took on the task of "de-reifying God," that is, of changing her conception/perception of God from "the supreme being" to a state of "Be-ing."[4] She proposed that women conceptualize God as Verb — as a force or energy rather than a masculine entity. The understanding of God, the Verb, as "Be-ing," provided the "essential leap" in the development of Daly's feminist journey. She explained,

The Naming of Be-ing as Verb — as intransitive Verb that does not require an "object" — expresses an Other way of understanding ultimate/intimate reality. The experiences of many feminists continue to confirm the original intuition that Naming Be-ing as Verb is an essential leap in the cognitive/affective journey beyond patriarchal fixations.[5]

Daly argued that "the unfolding of God . . . is an event in which women participate as [they] participate in [their] own revolution. The process involves the creation of new space, in which women are free to become who [they] are. . . ."[6] She reasoned that who or what "God" was would only unfold as women began to name and create their own reality. It was in this book that she summarized the feminist thesis: "to exist humanly is to name the self, the world, and God." Had Daly not been hurt so deeply by the institutionalized Church, she may have attempted to formulate her evolving views as theology, justified by Christianity. But because of the pain and rejection she had experienced, Daly turned her back on the Church completely, choosing instead to complete her journey outside its doors.

Mary Daly had an analytical mind and had always been careful in her use of language. However, as she became more convinced that claiming the right to name and define reality was the key to woman's liberation, she became even more particular with her use of words. Daly's third book, *Gyn/Ecology: The Metaethics of Radical Feminism*, demonstrates this. To begin, Daly pointed out that going beyond *Beyond God the Father* involved, for her, two things:

> First, there is the fact that be-ing continues. Be-ing at home on the road means continuing to Journey. This book continues to Spin on, in other directions/dimensions. It focuses beyond Christianity in Other ways. Second, there is some old semantic baggage to be discarded so that Journeyers will be unencumbered by malfunctioning (male-functioning) equipment.[7]

First, Daly saw the unfolding of God — of Be-ing — as a continuing process requiring an extended journey toward a higher consciousness. Second, she saw the process of "naming" as necessary for this journey. By claiming the right to use and define words, Daly believed that women exercised their right to claim and define reality. Daly critiqued her own use of language in previous books. Three words which she found necessary to purge from her vocabulary were *God*, *androgyny*, and *homosexuality*. I include the following quote to give you a taste of the way in which Daly's language was evolving, and also to point out that claiming the power to name had had bearing upon Daly's views on morality.

> There are some words which appeared to be adequate in the early seventies, which feminists later discovered to be false words. Three such words in *Beyond God the Father* which I cannot use again are *God*, *androgyny*, and *homosexuality*. There is no way to remove male/masculine imagery from *God*. Thus, when writing/speaking "anthropomorphically" of ultimate reality, of the divine spark of be-ing, I now choose to write/speak gynomorphically. I do so because *God* represents the necrophilia of patriarchy, whereas *Goddess* affirms the life-loving be-ing of women and nature. The second semantic abomination, *androgyny*, is a confusing term which I sometimes used in attempting to describe integrity of be-ing. The word is misbegotten — conveying something like "John Travolta and Farrah Fawcett-Majors scotch-taped together" — as I have reiterated in public recantations. The third treacherous term, *homosexuality*, reductionistically "includes," that is, excludes, gynocen-

tric be-ing/Lesbianism. . . . The Journey of this book, therefore, is . . . "for the Lesbian Imagination in All Women." It is for the Hag/Crone/Spinster in every *living* woman. It is for each individual Journeyer to decide/expand the scope of this imagination within her. It is she, and she alone, who can determine how far, and in what way, she will/can travel. She, and she alone, can discover the mystery of her own history, and find how it is interwoven with the lives of other women.[8]

Daly's attention to words was also demonstrated by her explanation of the title of her book. "*Gyn/Ecology*," she explained, "says exactly what I mean it to say."[9] *Ecology* was about the "complex web of interrelationships between organisms and their environment," and *Gyn* meant of or for women.[10] Daly used the term *Gyn/Ecology* to play against the traditional term *Gynecology*. "It is a way of wrenching back word power." Daly noted that the *Oxford Dictionary* defined gynecology as "that department of medical science which treats of the functions and diseases peculiar to women; also loosely, the science of womankind."[11] Daly argued that "loosely" the science of womankind had been totally male-defined. She claimed her right to define Gyn/Ecology *loosely*, as the science, or "the process of knowing" for women. According to Daly, Gyn/Ecology was about "*weaving world tapestries of our own kind.*"[12] She explained that it was about "discovering, developing the complex web. . . . It is dispossessing our Selves, enspiriting our Selves, hearing the call of the wild, naming our wisdom, spinning and weaving world tapestries out of genesis and demise. In contrast to gynecology, which depends upon fixation and dismemberment, Gyn/Ecology affirms that everything is connected."[13] In the subtitle of *Gyn/Ecology* — *The Metaethics of Radical Feminism*, Daly sought to convey that feminist ethics were "meta," that is, of a higher logical and deeper intuitive type than others.[14]

Gyn/Ecology described Daly's journey further away from the external God of Judeo-Christianity toward the goddess of be-ing which she had begun to locate within the self. She maintained,

> Journeying centerward is Self-centering movement in all directions. It erases implanted pseudodichotomies between the Self and "other" reality, while it unmasks the unreality of both "self" and "world" as these are portrayed, betrayed, in the language of the father's foreground. . . . Moving into the Background/Center is not navel-gazing. It is be-ing in the world. . . . The Journey is itself participation in Paradise.[15]

Daly concluded her third book by proclaiming:

> In the beginning was not the word. In the beginning is the hearing. Spinsters spin deeper into the listening deep. We can spin only what we hear, because we hear, and as well as we hear. We can weave and unweave, knot and unknot, only because we hear, what we hear, and as

well as we hear. Spinning is celebration/cerebration. Spinsters Spin all ways, always. Gyn/Ecology is Un-Creation; Gyn/Ecology is Creation.[16]

As Daly focused on the use of language, spinning a uniquely women's language that would leave patriarchy far behind, she also left many of the mainstream feminist audience behind. Most women found it difficult to sift through Daly's words in order to discover where her journey of consciousness was leading. But for those who persevered in following her train of thought, Daly was glaringly consistent with her presuppositions. Her sharp mind did not compromise her journey, but vigorously pursued it to its logical end.

Pure Lust was Daly's next step. In this book, she further changed words so as to alter their meaning and thereby affect reality. In *Pure Lust*, Daly focused on the "traditional Deadly Sin of lust."[17] She proclaimed that male lust was a "phallic, life-hating obsession" that raped and killed.[18] According to Daly, pure lust was the "vigorous, life-affirming force" that helped women "connect with the wild in Nature and ourSelves."[19] She explained that it was "the vigor, eagerness, and intense longing that launch(ed) Wild women on Journeys beyond the State of Lechery."[20]

> Primarily, then, Pure Lust Names the high humor, hope, and cosmic accord/harmony of those women who choose to escape, to follow our hearts' deepest desire and bound out of the State of Bondage, Wanderlusting and Wonderlusting with the elements, connecting with auras of animals and plants, moving in planetary communion with the farthest stars. This Lust is in its essence astral. It is pure Passion: unadulterated, absolute, simple sheer striving for abundance of be-ing. It is unlimited, unlimiting desire/fire. One move by its magic is Musing /Remembering. Choosing to leave the dismembered state, she casts her lot, life, with the trees and the winds, the sands and the tides, the mountains and moors. She is Outcast, casting her Self outward, inward, breaking out of the casts/castes of phallocracy's fabrications/fictions, moving out of the maze of mediated experience. As she lurches/leaps into starlight her tears become tidal, her cackles cosmic, her laughter Lusty . . . Elemental female Lust is intense longing/craving for the cosmic concrescence that is creation.[21]

In *Pure Lust* Daly encouraged women to throw off all inhibitions — to be driven "out of control" — in their revolt against the male system of Judeo-Christian patriarchy. In order to overcome their oppression, Daly argued that women would need to break the rules of morality, spirituality, and ethics. She proposed that women should be free to indulge in any form of physical pleasure (sexuality-lesbianism) or spiritual experience (witchcraft-paganism) they wished. Things which were formally considered taboo were endorsed by Daly as justified by a higher feminist consciousness.

She believed that the right to claim and name reality freed women from all boundaries.

Daly's latest book is entitled *Webster's First New Intergalactic Wickedary of the English Language*. The book cover proudly proclaimed that it was "conjured" rather than "written" by Mary Daly. Again, in this work Daly claimed the right to name. Common English definitions forwarded by *Webster's Dictionary* were replaced — for those with a raised consciousness — by those in the *Intergalactic Webster's Wickedary*. *Exorcism,* for instance, was defined as a "series of A-mazing Acts of Dispossession, expelling both internal and external manifestations of the godfather; Naming the demons who block each passage of the Otherworld Journey and thereby ousting these obstacles to the Ecstatic Process."[22] *The Incarnation* was defined as the "supremely sublimated male sexual fantasy promulgated as sublime christian dogma; mythic super-rape of the Virgin Mother, who represents all matter; symbolic legitimation of the rape of all women and all matter."[23] *The Original Sin of Women* was the "Original be-ing of women, from which patriarchal religion attempts to 'save' us, but which is inherently Untouchable, Inviolable, and Wild."[24] Daly's definition of Yahweh God contained such expletive language that I consider it inappropriate to repeat it.[25]

Daly's journey is ending far from where it began. Spinning her own definition of reality — based on the goddess that she has found within — Daly has woven a system of be-ing that is antithetical to the God of the Bible. Daly no longer has any need for Jehovah God. Her acceptance of the feminist thesis has naturally progressed toward a total rejection of Him.

Rosemary Radford Ruether

According to Rosemary Radford Ruether, she was always "implicitly a feminist," for even as a small child she instinctively rejected others' efforts to define her in a traditional female role.[26] She reasoned that this could have been due, in part, to the legacy of strong, independent women to which she was exposed, and also due to the absence of contact with males. Rosemary's father was an Anglican, a Republican, and "a Virginia gentleman."[27] Rosemary described him as a "shadowy figure" who was away in the Second World War for much of her grade-school years and who left again shortly after returning home. Ruether's father died when she was just twelve years old. At that time, her family became a "community of mother and daughters who had to make it together."[28]

Following the death of her husband, Rosemary's mother took Rosemary and her sisters back to her childhood home in California. There, surrounded by her mother's college girlfriends, Rosemary had strong role models of independent women of an earlier feminist generation. These women were an important reference group for Rosemary's development. All were vigorous, intellectually active and socially concerned, and all were interested in religion — keenly reading religious classics from all times and cultures. Aside from an uncle, all role models and authority figures that were operative in Rosemary's formative years were women. In her local Catholic school, those in charge from the top administration down to the classroom teacher were female. There were no boys in her classrooms, and priests were rare and distant figures. She recalled that "even the divine appeared to be immediately represented by a female, Mary. God and Christ were somewhere in the distance, like the priests, but Mary was the one you talked to if you wanted to pray."[29] So, too, the local convent where her Catholic mother went daily to Mass was a female world of elderly patients and sprightly nuns. Ruether summarized this impression of her childhood: "The role models and means of on-going life lay in communities of women, widows and daughters. When men appeared, back from some distant war or conflict, the women grew silent and respectful. A certain homage was paid to these almost godlike creatures. But one managed effectively on a day-to-day basis without them."[30]

After high school, Rosemary enrolled in Scripps College, in Claremont, California. Her early exposure to the classics of religion had piqued her interest and she became a classics major. Although she was not fanatically religious, Rosemary was fascinated by "the puzzle of Christianity's rise and triumph in the world."[31] Her B.A. thesis was centered on eschatology and intertestamental literature, her M.A. on classics and Roman history, and her Ph.D. in classics and patristics. Rosemary married Herman Ruether at the end of her junior year in college. She was twenty years old at the time. Both she and her husband continued to work on their education after their marriage, both earning doctorates and moving into teaching professions.

It was at this time that Rosemary experienced the first major and serious assault upon her well-being as a woman in the world. She reported that the chief strain came in coping with the Catholic Church's position on contraception. From all sides, Rosemary received messages that her destiny in life was to become pregnant and care for children. She received messages that her "salvation lay in passive acquiescence to God and biological destiny" and that "any effort to interfere with 'nature' was the most heinous crime."[32] Pressure was exerted, from all corners, for her to relinquish her educational pursuits for the higher calling of Motherhood. This she was unprepared to do.

> Shortly after our marriage, [my husband] and I visited the crusty old Monsignor of his parish church in Cincinnati. Roughly he informed us that if I wasn't pregnant within a year, he would know that we were "living in sin." I was outraged. It was as though the entire society was suddenly bent on destroying the entire identity and future that I had constructed for myself. The entire system of communities around me was engaged in a passive collaboration with this assault on my being.[33]

Ruether did eventually become pregnant. In fact, in a period of six years she bore three children, finished her B.A., M.A. and Ph.D., and embarked on her first book, a criticism of the doctrine of the Church (*The Church*

Against Itself, Herder and Herder, 1967). She was determined not to be forced into a traditional woman's role and worked herself to exhaustion to prevent it. She related that "this meant that an enormous amount of energy in the first ten years of marriage went into simply defending myself against this assault, trying to juggle children, marriage, housework, teaching, and graduate work."[34]

A second incident, in the maternity ward where she gave birth to her daughter in 1963, galvanized Ruether's commitment to fight the Church on its position regarding contraception. In the bed next to Ruether there lay a Mexican-American woman who had just given birth to her ninth child. The doctor had just left her bedside after tactfully recommending that she not return home without some adequate means of contraception. Tearfully, the woman described to Ruether the impoverished conditions into which she would take this ninth child: The house was without central heating, there was little food, and her husband beat her. But when urged to take some measures against a tenth pregnancy, she could only reply that her priest did not allow it, nor did her husband.

According to Ruether, "this incident precipitated my private struggle and dissent onto the public plane."[35] Her first feminist writing of the mid-sixties thus focused on a criticism of the Catholic views of sexuality and reproduction. Gradually, though, it became clear to her that these views themselves were "an integral part of a sexist ideology and culture whose purpose is to make women the creatures of biological destiny."[36] Her final thesis was shaped by some other important events that occurred in her life.

In the summer of 1965, Rosemary Ruether went through what she described as "a watershed experience."[37] A group of students and staff, organized by the college chaplains at the Claremont colleges, had decided to work for that summer in Mississippi with the Delta Ministry. One of their primary tasks was organizing blacks to come out and vote for the civil rights bill that would, among other things, protect their voting rights. For the first time Ruether experienced America "from the other side." She began to look with fear on carloads of whites or white policemen; she had church doors slammed in her face, and she was refused entrance to stores on account of her black companions. On one occasion she even encountered the infamous Ku Klux Klan. Others involved in the Delta Ministry were actually shot at by this group. The racism and hostility that she encountered affected her deeply, and she became very politically active for the rights of the oppressed. After moving to Washington in 1966 to teach at Howard University, Ruether was heavily involved in the peace and anti-imperialist movements. She reported that "it would be hard to count how many marches I participated in; how many sing-ins, pray-ins, and die-ins won me brief stays in Washington jails during that period."[38]

Much of Ruether's political effort was directed through church-related groups: St. Stephen's and the Incarnation Episcopal Church; the Community of Christ, an ecumenical, covenanted community; and the Community for Creative Non-Violence, most of whom were Catholic radicals. Through her involvement during this period of time, Ruether became aware of "a global system of Western colonialism and imperialism" which had stretched back for centuries. She became convinced that the triangle of trade that linked Europe, Africa, and the Americas had been built upon slave labor and extraction of rich resources under exploitive conditions.

In the early seventies, Ruether's interest turned increasingly toward Latin America. Her mother had been born in Monterey, Mexico, and had spoken Spanish fluently. As early explorers in California, her relatives had intermarried with the Mexican governor's family in Santa Barbara. The Latin American culture was interwoven with Ruether's own family biography and she was therefore drawn to the Latin American liberation theology which promised freedom from the effects of American neocolonialism.

It is at this point in time that Rosemary Radford Ruether began her most well-known contributions to theology, and it is as this point where we first encountered her through her 1972 work: *Liberation Theology: Human Hope Confronts Christian History and American Power*. In *Liberation Theology*, Ruether attacked the aspects of Christian and American history that oppressed Jews, blacks, women and Latin Americans. Ruether's initial focus was broad, attacking all the oppressive conditions which she had been exposed to in her life. Her following work, *New Woman, New Earth: Sexist Ideologies & Human Liberation*, focused specifically on the oppression of women. Published shortly after Letty Russell's *Human Liberation in a Feminist Perspective — A Theology*, Ruether's book gained an immediate audience, and Ruether thus discovered her niche. After that time her writings focused almost exclusively on the liberation of women. She credited her success in teaching, publishing, and lecturing to a timely congruence between her own personal concerns and the concerns of "a progressive sector of the churches and society."[39]

The development of Rosemary Radford Ruether's theology can be traced quite comprehensively throughout the first three sections of this book. It was, most often, at the cutting-edge of religious feminism. Ruether is unique, however, in that she was never faithfully committed to any one form of religion — not even the Roman Catholic Church with whom she had had the most contact. Indeed, her background in Christianity was more from the perspective of classical analysis and social activism than from a personal relationship with God. Nevertheless, Ruether profoundly influenced both liberal and conservative church theology. Furthermore, even though her views on the Bible and Christian equality for women were liberal to begin with, it is clear that she moved further and further away from her initial stance as time progressed, ending at a point so radical that it was congruent with the pagan goddess worship of secular feminism.

In 1982 Ruether scathingly criticized Mary Daly for Daly's feminist separatism.[40] She was also extremely skeptical of goddess worship, which she called "feminist romanticism."[41] Ruether regarded Mary Daly and the other secular feminists who were at that time beginning to explore feminist spirituality as "radical" and "countercultural" extremists."[42] On the other hand, she regarded herself and the other feminists who were working to transform the Judeo-Christian faith from within as rational "reformists." However, it is interesting that just a few short years later, Ruether was encouraging women to withdraw from men into Women-Church, and that she had integrated goddess worship into her rituals and liturgies. Ruether began from a religious social-activist background, but she, like Daly, was destined to follow the natural progression of the feminist presupposition. She, too, was drawn towards a total rejection of God.

Virginia Mollenkott

Virginia Mollenkott was a religious feminist with a strong evangelical heritage. She was brought up in American fundamentalism and received her undergraduate degree from Bob Jones University. In 1975, she wrote a two-part article for the *Reformed Journal* which passionately argued for women's equality in the Church, which would be evidenced by woman's "access to all privileges and responsibilities of governance and the ministry."[43] In the first installment of her essay, Mollenkott dealt with a number of the Scriptural texts that were often used as injunctions for woman's equal inclusion. In the second installment, she sought to illuminate the Church to the advantages of full female participation. Her book *Women, Men & the Bible*, published in 1977, expanded her thesis on the Biblical doctrine of human equality. At that time, Mollenkott argued that "Biblical feminism must root itself firmly in the major Bible doctrines of the Trinity, of creation in the image of God, of the incarnation, and of regeneration."[44] Therefore, at the start, Mollenkott was no different from any other Bible-believing evangelical Christian, except in her views regarding the Bible's teaching regarding the roles of female and male.

By the late 1970s, Mollenkott had expanded her equality concerns to include the issue of inclusive language. As a professor of English, linguistic use was of particular interest to her. She wrote another book, *Speech, Silence, Action*, and began to actively campaign for inclusive language in the Church. In a 1981 article, "The Bible & Linguistic Change," Mollenkott noted:

> Linguistic change has important political repercussions. Although social change modifies imagery, imagery also modifies society. As we think, so we are; as we are, so we speak. For that very reason, Jesus warned us that when our life-styles are judged, by our *words* we will be acquitted and by our *words* condemned (Matt. 12:37).
> The language issue is anything but trivial.[45]

Mollenkott was invited to join the Committee for the Production of the Inclusive Language Lectionary for the National Council of Churches. Her involvement on the committee furthered her interest in inclusive language and the image of God. By 1983 she had written another book, *The Divine Feminine: The Biblical Imagery of God as Female*. By this time Mollenkott was convinced that naming her own faith with inclusive God-language was necessary for the liberation of women in the Church.[46] Furthermore, she noted, inclusive God-language would be a step in the direction of the reconciliation of the patriarchal dichotomies of masculine/feminine, superior/inferior, logic/emotion, etc. At the conclusion of this work, Mollenkott suggested that God be referred to in an all-inclusive way, as the force in all things and all people.

> We can resolutely learn to speak of God in an all-inclusive way. I like Schubert M. Ogden's definition of God as "The Thou with the greatest conceivable degree of real relatedness to others — namely, relatedness to *all* others." For this reason, God is the most truly absolute Thou any mind can conceive. This *Thou*, this Absolute Relatedness, may be referred to as *He, She,* or *It* because this Thou relates to everyone and everything.... This Thou is a jealous God — not jealous in the sense of one prideful Potentate who insists on having all attention focused on Himself, but jealous instead that He/She/It be recognized everywhere in everyone and everything.

As a result of Mollenkott's commitment to feminism, her view of God was changing. This trend was even more evident in her subsequent work, *Godding: Human Responsibility and the Bible* (Crossroad, 1988). Mollenkott had claimed the feminist right to name. Consequently, she radically changed her ideas about what Christianity is and who "God" is.

> What a relief, then, to discover that my true goal is not be perfect, but merely to be whole, to be perfectly myself, made in the image of a God who is not Totally Other, but rather is all encompassing, encompassing even me, within me as well as far beyond what I can grasp or understand! What a relief to discover that I am rooted in the divine nature so inseparably that none of my delusions of separateness could ever be able to separate me even one little bit from the nature of God! What a relief to realize that roots grow and thrive in dirt, in the moist cold darkness of the earth, and therefore suggest that God, the Ground of our Being and Becoming, is darkness as well as light![47]

In *Godding*, Mollenkott followed the feminist presupposition further towards its logical end. She began to see herself as God. She proclaimed,

> I am a manifestation of *God*. God Herself! God Himself! God Itself! Above all. Through all. And in us all.[48]

It is noteworthy that Mollenkott also departed from other evangelical views. She argued that Christianity should yield its "exclusive claim" of Christ being the only way to God.[49] Finally, Mollenkott advocated an inclusive morality. According to Mollenkott, Christians should not condemn those who find sexual fulfillment outside of the context of marriage, nor should they condemn homosexuality. She reasoned that:

> When Scripture seems to be condemning homosexuals, it is actually condemning the loss of male sperm in a culture that needed population; or it is condemning pagan rituals, or prostitution, or exploitative lust, or the use of sex by some males to humiliate other males, as in the Sodom story. It is time for the heterosexuals in the church to . . . educate themselves about human sexuality so that they cease bearing false witness against their gay and lesbian neighbors.[50]

The journey of this evangelical feminist started from a different denominational perspective from the first two cited, and yet led toward the exact same end. Mollenkott had claimed the right to name herself, her world, and God. Ultimately, this led her to a total rejection of the Judeo-Christian God of the Bible. Furthermore, her rejection of God's pattern for male and female roles led to a rejection of Biblical morality. Mollenkott's story demonstrates that in accepting the feminist precept of the right to name, an individual places her/himself on a slippery slope that may lead toward a total alteration or rejection of the Bible.

NO MAN CAN SERVE TWO MASTERS

I have cited only three examples of the progressive nature of the feminist presupposition. I could cite many more. Carol Christ, Judith Plaskow, Letha Scanzoni, Nancy Hardesty, Elisabeth Schüssler Fiorenza, Sallie McFague, Christine Downing — all these and more bear witness to the nature of feminism. Many who were conservative have now adopted radical views, and many who once called themselves "Biblical feminists" are now far from the Bible. This is because feminism and Christianity are antithetical. Accepting the feminist precept into one's worldview immediately initiates a change in one's view of truth and absolutes. It places an individual upon a slippery slope which can lead, and usually does lead, far away from God. My point is not that every individual who calls her or himself a feminist is damned to Hell. I am not implying guilt by association. What I am saying is that the presupposition of feminism is not in harmony with the Bible. Accepting the feminist precept, even to a small degree, necessitates some degree of compromise. Although for a particular individual, this may not lead to a total rejection of the Bible and God, such is the logical and immanent end.

Another point I would like to make is that compromise of the Word of God is not restricted to feminism. Feminism is but one of Satan's many lies with which we are beguiled. Many other philosophies and theories and even our own human nature tempt us to entertain the question, as Eve did, "Did God really say . . . ?" I would be naive to assume that I am exempt from this error. I do not wish to self-righteously point my finger at feminists and fail to acknowledge that there are fingers pointing back at me. Whenever we remove ourselves from submitting to God's revealed standard and pattern for living, claiming that our knowledge is higher or loftier than that which God has revealed in His Word, we come under the influence of the other one who is vying for our souls. This is feminism's key error, but it is a tendency that we *all* possess.

Phyllis Trible said "if no man can serve two masters, no woman can serve two authorities, a master called scripture and a mistress called feminism." Trible viewed the statement as an oxymoron — a wise saying which at first glance appears foolish. Christians, she argued, *can* serve Scripture and feminism at the same time. I counter that Trible's assertion is, in fact, a foolish statement which at first glance appears wise. Women cannot serve two authorities; they *cannot* serve a master called Scripture and a mistress called feminism. Seeking to do so creates a tension of conflicting loyalties. The infidelity will eventually force her to leave one and cleave to the other. Such has been the history of those who have traveled feminism's path.

21

Fighting on Two Fronts

*In this fallen world, things constantly swing like a pendulum,
from being wrong in one extreme way to being wrong in
another extreme. The devil never gives us the luxury of fighting on only one front, and this will always be the case.*

Francis Schaeffer

THE "BLUE-JEAN" MENTALITY

In the 1960s, droves of young people rebelled against the materialistic values of their parents. They were rebels, and they wore the rebel's mark —
worn-out blue jeans. But they did not seem to notice that the blue jeans had
become a mark of accommodation — that indeed, everyone was in blue
jeans. Francis Schaeffer identified this phenomenon as "the Blue-Jean mentality."[1] In seeking to correct the sins of their parents, the rebels had swung
the cultural pendulum to the opposite but equally flawed extreme. They had
rebelled against one cultural icon only to create another.

All too often, the blue-jean syndrome affects Christians. In dealing with
contemporary issues, Christians merely don the blue jeans which are being
put on by everyone else. They do not address current popular topics from
a balanced, uniquely Christian worldview. With respect to women's issues,
I fear that Christians are responding to feminist concerns by merely adopting the fashion of the day rather than dressing themselves in revolutionary
Kingdom apparel. As Schaeffer points out, "It is so easy to be a radical in
the wearing of blue jeans when it fits in with the general climate of wearing
blue jeans."[2]

THE CHALLENGE OF FEMINISM

By now, some readers may have dismissed me as a "traditionalist." They
will have drawn the conclusion that I am against women, that I discredit
the validity of the problems identified by the feminist movement, or that I
reinforce or support domineering, overbearing abusive relationships

between men and women. Nothing could be farther from the truth. In this book I have had to concentrate on fighting on one front. My heart, however, has often been drawn to the other.

I am a woman. I have experienced the scorn and prideful superiority with which men have, at times, treated me. I have listened to insults against my capabilities, my intelligence, and my body. I have burned with anger as I have wiped the blood from a battered woman's face. I have wept with women who have been forcefully, brutally raped — violated to the very core of their being. I have been sickened at the perverted sexual abuse of little girls. I have boycotted stores which sell pornographic pictures of women. I have challenged men who sarcastically demean women with their "humor." And I have walked out of church services where pastors carelessly malign those whom God has called holy. I am often hurt and angered by sexist, yes, SEXIST demeaning attitudes and actions. And I grieve deeply at the distortion of the relationship that God created as harmonious and good. As a woman I feel the battle. I feel the sin. Feminism identifies real problems which demand real answers.

Biblical feminists are responding to the challenge of feminism by adopting feminist philosophy. They are reacting against the problems of sexism in the Church in the same way that secular women are seeking to overcome society's abuses. These Christian rebels are seeking to redefine Biblical texts in order to support the obliteration of male and female role distinctions in the home and Church. But in interpreting the Bible through feminism's lens rather than interpreting feminism's quest for equality through the Bible's, Biblical feminists are unwittingly claiming the right to name themselves and their world. Furthermore, they are stepping outside of the only framework that can provide adequate answers. The problems that feminists identify in the Church are real. But in addressing those problems, Biblical feminists have succumbed to the blue-jean mentality of thinking they are being courageous and radical, when in fact they are really only fitting into what is the accepted thought-form of the age around them.

Larry Crabb, in his recent book *Men & Women: Enjoying the Difference*, has said, "We need new thinking that is as old as the Bible itself. . . ."[3] The Bible is the standard by which we must scrutinize all patterns of male and female behavior. The feminist pattern must be subjected to the test of the Bible as must the "traditional" pattern to which society has grown accustomed. We do need new thinking. But that thinking must return to what is old. *"We need new thinking that is as old as the Bible itself."*

EVALUATING THE RIGHT TO NAME

Mary Daly encapsulated the basic premise of feminism as the self-appointed right to name the self, the world, and God. To this basic premise, Christians must say "no." It is not our right to name ourselves, the world, and the Creator. Rather it is God's right to name Himself, the world, and the people He has created. God provides the only reliable measure for a true interpretation of reality. It is from *Him* — not psychology, sociology, anthropology or any other human science — that we gain a proper framework for understanding ourselves, our world, and God Himself. If we look to ourselves for the framework, as feminism does, we will undoubtedly distort the pattern.

The philosophy of feminism accuses men of shaping truth and reality to suit their own pleasure. In this, feminism has observed a basic human tendency from which women are not exempt. Men *have* self-centeredly attempted to shape truth and reality. But their actions do not overturn reality, and their error does not justify feminism's quest to do the same. The reality of God exists independent of our human distortion of that reality. God's pattern exists even if not one male or female on the face of this earth ever acknowledges it or lives by it. Furthermore, God did not leave us on our own to blindly grope about for the answers to our existence. He *has* revealed Himself. Though we may only see dimly "as through a glass," we do have a grid to follow.

> For this is what the Lord says — he who created the heavens, he is God; he who fashioned and made the earth, he founded it; he did not create it to be empty, but formed it to be inhabited — he says:
> "I am the Lord, and there is no other. I have not spoken in secret from somewhere in a land of darkness; I have not said to Jacob's descendants, 'Seek me in vain.' I the Lord, speak the truth; I declare what is right." (Isaiah 45:18, 19)

God has revealed Himself to us. From Him we glean the clearest picture of God, the world, and ourselves that our fallen human minds are able to fathom. Daly started by naming herself and ended by naming her god. In doing so, she turned the proper sequence upside down. We must begin by letting God name Himself. We can then move on to discover how God has ordered and named His creation and finally us — His people.

God Has Named Himself

It is important to understand that it is not we who name God, but it is God who names Himself by showing us who He is.[4] In the Book of Exodus, God calls Himself "I am who I am" (Exod. 3:14). He also reveals Himself as Lord and Master (*Adonai*), Self-existent One (*Jehovah Yahweh*), God Most High (*El Elyon*), and the Everlasting God (*El Olam*). In the New Testament, Jesus Christ is revealed as Lord (*Kyrios*) and Son, and the first person of the Trinity is called Father and *Abba* (dear Father). The names of God are God's self-designation of His person and being. Such names do not tell us who God is exhaustively, but they are informative symbols having a basis in revelation itself.[5]

In the Bible the name of God represents the very reality and being of God. It is in His name that He reveals Himself and saves us. "Our help is in the *name* of the Lord, the Maker of heaven and earth" (Ps. 124:8). "Those who know your *name* will trust in you" (Ps. 9:10). "You are to give him the *name* Jesus, for he will save his people from their sins" (Matt. 1:21). "Salvation is found in no one else, for there is no other *name* under heaven given to men by which we must be saved" (Acts 4:12). Jesus promised that wherever two or three were gathered together in His *name*, there would He be in the midst of them (Matt. 18:20). The name of God is holy, trustworthy, known by God's people, and the mark of God's people. "We trust in his holy *name*" (Ps. 33:22). "My people will know my *name*"(Isa. 52:6). "They will see his face, and his *name* will be on their foreheads" (Rev. 22:4). God's name is "mighty in power" (Jer. 10.6), and it is for the sake of His name that God intercedes on behalf of His people (Ps. 79:9; 109:21; Ezek. 20:44; Rom. 1:5).

God considers His own name sacred. "For you have exalted above all things your name and your word"(Ps. 138:2). So it is not surprising that His adversaries misuse His name (Psa. 139:20), and people dishonor and blaspheme His name when they sin (Prov. 30:9; Jer. 3:17; Amos 2:17; Rom. 2:24). In John's vision as recorded in Revelation, the beast was "given a mouth to utter proud words." The first thing that the beast does, upon opening his mouth, is to blaspheme God and slander His name (Rev. 13:5, 6). But God's name will endure forever (Ps. 135:13), and His name, "KING OF KINGS AND LORD OF LORDS," will be written on His robe and on His thigh when Heaven opens and Christ descends upon a white horse to redeem His own, those mortals who bear the name of the most holy God (Rev. 19:11-16).

God has a name, "I AM who I AM" (Exod. 3:14). The name of God is important. The symbols of faith that compose the Biblical witness — in the form of God's own name — have been elected by God as means of revelation and salvation.[6] To challenge or change the name of God as God has revealed it is a denial of God. It is a denial of *who God is*. It is by God's name that we know Him, it is by His name that we are saved, and it is by His name that we are identified. Feminism's attempt to rename God is a blasphemy that comes out of the very depths of Hell. We have no right to name God. The only right we have, as created beings, is to submit to addressing God in the manner He has revealed as appropriate. It is not we who name God, it is God who names Himself.

God Has Named Creation

A short time ago, I had an interesting exchange with my four-year old son. Matthew burst into my study demanding an answer to a question. Apparently my answer did not satisfy him, for he defiantly challenged me with the sarcastic statement, "Well, Mommy, *you* don't know *everything* in the whole world!"

"Oh?" I replied, amused, "How do *you* know that I don't know everything in the whole world?"

His retort was prompt and reflected a simple yet profound childlike wisdom.

"*Well,*" he countered, with hands on hips, "you didn't *make* the whole world, did you?"

I couldn't help but laugh. "No, Matthew, I didn't *make* the whole world, and you are right . . . I don't *know* everything in the whole world."

My four-year-old perceives a truth that many adults fail to acknowledge. The One who created — "made" — the world naturally and logically possesses all knowledge about His creation. The Bible draws the same conclusion. One has only to read God's words in Job chapters 38 – 41 to realize that the knowledge God has regarding His creation is incomprehensible to humans. God asks:

Where were you when I laid the earth's foundation? Tell me, if you understand. Who marked off its dimensions? Surely you know! . . . Who cuts a channel for the torrents of rain, and a path for the thunderstorm. . . . Can you bind the beautiful Pleiades? Can you loose the cords of Orion? Can you bring forth the constellations in their seasons or lead out the Bear with its cubs? Do you know the laws of the heavens? Can you set up God's dominion over the earth?[7]

The fact that God created the world is referred to repeatedly throughout Scripture. When the people of Israel rebelled against God's laws and His revealed pattern for their lives, they were confronted with the fact of creation: "O foolish and unwise people — Is he not your Father, your Creator, who made you and formed you?" (Deut. 32:6). King Solomon claimed that humans could not fathom the ways of God because they did not have a part in creation: "You do not know the path of the wind, or how the body is formed in a mother's womb, so you cannot understand the work of God, the Maker of all things" (Eccl. 11:5). Solomon goes on to admonish people to "remember" their Creator (Eccl. 12:1).

Those who fail to acknowledge God as Creator of all — distinct, separate, and above all that is created — misplace the focus of their worship to someone or something other than God. They may "know God," but in their self-proclaimed wisdom about the world, they exchange the truth about God for a lie. Claiming to be wise, they become fools:

For although they knew God, they neither glorified him as God nor gave thanks to him, but their thinking became futile and their foolish hearts were darkened. Although they claimed to be wise, they became fools and exchanged the glory of the immortal God for images made to look like mortal man and birds and animals and reptiles. Therefore God gave them over in the sinful desires of their hearts to sexual impurity for the degrading of their bodies with one another. *They exchanged the truth of God for a lie, and worshiped and served created things rather than the Creator* — who is forever praised. Amen. Because of this, God gave them over to shameful lusts. Even their women exchanged natural relations for unnatural ones." (Rom. 1:21-26)

Feminism seeks to name the world. It seeks to formulate interpretations and boundaries for behavior independent of the Creator. In doing so, feminism exchanges the truth of God for a lie, and begins to worship and serve created things rather than the God who created them.

God Has Named Man and Woman

In the beginning God created man in his own image, in the image of God he created him; male and female he created them. (Genesis 1:26)

We are created beings. We have been created male and female. This fact is not inconsequential; it means something. The Bible informs us that there was an essential difference in the manner and the purpose of the creation of the two sexes. The New Testament reiterates that there are basic differences between men and women that are to be honored as part of God's design. By refusing to honor these differences, or by defiantly stating that "It cannot be so," we are claiming the right to define our own existence. That is a right which belongs to God. It is God who made the earth and created mankind upon it, and we have no right to question the wisdom of His directives for our behavior. God spoke through Isaiah:

Woe to him who quarrels with his Maker, to him who is but a potsherd [a broken piece of pottery] among the potsherds on the ground. Does the clay say to the potter, "What are you making?" Does your work say, "He has no hands"? . . . Concerning things to come, do you question me about my children, or give me orders about the work of my hands? It is I who made the earth and created mankind upon it. (Isa. 45:10-12)

Paul repeats the admonition in Romans:

But who are you, O man, to talk back to God? "Shall what is formed say to him who formed it, 'Why did you make me like this?'" Does not the potter have the right to make out of the same lump of clay some pottery for noble purposes and some for common use? (Rom. 9:20-21)

The Creator fashioned the two sexes differently. This is a fact that we dare not overlook or trivialize. In 1 Corinthians 11:9-12 we are told that "the man did not come from the woman, but woman from man; neither was man created for woman, but woman for man." Furthermore, "woman is not independent of man, nor is man independent of woman. For as woman came from man, so also man is born of woman. But everything comes from God." Numerous other texts in the Bible deal with differences in both the creation and roles of male and female.

The two sexes were created differently. The Bible provides important information as to how these differences are to be evidenced. It does not, as some have argued, provide a stereotyped checklist of which sex does what (e.g., men fix the cars, women do the baking), but it *does* teach us how we relate to one another. The Biblical framework teaches us to know and understand ourselves as men and women. Furthermore, our identity as male and female has an important symbolic aspect. It teaches us about the relationship between ourselves as God's people (the Church) and God. It also teaches us something of the inter-trinitarian relationship within the Godhead itself.[8]

The reality of who we are, how the world works, and who God is, is not hidden. It is revealed to us through the symbols and images of God, and of male and female. If we lose these fundamental images, we will lose ourselves. As Leanne Payne observes:

> Reality is simply far too great to be contained in propositions. That is why humans need gestures, pictures, images, rhythms, metaphor, symbol, and myth. It is also why we need ceremony, ritual, customs and conventions: those ways that perpetuate and mediate the images and symbols to us. . . . Man and woman, apart from their symbols, die.[9]

Mary Daly realized that the act of naming conveyed power to the one who does it. When Daly accepted the feminist precept regarding the individual's right to name, she removed herself from under God's authority and claimed authority for herself. In doing so, she submitted herself to the influence of the Evil One. This is the danger of feminist philosophy. As Christians, we must allow *God* to name Himself, to name His creation, and to name us. Then — and only then — will we gain a proper, undistorted understanding of ourselves, the world, and, most importantly, understanding about God.

FIGHTING ON TWO FRONTS

> In this fallen world, things constantly swing like a pendulum, from being wrong in one extreme way to being wrong in another extreme. The devil never gives us the luxury of fighting on only one front, and this will always be the case.[10]

The core philosophy of feminism is wrong. But it is a pendular reaction to the equally wrong "traditional" model of abusive male superiority and female inferiority. I therefore find myself in the difficult position of fighting a battle on two fronts. On the one hand, I must, as I have attempted to do in this book, stand unswervingly under the authority of the Word of God. The philosophy of feminism is an affront to that authority and must be exposed as such. On the other hand, I must fight against an equally destructive tendency in some quarters to use the Word of God to justify a legalistic religion that erects boundaries and restrictions foreign to the gospel.

The Bible does not teach the inequality of men and women. Each person, man or woman, stands before God as an individual created in the image of God, and at the same time as a sinner in need of salvation. Therefore, each person, whether male or female, has at the same time both an *infinite equality of worth* before God and one another, and a *total equality of need* for Jesus Christ as Savior.[11] However, the equality of man and woman does not undermine the difference between the sexes. It allows for the realization and fulfillment of this difference. Biblical equality affirms that although both male and female are created in the image of God, they exist as *complementary expressions of the image of God.*[12] In this wonderful complementarity there is an enormous range of diversity. But at the same time, it is not a freedom without form. The Bible grants freedom to men and women within the bounds of Biblical truth and within the bounds of what it means to be complementary expressions of the image of God.[13] Those who have unduly restricted the Biblical freedom of women are just as guilty of abusing God's pattern as those who have cast aside all boundaries. The battle against falsehood regarding the role of men and women is raging on two fronts. It must be fought on two opposite extremes.

22

The Future of Feminism

The women . . . had neither adopted nor rejected feminism. Rather, it had seeped into their minds like intravenous saline into the arm of an unconscious patient. They were feminists without knowing it.[1]

The mauve and gray seminar room is filled with women dressed in pastel silk coordinates and business suits. An oblong table, draped with lace cloth, is positioned on a slightly raised platform in the center of the room. Were it not for the tall candles, the heady aroma of incense, and the music emanating from sophisticated stereo speakers, this would appear to be nothing more than a respectable professional conference or executive business meeting. But the table looks suspiciously like an altar, and the lyrics sung by the flute-accompanied female chorus intimate the true purpose of this gathering:

> *Oh, great spirit, earth, sun, sky and sea.*
> *You are inside and all around me.*

The anthem softly echoes over and over again, until a woman — smartly dressed in a black skirt and coordinating pink and black jacket — takes her place in a director's chair in front of the altar.

"This is the third Women's Empowerment Night," she says. "We will start with the closed-eye process."

On cue, all the women in the room close their eyes while the music picks up again and a new choir sings:

> *Goddess of grace, goddess of strength,*
> *keeper of the creative force. . . .*
> *Goddess of Love, I long to be one with you.*
> *Teach me to be a goddess too.*[2]

This snapshot is not of a leather-fringed, metal-studded, or nude countercultural group of social misfits partaking in some ritual in a hidden enclave. All these women, aged twenty-five to forty-five, are highly educated middle- and upper-class professionals. They have each paid $20 to enter this respected center of education. The Omega Centre of Self-Discovery, with its bookstore and seminar rooms decked out with tweed and chrome armchairs, is on the edge of Toronto's high-rent Yorkville district, across the road from a Mercedes Benz service center and two minutes from the posh department store Holt Renfrew.

The Women's Empowerment Night in Toronto is one of thousands of events that take place every day across the continent. The Big Sisters Association of Ontario does exercises in "brain gym" at their annual conference. The Cancer Society runs "creative visualization" classes. The Y.W.C.A. sponsors women's empowerment retreat weekends. Law classes at universities educate prospective lawyers in women's concerns and help them contact their "deep selves." The feminist phenomenon is not restricted to secular society. Inclusive language, revised lectionaries, and feminist rituals can be found in many mainstream churches. Christian seminaries and Bible schools offer women's studies courses, and church leaders can have their "consciousness raised" to a feminist perspective through Christian feminist conferences. Feminism, goddess worship, and feminist mysticism are no longer confined to a select radical few. They have gone mainstream.

MAINSTREAMING THE AGENDA

The social and political agenda of the feminist movement expanded as the philosophy of the movement evolved. Women initially wanted to overcome their biological differences in order to be equal with (i.e., the same as) men. They thus sought legal freedom for abortion, changes in marriage and divorce law, tax reform, universal day care, pay equity, affirmative action in employment, and changes in language. In the second phase of development, their agenda expanded. Women were becoming proud of their differences. Women expanded their attention from naming themselves to naming their world. They emphasized female strengths — women's capacity for love, acceptance, peace and empathy — and added issues such as nuclear disarmament, militarism, homosexual rights, aboriginal rights, women's art, women-centered politics, and feminist interpretive law to the list. Finally, feminism moved into a third phase of spiritual awareness. Esoteric metaphysics, which asserts woman's divine connectedness with nature, motivated feminist women to direct their energy toward saving the earth. Ecological awareness, pollution, animal rights, and rain forest preservation were therefore also added to the feminist agenda.

By the time feminism had reached its third phase of development, its earlier goals were well on their way to being realized. North American society had moved toward accepting and integrating the feminist view of abortion, day care, divorce, sexual liberty, and affirmative action into common policy. The agenda of the second phase, while not yet as widely accepted by society, had also progressed toward mainstream integration. The mainstream acceptance of the feminist agenda caused the movement to lose its distinction. Further distinction was lost as third phase feminists turned their attention to other problems that could not be categorized as "belonging to women."

Feminists are becoming difficult to identify, not because they do not exist, but because their philosophy has been integrated into mainstream society so thoroughly. The philosophy is almost unidentifiable as *feminist*, for it is virtually indistinguishable from *mainstream*. This is not to say that there has been a decline in feminism. Far from it! Organized secular feminist groups still exist. They are in large measure funded by government dollars and justify their existence (and their funding) by addressing the remaining legal and social barriers for the phase one and two feminist agendas. But more significantly, feminist philosophy has been effectively integrated into the minds of this generation and into the precepts of contemporary society.

FEMINISM IN DECLINE?

Within the past few years, "The Decline of Feminism" has been the tedious subject of afternoon talk shows and long, emotive articles in women's magazines. In 1989, a publisher approached twenty-seven-year-old writer Danielle Crittenden to write a book about why feminism had lost its appeal, particularly to women under thirty — the "daughters of the revolution," those on whose behalf liberation had been sought but who appeared to be "rather ungratefully bored by the whole thing."[3]

Crittenden, in order to reveal the state of the feminist movement, drove around eastern Canada and the northeastern United States interviewing young female students — mostly at universities. She found that most young women ardently reacted to the label "feminist" — "as if it were an orange bell-bottomed pantsuit found at the back of their mother's closets."[4] Few of these women had read Betty Friedan's *The Feminine Mystique*, or any other feminist pop classic for that matter. Nor did they belong to any feminist organizations. But, according to Crittenden, they were feminists nonetheless.

> The young people of their generation had been made the laboratory mice for the numerous social experiments of the past 20 years: infant day care and no-fault divorce; textbooks illustrated with little girls flying planes and little boys doing the vacuuming; coed shop classes instead of home economics; the frank discussions about condoms with high school gym teachers. Their brains, meanwhile, had been irradiated with a mishmash of feminist cultural messages, from the proudly menstruating teenage heroines of Judy Blume novels to the supportive articles about single mothers in the Sunday life-style section to the audience applause on

Donahue for the woman who left her husband and three kids in Minnesota to realize herself as a potter in Santa Fe.

The women I interviewed had neither adopted nor rejected feminism. Rather, it had seeped into their minds like intravenous saline into the arm of an unconscious patient. *They were feminists without knowing it.*[5] (emphasis added)

The apparent lull in feminism's activism should not be interpreted as a decrease in feminism's overall social power. Feminism as a popular movement seems in decline only because it has been so wildly effective. All the major institutions of society — businesses, government, universities — have absorbed feminism's tenets. There are women's studies departments at universities, provincial women's directorates, status of women councils, sex-harassment boards, and board of education committees on "gender-free" curricula in the school system. Ideas that were once considered radical or bizarre are now considered conventional. Feminist wisdom is even being forwarded by officials in the highest level of the judicial system. For example, Canadian Supreme Court Justice Bertha Wilson, in a speech to the Osgoode Hall Law School in February of 1990, called for the transformation of the law along feminist principles and for the reeducation of her male colleagues in "summer schools on sexism." She endorsed the idea, proposed by second-phase feminist philosophers, that women are more caring and inherently "nicer" than men, and that they are less concerned than men with abstract notions of justice, less preoccupied with what is "right" and "wrong," and hence less inclined to separate their feelings from their thinking. She went on to chastise her fellow judges for relying too much on the evidence of a case instead of entering "into the skin of the litigant and making his or her experience part of your experience and only when you have done that, to judge."[6] According to Wilson, a woman who had suffered at the hands of a particular man could not readily be judged as guilty in the murder of that man. The implications of these feminist notions are radical and drastic to the traditional practice of law and justice, and yet they hardly met a raised eyebrow. Little public debate resulted, just a praising article in a leading national newspaper.

In feminism, as in any major social/political/religious movement, the radical end of the philosophy provides the driving impetus. Furthermore, the thoughts that are radical at one point become the accepted, integrated norm for future generations. The feminist philosophy proposed by first-phase feminism — radical as it was — has now become conventional wisdom. Phase-two women-centered analysis, though not yet totally integrated, is also broadly accepted by society. Furthermore, the feminist spirituality — which seemed so brash when introduced in the late 1970s — has progressed from being viewed as radical and deviant to being included in the spectrum of tolerated normal behavior. Future generations will perhaps accept it as normative truth. For the evangelical Church, the acceptance of feminist precepts lags behind secular society and liberal theology by about ten years. But the process is also well established. Is feminism in decline? Perhaps to the casual observer it may seem so. But the truth is, feminism only appears to be in decline because we have accepted it so thoroughly into into our own psyches and lifestyles. We all, to varying degrees, are feminists ourselves.

SAILING BETWEEN SCYLLA AND CHARYBDIS

The Strait of Messina lies between Sicily and the southwestern tip of Italy connecting the Ionian and Tyrrhenian seas. Historically, it was an important route for Roman and Greek trade. The channel is narrow, spanning only two miles in width, and is treacherous to navigate because of a rocky coast on the one side and a massive, churning whirlpool on the other. According to mythology, Scylla, a sea monster who was part woman and part fish, lived in a cave above the Strait of Messina opposite the whirlpool Charybdis. She and Charybdis harassed ships in the Strait of Messina and seized and ate sailors that came too close. Sailors tried to steer a middle course between Scylla and Charybdis, but it was incredibly difficult to avoid the danger of one without encountering the danger of the other.

Likewise, it is difficult for us, as Christians, to navigate between the two dangers that confront us. We must avoid the traditional whirlpool of Charybdis which can trap us in restrictive, abusive, stereotyped roles, but we must also be careful, in avoiding the danger of Charybdis, not to be shipwrecked on the deadly rocks of feminist Scylla. It is difficult, but I believe God's Word provides the directions for safely sailing between the two. If we return to the Bible for new thinking about male and female roles, and allow God to name Himself, His world, and us, His people, then we will avoid danger and chart a course that will bring us safely to our ultimate destination.

The world-philosophy of feminism stands in antithesis to the philosophy of the Bible. Sadly, many Christians are seeking to unite the two. The Christian community *must* answer the questions with which it has been challenged, but it must find new answers which are as old as the Bible itself. It must resist the temptation to succumb to the "blue-jean mentality" of accepting the solutions that are being proposed by the world. In order to live as Christian believers, we need to accept the model of male and female, the world, and God that are presented in the Bible. Apart from this framework, the quest for true wholeness, fulfillment, and equality is futile. The Bible, and *only* the Bible, contains the real hope for the liberation of women. It is my hope that this work will serve as a buffer against the tremendous pressure that is being exerted upon the evangelical Church to compromise the Bible in the area of male and female roles. Looking to Christ for strength, as our whole culture is against us at this point, we must reject the infiltration of feminism in theology and in life equally. We, as the Bride of Christ, need to remain pure by rejecting this unholy union.

APPENDIX

Charts Depicting the Development of Feminism

The charts on the following pages depict the progression of feminist theology and theory in the 1960s, 1970s, and 1980s. Study of these diagrams will assist in the understanding of the stages which have led to the feminist movement in its present state.

THE HISTORICAL DEVELOPMENT OF FEMINIST THEOLOGY

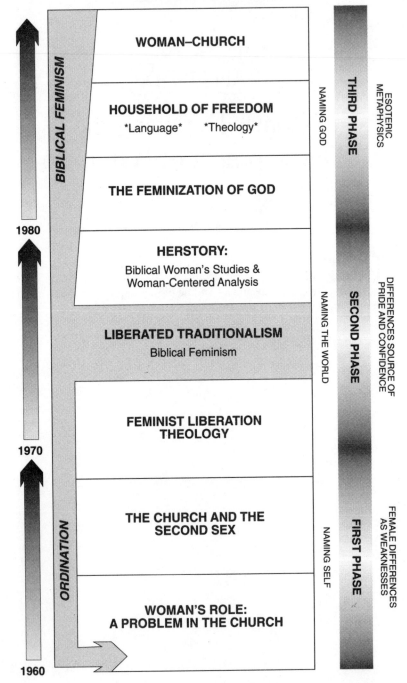

THE HISTORICAL DEVELOPMENT OF FEMINIST THEORY

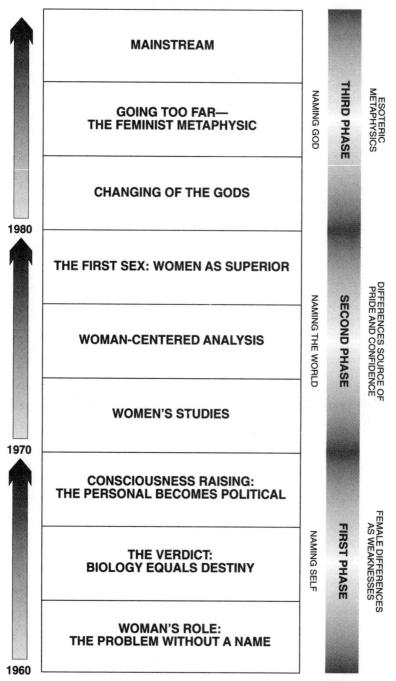

NOTES

CHAPTER ONE: *The Problem Without a Name*

1. Josephine Donovan, *Feminist Theory — The Intellectual Traditions of American Feminism* (New York: Frederick Ungar Publishing Co., 1985), p. 1.
2. Donavan noted that couverture also gave the husband power to deprive his wife of liberty and to administer chastisement as he saw fit. *Ibid.*, p. 7.
3. Donovan, *ibid.*
4. Women's educational opportunities gradually expanded throughout the 1800s. In 1821, Emma Willard, an American teacher, founded the Troy Female Seminary (now the Emma Willard School) in Troy, N.Y. Her school was one of the first institutions to offer girls a high-school education. In 1833, Oberlin Collegiate Institute, now known as Oberlin College, opened as the first coeducational college in the United States. By 1900, some major European and American universities began to follow suit and accepted women for advanced study and professional training.
5. Donovan, *Feminist Theory*, p. 27.
6. Mary Evans, *Feminist Theorists: Three Centuries of Key Women Thinkers*, ed. Dale Spender (New York: Pantheon Books, 1983), p. 349.
7. Simone deBeauvoir, *The Second Sex* (New York: Random House, 1952), p. xix.
8. *Ibid.*
9. *Ibid.*, pp. xxiv, xviii.
10. *Ibid.*, p. xxvii.
11. *Ibid.*, p. xviii.
12. *Ibid.*, p. xxxiv.
13. *Ibid.*, p. xxxiii.
14. *Ibid.*, p. xxii.
15. *Ibid.*, pp. xxii-xxiii.
16. *Ibid.*, p. 797.
17. *Ibid.*
18. *Ibid.*
19. *Ibid.*, p. 126.
20. *Ibid.*, p. 806.
21. Betty Friedan, *The Feminine Mystique* (New York: Dell Publishing Co., 1963), p. 6.
22. *Ibid.*, p. 7.
23. *Ibid.*, p. 22.
24. *Ibid.*, p. 44.
25. *Ibid.*, p. 16.
26. *Ibid.*, pp. 36, 66.
27. *Ibid.*, p. 18.

28. *Ibid.*, p. 77.
29. *Ibid.*, p. 312.
30. *Ibid.*, p. 344.
31. *Ibid.*, p. 19.
32. *Ibid.*, p. 311.
33. *Ibid.*
34. Adrienne Rich, *Of Women Born* (New York: Bantam Books, 1976), pp. 57, 58.

CHAPTER TWO: *A Problem in the Church*

1. Gertrud Heinzelmann, "The Priesthood and Women," *Commonweal*, Vol. 81, No. 16 (January 15, 1965), p. 504.
2. Katherine Bliss, *The Service and Status of Women in the Church* (London: SCM Press, 1952).
3. *Ibid.*, p. 10.
4. *Ibid.*
5. I believe that the major contributing factor to the presence of feminism in the Church is a wrong enactment of Biblical leadership and a wrong concept of Church structure. I agree with feminists that the Church abuses and oppresses its women. I cannot, however, support the course religious feminists have chosen for correcting the problem. For further discussion, please refer to my first book — *Women, Creation and the Fall* (Crossway, 1990).
6. Mary Daly, "A Built-In Bias," *Commonweal*, Vol. 81, No. 16 (January 15, 1965), p. 511.
7. William Douglas, "Women in the Church," *Pastoral Psychology* (1961), p. 15.
8. *Ibid.*, p. 14.
9. F. S. Smith, "Fairness for the Fair Sex," *Christianity and Crisis* (September 17, 1962), pp. 146-7.
10. Polly Allen Robinson, "Women in Christ," *Union Seminary Quarterly Review*, Vol. 19 (March, 1964), p. 193.
11. Arlene Swidler, "An Ecumenical Question: The Status of Women," *Journal of Ecumenical Studies*, Vol. 4 (1967), p. 114.
12. *Ibid.*, pp. 113-115.
13 Rugh E. Hartley, "Some Implications on Current Changes in Sex Role Patterns," *Pastoral Psychology*, Vol. 12 (November, 1961), pp. 7-9.
14. Valerie Saiving Goldstein, "Where Is the Woman," *Theology Today*, Vol. 19 (1962), pp. 111-14.
15. James Ashbrook, "The Church as Matriarchy," *Pastoral Psychology*, Vol. 14 (1963), pp. 38-49.
16. R. A. Schmidt, "Second Class Citizenship in the Kingdom of God," *Christianity Today*, Vol. 15 (January 1, 1971), pp. 13-4.
17. Douglas, "Women in the Church," *Pastoral Psychology*, p. 13.
18. *Ibid.*, p. 19.
19. St. Joan's International Alliance, for example, a women's group founded in 1931, suggested at a 1963 meeting that diaconal duties be entrusted to women as well as men and noted that women would be willing and eager to serve as priests.
20. As quoted by Rosemary Lauer, "Women and the Church," *Commonweal*, Vol. 79, No. 13 (1963), p. 366.
21. *Ibid.*
22. *Ibid.*
23. *Ibid.*
24. Charles Trombley, *Who Said Women Can't Teach?* (South Plainfield, NJ: Bridge Publishing, 1985), p. 29.
25. Lauer, "Women and the Church," *Commonweal*, p. 17.

26. Douglas, "Women in the Church," *Pastoral Psychology*, p. 16.
27. Mary Daly, "A Built-In Bias," *Commonweal*, Vol. 81, No. 16 (January 15, 1965), p. 509.
28. *Ibid.*
29. Lauer, "Women and the Church," *Commonweal*, p. 367.
30. *Ibid.*
31. *Ibid.*
32. *Ibid.*
33. *Ibid.*, p. 366.
34. *Ibid.*
35. Daly, "A Built-In Bias," *Commonweal*, p. 510.
36. Margaret Mead, *Male and Female* (New York: William Morrow and Company, 1949); *Sex and Temperament* (New York: William Morrow and Company, 1935).
37. Ashbrook, "Church as Matriarchy," *Pastoral Psychology*, p. 41.
38. Mead's work has been refuted by Derek Freeman, *Margaret Mead and Samoa* (Cambridge: Harvard University Press, 1983).
39. Lauer, "Women and the Church," *Commonweal*, p. 367.
40. Valerie Saiving Goldstein, "The Human Situation: A Feminine Viewpoint," *Journal of Religion*, Vol. 40, No. 2 (April, 1960).
41. Goldstein, "The Human Situation: A Feminine Viewpoint," published in *The Nature of Man*, ed. Simon Doniger (New York: Harper & Brothers, 1962), reprinted in *Pastoral Psychology*, Vol. 17 (1966) pp. 29-41.
42. Goldstein, *Pastoral Psychology*, p. 38.
43. *Ibid.*, p. 39.
44. *Ibid.*, p. 36.
45. *Ibid.*, p. 41.
46. Monolithic equality is a term used by Dr. Francis Schaeffer to represent the type of equality that is pursued by feminism. Monolithic equality is "freedom without form." It is an androgynous state in which no boundaries are placed on roles. See Dr. Francis Schaeffer, *The Great Evangelical Disaster* (Wheaton, IL: Crossway Books, 1984), pp. 130-140.
47. Douglas, "Women in the Church," *Pastoral Psychology*, p. 20.

CHAPTER THREE: *The Church and the Second Sex*

1. Mary Daly, *The Church and the Second Sex* (Boston: Beacon Press, 1968), p. 58.
2. *Ibid.*
3. *Ibid.*
4. *Ibid.*
5. *Ibid.*
6. *Ibid.*, p. 59.
7. *Ibid.*
8. *Ibid.*, p. 60.
9. *Ibid.*, p. 61.
10. *Ibid.*
11. *Ibid.*, p. 63.
12. *Ibid.*
13. *Ibid.*
14. *Ibid.*, p. 64.
15. *Ibid.*, p. 65.
16. *Ibid.*
17. *Ibid.*, p. 180.
18. Mary Daly, *Beyond God the Father* (Boston: Beacon Press, 1973), p. 19.

19. Daly, *The Church and the Second Sex*, p. 182.
20. *Ibid.*
21. *Ibid.*
22. *Ibid.*, p. 188.
23. *Ibid.*, p. 180.
24. *Ibid.*, p. 183.
25. *Ibid.*
26. *Ibid.*, pp. 74-75.
27. *Ibid.*
28. *Ibid.*, p. 184.
29. *Ibid.*, p. 185.
30. *Ibid.*, p. 188.
31. *Ibid.*, p. 184.
32. *Ibid.*, p. 185.
33. *Ibid.*
34. *Ibid.*
35. *Ibid.*, p. 186.
36. *Ibid.*

CHPATER FOUR: *Biology Equals Destiny*

1. Shulamith Firestone, *The Dialectic of Sex: The Case for Feminist Revolution* (New York: William Morrow and Company, Inc., 1970), p. 81.
2. *Ibid.*, p. 8.
3. *Ibid.*, p. 14.
4. *Ibid.*, pp. 8, 9.
5. *Ibid.*, p. 10.
6. *Ibid.*, p. 2.
7. *Ibid.*, p. 12.
8. *Ibid.*, p. 83.
9. *Ibid.*, p. 12.
10. Juliet Mitchell, *Woman's Estate* (New York: Random House Inc., 1971), p. 109.
11. *Ibid.*, p. 107.
12. *Ibid.*, pp. 101-122.
13. Susan Brownmiller, *Against Our Will* (New York: Bantam Books, 1975), p. xiii.
14. *Ibid.*, pp. 7, 8.
15. Hester Eisenstein, *Contemporary Feminist Thought* (Boston: G. K. Hall & Co.), p. 32; Susan Griffin, "Rape: the All-American Crime," *Ramparts*, Vol. 10 (September 1971), pp. 26-35.
16. Susan Brownmiller, *Against Our Will*, p. 5.
17. *Ibid.*, p. 7.
18. *Ibid.*, p. 6.
19. *Ibid.*, pp. 7, 8.
20. Eisenstein, *Contemporary Feminist Thought*, p. 81.
21. Ti-Grace Atkinson, *Amazon Odyssey* (New York: Links Books, 1976), p. 1.
22. Firestone, *The Dialectic of Sex: The Case for Feminist Revolution*, p. 12.
23. The marches were referred to as "burn the bra" marches even though bras were never actually burned.
24. National Organization for Women (N.O.W.) was established in the U.S.A. by Betty Friedan in 1966. Laura Sabia established the National Action Committee (N.A.C.) in Canada in 1972.
25. Firestone, *The Dialectic of Sex: The Case for Feminist Revolution*, pp. 233-236.
26. Germaine Greer, *The Female Eunuch* (Great Britain: MacGibbon & Kee Ltd., 1970), p. 14.

27. *Ibid.*, p. 33.

CHAPTER FIVE: *Feminist Liberation Theology*

1. Letty Russell, *Human Liberation in a Feminist Perspective: A Theology* (Philadelphia: Westminster Press, 1974), pp. 11, 17.
2. *Ibid.*, p. 45.
3. *Ibid.*, p. 20.
4. As quoted by Michael Novak, *Will It Liberate?* — *Questions About Liberation Theology* (New York: Paulist Press, 1986), p. 23.
5. Russell, *Human Liberation in a Feminist Perspective*, p. 104.
6. Novak, *Will It Liberate?*, p. 26.
7. *Ibid.*, p. 27.
8. Russell, *Human Liberation in a Feminist Perspective*, p. 104.
9. Novak, *Will It Liberate?*, p. 25.
10. *Ibid.*
11. Russell, *Human Liberation in a Feminist Perspective*, p. 29.
12. Valerie Saiving Goldstein, "Where Is the Woman?," *Theology Today*, Vol. 19 (1962), p. 111.
13. Rosemary Radford Ruether, *Liberation Theology: Human Hope Confronts Christian History and American Power* (New York: Paulist Press, 1972), p. 16.
14. *Ibid.*, p. 17.
15. *Ibid.*
16. *Ibid.*, p. 20.
17. *Ibid.*, p. 21.
18. *Ibid.*, p. 22.
19. *Ibid.*
20. Russell, *Human Liberation in a Feminist Perspective*, p. 27.
21. Ruether, *Liberation Theology*, p. 124.
22. *Ibid.*
23. Russell, *Human Liberation in a Feminist Perspective*, p. 25.
24. *Ibid.*, p. 26.
25. *Ibid.*, p. 30.
26. *Ibid.*, p. 32.
27. *Ibid.*
28. *Ibid.*
29. *Ibid.*, p. 33.
30. *Ibid.*, p. 45.
31. *Ibid.*, p. 28.
32. Ruether, *Liberation Theology*, p. 189.
33. Russell, *Human Liberation in a Feminist Perspective*, p. 19.
34. Ruether, *Liberation Theology*, pp. 124, 125.
35. *Ibid.*, p. 126.
36. Russell, *Human Liberation in a Feminist Perspective*, pp. 34, 77.

CHAPTER SIX: *The Personal Becomes Political*

1. Congress passed the Civil Rights Act in 1964. Title VII prevents sex discrimination in employment in businesses of twenty-five or more employees. The Equal Employment Opportunity Commission was established to monitor the Civil Rights Act.
2. Regulation regarding the employment of stewardesses demanded that stewardesses be fired if they married or when they reached thirty-two years of age.
3. More details regarding the events of the women's movement can be found in Marcia Cohen, *The Sisterhood: The Inside Story of the Women's Movement and*

the Leaders Who Made It Happen (New York: Ballantine Books, division of Random House, 1988).

4. The Oak Room, at the Plaza Hotel in New York, had a policy that barred women entrance at lunchtime — from twelve to three o'clock. On February 12, 1969 a group of women invaded the Oak Room and demanded service. Service was refused. The media, it is estimated, outnumbered demonstrators by a count of two to one.

5. Claudia Dreifus, *Woman's Fate: Raps from a Feminist Consciousness-raising Group* (New York: Bantam Books, 1973), pp. 3-4.

6. The technique was described in Kathie Sarachild, "A Program for Feminist Consciousness Raising, Notes from the Second Year," cited in Alex Kate Shulman, "Sex and Power: Sexual Bases of Radical Feminism," *Signs*, Vol. 5 (Summer, 1980), p. 594.

7. Dreifus, *Woman's Fate: Raps from a Feminist Consciousness-raising Group*, p. 12.

8. *Ibid.*, pp. 12, 13.

9. For more specific information on CR groups, see: Virginia Coover, Charles Esser, Ellen Deacon and Christopher Moore, *Resource Manual for a Living Revolution* (Philadelphia: New Society Publishers, 1977); Linda Donnan and Sue Lenton, *Helping Ourselves* (Toronto: Women's Press, 1985); Liz Stanley and Sue Wise, *Breaking Out: Feminist Consciousness and Feminist Research* (London: Routledge and Kegan Paul, 1983); Pamela Allen, *Free Space: A Perspective on the Small Group in Women's Liberation* (New York: Times Change Press, 1970); Greta H. Nemiroff, *Power and the Empowerment of Women* (Montreal, Quebec: New School of Dawson College, 1981); Maxine Nunes and Deanna White, *The Lace Ghetto* (Toronto: New Press, 1973); Luise Eichenbaum and Susie Orbach, *Understanding Women: A Feminist Psychoanalytic Approach* (New York: Basic Books, 1983); Vivian Gornick, "Consciousness," in *Essays in Feminism* (New York: Harper & Row, 1978).

10. Maren Lockwood Carden, *The New Feminist Movement* (New York: Russell Sage Foundation, 1974), p. 33.

11. *Ibid.*, p. 36.

12. Jo Freeman, *The Politics of Women's Liberation* (New York: Longman, 1975), p. 118.

13. Carden, *The New Feminist Movement*, p. 33.

14. *Ibid.*

15. Hester Eisenstein, *Contemporary Feminist Thought* (Boston: G. K. Hall & Co., 1983), p. 36.

16. Juliet Mitchell, *Woman's Estate* (New York: Random House, 1971), p. 59.

17. *Ibid.*, p. 61.

18. Robin Morgan, ed. *Sisterhood Is Powerful: An Anthology of Writings from the Women's Liberation Movement* (New York: Vintage, 1970).

19. Susan Brownmiller, "Sisterhood Is Powerful — A Member of the Women's Liberation Movement Explains What It's All About," *New York Times*, March 15, 1970.

20. Hester Eisenstein, *Contemporary Feminist Thought*, p. 38.

21. Marcia Cohen, *The Sisterhood: The Inside Story of the Women's Movement and the Leaders Who Made It Happen*, p. 286.

CHAPTER SEVEN: *Woman-centered Analysis*

1. Dale Spender, *For the Record: The Making and Meaning of Feminist Knowledge* (London: The Women's Press, 1985).

2. Mary Daly, *Beyond God the Father: Towards a Philosophy of Women's Liberation* (Boston: Beacon Press, 1973), p. 9.
3. Robin Lakoff, *Language and Woman's Place* (New York: Harper & Row, 1975), p. 4.
4. *Ibid.*, p. 2.
5. *Ibid.*, p. 6.
6. *Ibid.*, p. 62.
7. Casey Miller and Kate Swift, *Words and Women: New Language in New Times* (Garden City, NY: Anchor Books/Doubleday, 1976); Dale Spender, *Man Made Language* (London: Routledge & Kegan Paul, 1980).
8. Elaine Showalter, *Feminist Criticism: Essays on Women, Literature & Theory* (New York: Pantheon Books, 1985), p. 5.
9. *Ibid.*, p. 3.
10. Spender, *Man Made Language*, p. 190.
11. Daly, *Beyond God the Father*, p. 8.
12. Jean Baker Miller, *Toward a New Psychology of Women* (Boston: Beacon Press, 1976), p. 94. Portions of this book were previously published in another form in the paper "Psychological Consequences of Sexual Inequality," in the *American Journal of Orthopsychiatry*, Vol. 41 (1971), pp. 767-775.
13. *Ibid.*, p. 7.
14. *Ibid.*
15. Phyllis Chesler, *Women and Madness* (Garden City, NY: Doubleday & Co., 1972), p. 104.
16. *Ibid.*, pp. 108, 109.
17. Miller, *Toward a New Psychology of Women*, pp. 18, 19.
18. *Ibid.*, p. 19.
19. *Ibid.*, p. 20.
20. *Ibid.*, p. 94.
21. Adrienne Rich, *Of Woman Born: Motherhood as Experience and Institution* (New York: W.W. Norton & Company, 1976), pp. 126, 127.
22. Spender, *For the Record*, p. 167.
23. *Ibid.*
24. As quoted in Spender, *For the Record*, p. 167.
25. Jules Mishelet as quoted by Chesler, *Women and Madness*, p. 102.
26. Rich, *Of Woman Born*, p. 13.
27. *Ibid.*, p. 284.
28. *Ibid.*
29. *Ibid.*, p. 75.
30. *Ibid.*, p. 42.
31. *Ibid.*
32. *Ibid.*, p. 13.
33. *Ibid.*, p. 42.
34. *Ibid.*, p. 99.
35. *Ibid.*, p. 94.
36. *Ibid.*, p. 68.
37. *Ibid.*, p. 280.
38. *Ibid.*, p. 93.
39. *Ibid.*, p. 284.
40. *Ibid.*, pp. 285, 286.
41. Ann Oakley, *The Sociology of Housework* (New York: Pantheon Books, 1974).
42. *Ibid.*, p. 4.
43. *Ibid.*, p. 19.
44. Spender, *For the Record*, p. 138.
45. Oakley, *The Sociology of Housework*, p. 195.

46. Sarah Lucia Hoagland and Julia Penelope, eds., *For Lesbians Only — A Separatist Anthology* (Tiptree, Essex, Great Britain: Only Women Press, 1988), p. 17.
47. Kate Millett, *Sexual Politics* (Garden City, NY: Doubleday, 1970).
48. As cited by Marcia Cohan, *The Sisterhood: The Inside Story of the Women's Movement and the Leaders Who Made It Happen* (New York: Fawcett Columbine, 1988), p. 236.
49. *Ibid.*, p. 246.
50. *Ibid.*, p. 249.
51. *Ibid.*
52. *Ibid.*, pp. 250, 251.
53. Hoagland and Penelope, *For Lesbians Only*, p. 21.
54. Jill Johnston, *Lesbian Nation: The Feminist Solution* (New York: Simon and Schuster, 1974), p. 278.
55. Hoagland and Penelope, *For Lesbians Only*, p. 19.
56. Johnston, *Lesbian Nation*, p. 278.
57. Charlotte Bunch, quoted by Josephine Donovan, *Feminist Theory: The Intellectual Traditions of American Feminism* (New York: Frederick Ungar Publishing Co., 1985), p. 164.
58. Adrienne Rich quoted by Donovan, *Feminist Theory*, pp. 166, 167.
59. *Ibid.*
60. *Ibid.*, p. 165.
61. Martha Shelley, "Notes of a Radical Lesbian," *Sisterhood Is Powerful*, ed. Robin Morgan (New York: Vintage, 1970), p. 308.
62. "Notes from the Third Year," *ibid.*, p. 26
63. Ti-Grace Atkinson, *Amazon Odyssey: The First Collection of Writings by the Political Pioneer of the Women's Movement* (New York: Links Books, 1974), p. 132.
64. Hoagland and Penelope, *For Lesbians Only*, p. 21.
65. Johnston, *Lesbian Nation*, p. 184.
66. Cohen, *The Sisterhood*, caption under photograph #68.
67. Elizabeth Gould Davis, *The First Sex* (Baltimore: Penguin Books,1972), pp. 335-337.

CHAPTER EIGHT: *Woman-centered Analysis of Theology*

1. Rosemary Radford Ruether, "Feminist Theology and Spirituality," *Christian Feminism*, ed. Judith L. Weidman (San Francisco: Harper & Row, 1984), pp. 10-11.
2. Rosemary Radford Ruether, "A Method of Correlation," *Feminist Interpretation of the Bible*, ed. Letty Russell (Philadelphia: Westminster Press, 1985), p. 115.
3. Letty Russell, *Human Liberation in a Feminist Perspective: A Theology* (Philadelphia: Westminster Press, 1974), p. 50.
4. *Ibid.*, p. 52.
5. *Ibid.*
6. *Ibid.*, p. 54.
7. *Ibid.*
8. *Ibid.*, p. 53.
9. *Ibid.*, p. 55.
10. *Ibid.*
11. *Ibid.*
12. *Ibid.*, p. 57.
13. *Ibid.*
14. *Ibid.*
15. *Ibid.*, p. 58.

16. *Ibid.*, p. 60.
17. *Ibid.*, p. 59.
18. *Ibid.*, p. 61.
19. *Ibid.*
20. *Ibid.*, p. 63.
21. *Ibid.*, p. 66.
22. *Ibid.*, p. 111.
23. *Ibid.*
24. *Ibid.*, p. 64.
25. *Ibid.*, p. 66.
26. *Ibid.*, p. 115.
27. *Ibid.*
28. As quoted by Russell, *ibid.*
29. *Ibid.*, p. 123.
30. Rosemary Radford Ruether, *Liberation Theology: Human Hope Confronts Christian History and American Power* (New York: Paulist Press, 1972), p. 13.
31. Russell, *Human Liberation in a Feminist Perspective*, p. 68.
32. *Ibid.*, p. 70.
33. *Ibid.*, p. 71.
34. Ruether, *Liberation Theology*, p. 183.
35. Russell, *Human Liberation in a Feminist Perspective*, p. 54.
36. Ruether, *Liberation Theology*, p. 3.
37. Russell, *Human Liberation in a Feminist Perspective*, p. 41.
38. *Ibid.*, p. 34.
39. *Ibid.*
40. *Ibid.*, p. 77.
41. *Ibid.*, p. 41.
42. *Ibid.*, p. 62.
43. *Ibid.*, p. 113.
44. *Ibid.*, p. 21.
45. Ruether, *Liberation Theology*, p. 125.
46. Russell, *Human Liberation in a Feminist Perspective*, p. 106.
47. *Ibid.*, p. 33.
48. Ruether, *Liberation Theology*, p. 183.
49. Russell, *Human Liberation in a Feminist Perspective*, p. 158.
50. *Ibid.*, p. 158.
51. *Ibid.*, p. 159.
52. *Ibid.*, p. 161.
53. *Ibid.*, p. 28.
54. *Ibid.*, p. 40.
55. *Ibid.*, p. 19.

CHPATER NINE: *The First Sex*

1. Elizabeth Gould Davis, *The First Sex* (Baltimore: Penguin Books, 1972), p. 66.
2. *Ibid.*, p. 65.
3. *Ibid.*, p. 21.
4. *Ibid.*, p. 23.
5. *Ibid.*, p. 25.
6. *Ibid.*, p. 29.
·7. *Ibid.*
8. *Ibid.*, p. 68.
9. *Ibid.*

10. Ashley Montague, *The Natural Superiority of Women* (New York: Macmillan Co., 1968), p. 74.
11. Davis, *The First Sex*, p. 34.
12. *Ibid.*, p. 35.
13. *Ibid.*
14. *Ibid.*
15. *Ibid.*, p. 17.
16. Mary Jane Sherfey, M.D., "A Theory on Female Sexuality," *Sisterhood Is Powerful*, ed. Robin Morgan (New York: Vintage, 1970), p. 251.
17. *Ibid.*, pp. 246, 247; Susan Lydon, "The Politics of Orgasm," *Sisterhood Is Powerful*, pp. 219-228.
18. Sherfey, "A Theory on Female Sexuality," *ibid.*, p. 250.
19. Davis, *The First Sex*, p. 36.
20. Sherfey, "A Theory on Female Sexuality," *Sisterhood Is Powerful*, p. 252.
21. Davis, *The First Sex*, p. 35.
22. *Ibid.*
23. *Ibid.*, p. 34.
24. *Ibid.*, p. 329.
25. *Ibid.*, p. 45.
26. *Ibid.*
27. *Ibid.*
28. *Ibid.*, p. 42.
29. *Ibid.*, p. 96.
30. *Ibid.*, p. 148.
31. *Ibid.*, pp. 34, 35.
32. *Ibid.*, pp. 37, 38.
33. Judith Antonelli, "The Politics of the Psyche," *The Politics of Women's Spirituality*, ed. Charlene Spretnak (Garden City, NY: Anchor Press/Doubleday, 1982), p. 401.
34. Davis, *The First Sex*, p. 18.
35. *Ibid.*, p. 338.
36. Gina Covina, "Rosy Rightbrain's Exorcism?," *The Lesbian Reader*, eds. Gina Covina and Laurel Galana (Oakland, CA: Amazon Press, 1975), pp. 94, 95.
37. *Ibid.*, p. 96.
38. Davis, *The First Sex*, p. 339.
39. *Ibid.*, p. 340.

CHAPTER TEN: *Herstory*

1. Mary Daly, *Beyond God the Father: Towards a Philosophy of Women's Liberation* (Boston: Beacon Press, 1973), p. 140.
2. Phyllis Trible, *God and the Rhetoric of Sexuality* (Philadelphia: Fortress Press, 1978), p. 200.
3. Letty Russell, *Human Liberation in a Feminist Perspective: A Theology* (Philadelphia: Westminster Press, 1974), pp. 18, 19.
4. *Ibid.*, p. 86.
5. Elisabeth Shüssler Fiorenza, "Interpreting Patriarchal Traditions," *The Liberating Word: A Guide to Nonsexist Interpretation of the Bible*, ed. Letty M. Russell (Philadelphia: Westminster Press, 1976), p. 60.
6. Elisabeth Shüssler Fiorenza, "Emerging Issues in Feminist Biblical Interpretation," *Christian Feminism: Visions of a New Humanity*, ed. Judith L. Weidman (San Francisco: Harper & Row, 1984), pp. 47-54. These themes are expanded in Elisabeth Schüssler Fiorenza, *In Memory of Her: A Feminist Theological*

Reconstruction of Christian Origins (New York: Crossroad Publishing Co., 1985).

7. J. Ellen Nunnally, *Fore-Mothers: Women of the Bible* (San Francisco: Harper & Row, 1981), p. 88.
8. Fiorenza, "Feminist Biblical Interpretation," *Christian Feminism*, pp. 50, 51.
9. *Ibid.*
10. Nunnally, *Fore-Mothers*, p. 9
11. *Ibid.*, p. 35.
12. *Ibid.*, p. 11.
13. Phyllis Trible, "The Pilgrim Bible on a Feminist Journey," *The Auburn News* (Spring 1988), p. 4.
14. Fiorenza, "Feminist Biblical Interpretation," *Christian Feminism*, p. 53.
15. *Ibid.*
16. Judith Plaskow, "The Coming of Lilith," in *Religion and Sexism: Images of Women in the Jewish and Christian Traditions*, ed. Rosemary Ruether (New York: Simon and Schuster, 1974), pp. 341-343
17. Russell, *Human Liberation in a Feminist Perspective*, p. 81.
18. *Ibid.*, p. 82.

CHAPTER ELEVEN: *Women's Studies*

1. Hunter College Women's Studies Collective, *Women's Realities, Women's Choices: An Introduction to Women's Studies* (New York: Oxford University Press, 1983), p. 3.
2. Cited by Marilyn J. Boxer, "For and About Women: The Theory and Practice of Women's Studies in the United States," *Feminist Theory: A Critique of Ideology*, eds. Nannerl O. Keohane, Michelle Z. Rosaldo, and Barbara C. Gelpi (Chicago: University of Chicago Press, 1982), p. 237.
3. Hunter College Women's Studies Collective, *An Introduction to Women's Studies*, p. 5.
4. Jane Williamson, *Women's Action Almanac*, eds. Jane Williamson, Diane Watson, Wanda Wooten (New York: William Morrow & Co., 1979), p. 336.
5. Boxer, "For and About Women: The Theory and Practice of Women's Studies in the United States," *Feminist Theory: A Critique of Ideology*, p. 237.
6. Gloria Bowles, *Theories of Women's Studies*, eds. Gloria Bowles and Renate Duelli (London: Klein Routledge & Kegan Paul, 1983), p. 28.
7. Sheila Ruth Houghton, *Issues in Feminism: A First Course in Women's Studies* (Boston: Mifflin Company, 1980), p. 7.
8. *Ibid.*, p. 24.
9. *Ibid.*, p. 23.
10. *Ibid.*, p. 24.
11. Mary Daly, as quoted in *Issues in Feminism*, p. 24.
12. Sandra Coyner, *Theories of Women's Studies*, p. 68.
13. *Ibid.*
14. Taly Rutenberg, *ibid.*, p. 73.
15. Gloria Bowles, *ibid.*, p. 22.
16. Marilyn J. Boxer, *Feminist Theory*, p. 248.
17. Taly Rutenberg, *Theories of Women's Studies*, p. 77.
18. Sheila Ruth Houghton, *Issues in Feminism*, p. 14.
19. *Ibid.*, p. 13.
20. *Ibid.*, p. 9.
21. *Ibid.*, p. 13.
22. *Ibid.*, pp. 13, 14.
23. *Ibid.*, p. 84.

24. Mary Daly as quoted in *Issues in Feminism*, p. 84.
25. Sheila Ruth Houghton, *ibid.*, p. 153.
26. *Ibid.*, p. 163.
27. *Ibid.*, p. 270.
28. *Ibid.*
29. *Ibid.*, p. 396.
30. *Ibid.*, p. 382.
31. *Ibid.*, p. 318.
32. *Ibid.*
33. *Ibid.*,p. 381.
34. Betty Schmitz, *Integrating Women's Studies into the Curriculum* (Old Westbury, NY: The Feminist Press, 1985), p. 2.
35. *Ibid.*, p. 3.
36. *Ibid.*, p. 33.

CHAPTER TWELVE: *The Feminization of God*

1. Mary Daly, *Beyond God the Father: Towards a Philosophy of Women's Liberation* (Boston: Beacon Press, 1973), p. 8.
2. Casey Miller and Kate Swift, *Words and Women — New Language in New Times* (Garden City, NY: Anchor Books/Doubleday, 1976), p. 64.
3. Letty Russell, *The Liberating Word: A Guide to Non-sexist Interpretation of the Bible*, ed. Letty Russell (Philadelphia: Westminster Press, 1976), p. 11.
4. *Ibid.*
5. *Ibid.*, p. 9.
6. *Ibid.*, p. 89.
7. *Ibid.*, p. 10.
8. *Ibid.*, p. 15.
9. *Ibid.*, pp. 16, 17.
10. *Ibid.*, p. 14.
11. *Ibid.*, p. 18.
12. *Ibid.*, p. 87.
13. Sharon Neufer Emswiler and Thomas Neufer Emswiler, *Women & Worship — A Guide to Nonsexist Hymns, Prayers, and Liturgies* (San Francisco: Harper & Row, 1974), p. 5.
14. Miller and Swift, *Words and Women*, p. 12.
15. *Ibid.*
16. *Ibid.*, p. 64.
17. Russell, *The Liberating Word*, p. 18.
18. Judith Weidman, *Christian Feminism: Visions of a New Humanity*, ed. Judith Weidman (San Francisco: Harper & Row, 1984), p. 1.
19. Emswiler and Emswiler, *Women & Worship*, p. 2.
20. Russell, *The Liberating Word*, p. 17.
21. Virginia Ramey Mollenkott, *The Divine Feminine: The Biblical Imagery of God as Female* (New York: Crossroad Publishing Co., 1988).
22. *Ibid.*, p. 61.
23. *Ibid.*
24. Russell, *The Liberating Word*, p. 17.
25. Rosemary Radford Ruether, "Feminist Theology and Spirituality," *Christian Feminism*, p. 16.
26. Krister Stendal, as quoted in *Words and Women*, eds. Casey Miller and Kate Swift, pp. 67, 68.
27. Fiorenza, "Interpreting Patriarchal Traditions," *The Liberating Word*, p. 39.

28. Letty Russell, *Human Liberation in a Feminist Perspective: A Theology* (Philadelphia: Westminster Press, 1974), p. 93.
29. Russell, *The Liberating Word*, p. 85.
30. *Ibid.*, p. 18.
31. *Ibid.*, pp. 86, 87.
32. *Ibid.*, p. 88.
33. *Ibid.*, p. 92.
34. Emswiler, *Women & Worship*, p. 93.
35. *Ibid.*, p. 92.
36. Krister Stendal, as quoted by Miller and Swift, *Words and Women*, pp. 67, 68.
37. Russell, *The Liberating Word*, p. 94.
38. As quoted by Leanne Payne, *The Healing Presence* (Wheaton, IL: Crossway Books, 1989), p. 126.
39. Donald Bloesch, *The Battle for the Trinity: The Debate over Inclusive God-Language* (Ann Arbor, MI: Servant Books, 1985), p. xviii.
40. *Ibid.*, p. 11.
41. *Ibid.*, p. 54.
42. Mollenkott, *The Divine Feminine*, p. 113.
43. Bloesch, *The Battle for the Trinity*, p. 35.
44. *Ibid.*
45. *Ibid.*
46. *Ibid.*
47. *Ibid.*, p. 36.
48. *Ibid.*
49. For comprehensive argument, see Bloesch, *The Battle for the Trinity*; also, Donald Bloesch, *Is the Bible Sexist?* (Wheaton, IL: Crossway Books, 1982); Vernard Eller, *Feminist Theology and the Language of Canaan* (Grand Rapids, MI: Eerdmans Publishing Co., 1982).
50. Emswiler, *Women & Worship*, p. 31.
51. Bloesch, *The Battle for the Trinity*, p. 46.
52. Payne, *The Healing Presence*, p. 128.
53. Bloesch, *The Battle for the Trinity*, p. 33.
54. Rita Nakashima Brock, "The Feminist Redemption of Christ," *Christian Feminism*, ed. Judith Weidman, pp. 68, 69.
55. Rosemary Radford Ruether, "Feminist Theology and Spirituality," *ibid.*, p. 17.

CHAPTER THIRTEEN: *Changing of the Gods*

1. Margot Adler, *Drawing Down the Moon: Witches, Druids, Goddess-worshippers, and Other Pagans in America Today* (Boston: Beacon Press, 1986), p. 223
2. Robin Morgan, *Going Too Far — the Personal Chronicle of a Feminist* (New York: Random House, 1977), p. 188.
3. Jean Mountaingrave, as quoted by Adler, *Drawing Down the Moon*, p. 183.
4. Mary Daly, *Beyond God the Father* (Boston: Beacon Press, 1973), p. 6.
5. *Ibid.*, p. 23.
6. *Ibid.*, p. 8.
7. *Ibid.*, p. 9.
8. *Ibid.*, p. 19.
9. Morgan, *Going Too Far*, p. 302.
10. Mary Daly, *Beyond God the Father*, p. 13.
11. Charlene Spretnak, *The Politics of Women's Spirituality: Essays on the Rise of Spiritual Power Within the Feminist Movement*, ed. Charlene Spretnak (New York: Anchor Press/Doubleday, 1982), p. xii.

12. Naomi Goldenberg, *Changing of the Gods: Feminism and the End of Traditional Religions* (Boston: Beacon Press, 1979), p. 41.
13. Daly, *Beyond God the Father*, p. 18.
14. *Ibid.*, p. 33.
15. *Ibid.*, p. 29.
16. *Ibid.*, p. 43.
17. Adler, *Drawing Down the Moon*, p. 223.
18. Goldenberg, *Changing of the Gods*, pp. 93, 94.
19. Quoted by Adler, *Drawing Down the Moon*, p. 192.
20. *Ibid.*, p. 188.
21. Mary Daly, "Sisterhood as a Cosmic Covenant," *The Politics of Women's Spirituality*, p. 353.
22. Dorothy Riddle, "Politics, Spirituality, and Models of Change," in *ibid.*, p. 374.
23. Starhawk, "Ethics and Justice in Goddess Religion," in *ibid.*, p. 415.
24. Spretnak, in *ibid.*, p. xxiii.
25. *Ibid.*, p. 398.

CHAPTER FOURTEEN: *Going Too Far: The Feminist Metaphysic*

1. Christine De Pisane was a feminist poet and philosopher, c. 1364-1431. Quoted by Robin Morgan in *Going Too Far: the Personal Chronicle of a Feminist* (New York: Random House, 1977), p. 290.
2. Carol P. Christ, "Why Women Need the Goddess: Phenomenological, Psychological, and Political Reflections," *The Politics of Women's Spirituality: Essays on the Rise of Spiritual Power Within the Feminist Movement*, ed. Charlene Spretnak (Garden City, NY: Anchor Press/Doubleday, 1982), p. 75.
3. *Ibid.*, p. 76
4. Starhawk, "Witchcraft as Goddess Religion," *ibid.*, p. 51.
5. Christ, "Why Women Need the Goddess," *ibid.*, p. 76.
6. Starhawk, "Witchcraft as Goddess Religion," *ibid.*, p. 51.
7. Margot Adler, *Drawing Down the Moon: Witches, Druids, Goddess-worshippers, and Other Pagans in America Today* (Boston: Beacon Press, 1986), pp. 204, 205.
8. Douglas Groothuis, *Unmasking the New Age* (Downers Grove, IL: InterVarsity Press, 1986), p. 18.
9. *Ibid.*
10. Starhawk, "Witchcraft as Goddess Religion," *The Politics of Women's Spirituality*, p. 50.
11. Groothuis, *Unmasking the New Age*, p. 20.
12. Charlene Spretnak, *The Politics of Women's Spirituality*, p. xvii.
13. Starhawk, "Witchcraft as Goddess Religion," *ibid.*, pp. 50, 51.
14. *Ibid.*
15. Z. Budapest, "The Vows, Wows, and Joys of the High Priestess," *ibid.*, p. 538.
16. Judith Antonelli, "Feminist Spirituality: The Politics of the Psyche," *ibid.*, p. 403.
17. Starhawk, "Consciousness, Politics and Magic," *ibid.*, pp. 177, 178.
18. Mary Daly, *Beyond God the Father* (Boston: Beacon Press, 1973), p. 40.
19. Carol Christ, "Rethinking Theology and Nature," *Weaving the Visions: New Patterns in Feminist Spirituality*, eds. Carol Christ and Judith Plaskow (San Francisco: Harper & Row, 1989), p. 322.
20. Starhawk, "Witchcraft as Goddess Religion," *The Politics of Women's Spirituality*, p. 50.
21. *Ibid.*
22. Baba Copper, "The Voice of Women's Spirituality in Futurism," *ibid.*, p. 505.
23. Barbara Starrett, "The Metaphors of Power," *ibid.*, p. 185.

24. Adler, *Drawing Down the Moon*, p. 192.
25. Carolyn R. Shaffer, "Re-powering Survivors of Sexual Assault," *The Politics of Women's Spirituality*, p. 468.
26. *Ibid.*
27. *Ibid.*
28. Adler, *Drawing Down the Moon*, p. 198.
29. *Ibid.*, p. 197.
30. *Ibid.*, p. 198.
31. *Ibid.*, p. 183.
32. *Ibid.*, p. 202.
33. *Ibid.*, p. 197.
34. Budapest, "The Vows, Wows, and Joys of the High Priestess," *The Politics of Women's Spirituality*, p. 540.

CHAPTER FIFTEEN: *Household of Freedom*

1. Burton Throckmorton, Jr. is a Maine professor of New Testament and a member of the National Council of Churches revision committee on the Revised Standard Version of the Bible. He is quoted by Virginia Byfield, in "The Move to Rewrite the Bible," *Alberta Report* (April 29, 1986), p. 36.
2. Letty Russell, *Feminist Interpretation of the Bible*, ed. Letty Russell (Philadelphia: Westminster Press, 1985), p. 17.
3. Katharine Doob Sakenfeld, "Feminist Uses of Biblical Materials," *ibid.*, p. 64.
4. Letty Russell, *Household of Freedom: Authority in Feminist Theology* (Philadelphia: Westminster Press, 1987), pp. 19, 20.
5. Margaret A. Farley, "Feminist Consciousness and the Interpretation of Scripture," *Feminist Interpretation of the Bible*, p. 43.
6. Russell, *ibid.*, p. 16.
7. *Ibid.*
8. Rosemary Radford Ruether, "A Method of Correlation," *ibid.*, p. 114.
9. *Ibid.*, pp. 114, 115.
10. *Ibid.*, p. 115.
11. *Ibid.*
12. Elisabeth Schüssler Fiorenza, "The Will to Choose or to Reject: Continuing Our Critical Work," *ibid.*, p. 128.
13. Rosemary Radford Ruether, "Feminist Theology and Spirituality," *Christian Feminism: Visions of a New Humanity*, ed. Judith Weidman (San Francisco: Harper & Row, 1984), p. 13.
14. Russell, *Household of Freedom*, p. 30.
15. Russell, *Feminist Interpretation of the Bible*, p. 138.
16. *Ibid.*, p. 144.
17. *Ibid.*, p. 139.
18. Ruether, "Feminist Theology and Spirituality," *Christian Feminism*, p. 12.
19. *Ibid.*, pp. 12, 13.
20. Rosemary Radford Ruether, *Womanguides: Readings Toward a Feminist Theology* (Boston: Beacon Press, 1985), p. xi.
21. *Ibid.*
22. *Ibid.*, p. 247.
23. *Ibid.*
24. Rosemary Ruether and Eleanor McLaughlin, eds. *Women of Spirit: Female Leadership in the Jewish and Christian Traditions* (New York: Simon and Schuster, 1979).
25. Susan Cady, Marian Ronan, and Hal Taussig, *Sophia: The Future of Feminist Spirituality* (New York: Harper & Row, 1986).

26. Barbara J. MacHaffie, *HerStory: Women in Christian Tradition* (Philadelphia: Fortress Press, 1986).
27. *Ibid.*, pp. 32, 33.
28. Elaine Pagels, *The Gnostic Gospels* (New York: Random House, 1981), pp. xiv, xv.
29. *Ibid.*, p. 171.
30. *Ibid.*, p. xviii.
31. As quoted by Pagels, *The Gnostic Gospels*, p. xix.
32. *Ibid.*, p. xx.
33. *Ibid.*, p. 69.
34. *Ibid.*, p. 66.
35. *Ibid.*, p. 38.
36. *Ibid.*, p. 28.
37. *Ibid.*
38. Fiorenza, "Word, Spirit and Power," *Women of Spirit*, pp. 41, 42.
39. *Ibid.*
40. *Ibid.*
41. *Ibid.*
42. MacHaffie, *HerStory*, p. 34.
43. Ruether, "Mothers of the Church," *Women of Spirit*, p. 72.
44. MacHaffie, *HerStory*, p. 44.
45. Ruether, "Mothers of the Church," *Women of Spirit*, p. 72.
46. Barbara Brown Zikmund, "The Feminist Thrust of Sectarian Christianity," *ibid.*, p. 206.
47. *Ibid.*, p. 209.
48. *Ibid.*
49. *Ibid.*, pp. 209, 210.
50. MacHaffie, *HerStory*, p. 124.
51. *Ibid.*, p. 126.
52. Zikmund, "The Feminist Thrust of Sectarian Christianity," *Women of Spirit*, p. 211.
53. *Ibid.*, p. 212.
54. *Ibid.*, p. 213.
55. MacHaffie, *HerStory*, p. 125.
56. Susan Cady, Marian Ronan and Hal Taussig, *Wisdom's Feast: Sophia in Study and Celebration* (San Francisco: Harper & Row, 1989).
57. *Ibid.*, p. 10.
58. *Ibid.*
59. *Ibid.*, p. 17.
60. *Ibid.*
61. *Ibid.*, p. 19.
62. *Ibid.*, p. 28.
63. *Ibid.*, pp. 33-46.
64. Joan Chamberlain Engelsman, *The Feminine Dimension of the Divine* (Philadelphia: Westminster Press, 1979), p. 119.
65. Cady, Ronan and Taussig, *Wisdom's Feast*, p. 29.
66. Engelsman, *The Feminine Dimension of the Divine*, p. 119.
67. Cady, Ronan and Taussig, *Wisdom's Feast*, p. 11.
68. *Ibid.*
69. *Ibid.*
70. *Ibid.*, p. 31.
71. *Ibid.*, p. 79.
72. *Ibid.*, p. 59.
73. *Ibid.*

74. *Ibid.*
75. *Ibid.*, p. 10.
76. *Ibid.*
77. *Ibid.*
78. Ruether, *Womanguides.*
79. Fiorenza, "Word, Spirit and Power," *Women of Spirit*, p. 57.
80. Zikmund, "The Feminist Thrust of Sectarian Christianity," *Women of Spirit*, p. 29.
81. Virginia Ramey Mollenkott, "An Evangelical Feminist Confronts the Goddess," *Christian Century*, Vol. 99 (October 20, 1982), p. 1043.
82. *Ibid.*, p. 1045.
83. *Ibid.*, p. 1046.
84. Elisabeth Schüssler Fiorenza, *In Memory of Her: A Feminist Theological Reconstruction of Christian Origins* (New York: Crossroad Publishing Co., 1985), p. 146.
85. Mollenkott, "An Evangelical Feminist Confronts the Goddess," *Christian Century*, p. 1046.
86. Rosemary Radford Ruether, "Asking the Existential Questions: How My Mind Has Changed," *Christian Century*, Vol. 97 (April 2, 1980), p. 374.
87. *Ibid.*

CHAPTER SIXTEEN: *Godding*

1. Virginia Ramey Mollenkott, *Godding: Human Responsibility and the Bible* (New York: Crossroad Publishing Co., 1988), p. 4.
2. *Ibid.*, p. 138.
3. *Ibid.*, p. 48.
4. *Ibid.*
5. *Ibid.*, p. 8.
6. *Ibid.*, p. 9.
7. *Ibid.*, p. 78.
8. *Ibid.*, p. 26.
9. *Ibid.*, p. 78.
10. *Ibid.*, p. 48.
11. *Ibid.*, p. 127.
12. Virginia Ramey Mollenkott, *The Divine Feminine: The Biblical Imagery of God as Female* (New York: Crossroad Publishing Co., 1988), p. 107.
13. Mollenkott, *Godding*, p. 109.
14. Susan Cady, Marian Ronan and Hal Taussig, *Wisdom's Feast: Sophia in Study and Celebration* (San Francisco: Harper & Row, 1989), p. 163.
15. Mollenkott, *The Divine Feminine*, p. 114.
16. Cady, Ronan and Taussig, *Wisdom's Feast*, p. 134.
17. *Ibid.*, p. 127.
18. *Ibid.*
19. Mollenkott, *The Divine Feminine*, pp. 113, 114.
20. Mollenkott, *Godding*, p. 5.
21. *Ibid.*, p. 4.
22. *Ibid.*
23. *Ibid.*, p. 6.
24. *Ibid.*, p. 30.
25. *Ibid.*, p. 45.
26. *Ibid.*, p. 40.
27. *Ibid.*
28. *Ibid.*, p. 2.

29. *Ibid.*, p. 80.
30. *Ibid.*, p. 10.
31. *Ibid.*, p. 46.
32. *Ibid.*, p. 48.
33. *Ibid.*
34. Rosemary Radford Ruether, *Women-Church: Theology and Practice of Feminist Liturgical Communities* (San Francisco: Harper & Row, 1985), p. 23.
35. Cady, Ronan and Taussig, *Wisdom's Feast*, p. 59.
36. *Ibid.*, p. 61.
37. *Ibid.*, p. 127.
38. Mollenkott, *Godding*, p. 32.

CHAPTER SEVENTEEN: *Women-Church*

1. Susan Cady, Marian Ronan and Hal Taussig, *Wisdom's Feast: Sophia in Study and Celebration* (San Francisco: Harper & Row, 1989), pp. 160, 161.
2. The rite is described in greater detail in *Women-Church*, by Rosemary Radford Ruether (San Francisco: Harper & Row, 1985), pp. 128-130.
3. Elisabeth Schüssler Fiorenza, *In Memory of Her: A Feminist Theological Reconstruction of Christian Origins* (New York: Crossroad Publishing Co., 1985), p. 343.
4. Ruether, *Women-Church*, p. 3.
5. *Ibid.*, p. 63.
6. Ibid., p. 56.
7. *Ibid.*, p. 61.
8. *Ibid.*, p. 39.
9. *Ibid.*
10. *Ibid.*, pp. 63, 64.
11. *Ibid.*, p. 86.
12. *Ibid.*, p. 92.
13. *Ibid.*, p. 93.
14. *Ibid.*
15. *Ibid.*, p. 104.
16. *Ibid.*, p. 145.
17. *Ibid.*, p. 214.
18. Rita Nakashima Brock, "The Feminist Redemption of Christ," *Christian Feminism: Visions of a New Humanity*, ed. Judith Weidman (San Francisco: Harper & Row, 1984), pp. 68, 69.

CHAPTER EIGHTEEN: *Biblical Feminism*

1. Virginia Mollenkott, in a letter to *His* magazine, June 1973 as quoted by Dorothy Pape, *In Search of God's Ideal Woman: A Personal Examination of the New Testament* (Downers Grove, IL: InterVarsity Press, 1978), p. 249.
2. Karl D. Barth, *Kirchliche Dogmatik*, III/1, pts. 2 and 3 (*Church Dogmatics*, Vol. III/1), trans. J. W. Edwards, O. Bussey and Harold Knight (Edinburgh: T. & T. Clark, 1958).
3. Pape, *In Search of God's Ideal Woman*, p. 173.
4. Letha Scanzoni and Nancy Hardesty, *All We're Meant to Be: A Biblical Approach to Women's Liberation* (Waco, TX: Word Books, 1974), p. 15.
5. *Ibid.*, p. 110.
6. *Ibid.*
7. Virginia Mollenkott, *Women, Men & the Bible* (Nashville: Abingdon Press, 1977), p. 137.
8. *Ibid.*

9. Paul Jewett, *Man as Male and Female: A Study in Sexual Relationships from a Theological Point of View* (Grand Rapids, MI: William B. Eerdmans, 1975), p. 71.
10. Mollenkott, *Women, Men & the Bible*, p. 90.
11. Jewett, *Man as Male and Female*, p. 131.
12. *Ibid.*, p. 134.
13. Mollenkott, *Women, Men & the Bible*, p. 119.
14. Scanzoni and Hardesty, *All We're Meant to Be*, p. 20.
15. Mollenkott, *Women, Men & the Bible*, p. 106.
16. Scanzoni and Hardesty, *All We're Meant to Be*, p. 20.
17. *Ibid.*, p. 72.
18. *Ibid.*, p. 99.
19. Mollenkott, *Women, Men & the Bible*, p. 93.
20. Jewett, *Man as Male and Female*, p. 130.
21. Mollenkott, *Women, Men & the Bible*, p. 95.
22. *Ibid.*, p. 105.
23. *Ibid.* Considering this author's aforementioned judgment on Paul and the subsequent applicability of his directives, it does seem ironic to me that she neglected to consider that perhaps *her* arguments reflected *her* personal struggle with *female submission and the Biblical definition of equality* and showed vestiges of *Western* philosophy (particularly humanism) and of the training *she* received from her *own* socialization and especially from the *secular feminist movement*.
24. Scanzoni and Hardesty, *All We're Meant to Be*, pp. 27, 28.
25. *Ibid.*, p. 28.
26. *Ibid.*, p. 53.
27. Jewett, *Man as Male and Female*, p. 113.
28. *Ibid.*, p. 136.
29. Mollenkott, *Women, Men & the Bible*, p. 98.
30. *Ibid.*, p. 101.
31. For a discussion of Biblical feminist hermeneutics refer to Mary Kassian, *Women, Creation and the Fall* (Wheaton, IL: Crossway Books, 1990), pp. 149-151.
32. Berkeley and Alvera Mickelsen, Philip Payne, Gilbert Bilezikian and Catherine Kroeger have recently argued that "*kephale*," the Greek work for "head," means "source" and therefore does not contain any implications for authority or an authority structure. For a detailed discussion regarding the meaning of *kephale*, and an interaction with their theory, refer to "The Meaning of *Kephale* (Head): A response to Recent Studies," by Wayne Grudem, published in *Recovering Biblical Manhood & Womanhood*, eds. John Piper and Wayne Grudem (Wheaton, IL: Crossway Books, 1991), pp. 425-468.
33. See Kassian, *Women, Creation and the Fall*, pp. 102, 103 for standard rules of hermeneutics in determining cultural applicability of Biblical directives.
34. Pape, *In Search of God's Ideal Woman*, p. 155.
35. Mollenkott, *Women, Men & the Bible*, p. 102.
36. Scanzoni and Hardesty, *All We're Meant to Be*, p. 72.
37. From the subtitle of her book, Mary Stewart VanLeeuwen, *Gender & Grace: Love, Work & Parenting in a Changing World* (Downers Grove, IL: InterVarsity Press, 1990).
38. *Ibid.*, p. 34.
39. *Ibid.*
40. *Ibid.*
41. *Ibid.*, p. 35.
42. *Ibid.*
43. *Ibid.*, p. 36.

44. She bases her arguments for the equality of male and female on the *imago Dei* — the image of God — a concept extensively argued by Paul Jewett in *Man as Male and Female.*
45. VanLeeuwen, *Gender & Grace*, pp. 41-43.
46. *Ibid.*, p. 46.
47. This is remarkably similar to Valerie Saiving Goldstein's contention that the sin of man is pride and selfishness, and the sin of woman not enough pride and not enough selfishness. Refer to Chapter Ten of this book to review Goldstein's theory.
48. VanLeeuwen, *Gender & Grace*, p. 70.
49. *Ibid.*, p. 244.
50. *Ibid.*, p. 182.
51. *Ibid.*, p. 183.
52. *Ibid.*, pp. 136-143.
53. *Ibid.*, p. 131.
54. Evangelical Women's Caucus, "Statement of Faith," *Evangelical Women's Caucus International Introductory Brochure*, available from P.O. Box 209, Hadley, NY 12835.
55. *Ibid.*
56. *Ibid.*
57. "Christian Feminists Form New Organization," *Christianity Today*, Vol. 31 (October 16, 1987), p. 44.
58. *Ibid.*
59. "Mutual submission" is a misnomer. Besides being a linguistic impossibility, it is a concept that is absent from the Bible. See my discussion of the term in *Women, Creation and the Fall*, pp. 36, 37.

CHAPTER NINETEEN: *The Inevitable Intersection*

1. Margot Adler, *Drawing Down the Moon: Witches, Druids, Goddess-worshippers and Other Pagans in America Today* (Boston: Beacon Press, 1986), p. 182.
2. Josephine Donovan, *Feminist Theory: The Intellectual Traditions of American Feminism* (New York: Frederick Ungar Publishing Co. Inc., 1985).
3. June Steffensen Hagan, ed. *Gender Matters, Women's Studies for the Christian Community* (Grand Rapids, MI: Academie Books, Zondervan Publishing House, 1990).
4. Mary Daly, *Beyond God the Father* (Boston: Beacon Press, 1973), p. 8.
5. Naomi R. Goldenberg, *Changing of the Gods: Feminism and the End of Traditional Religions* (Boston: Beacon Press, 1979), pp. 8, 9.
6. *Ibid.*
7. *Ibid.*, p. 4.
8. *Ibid.*, p. 19.
9. *Ibid.*, p. 20.
10. *Ibid.*, pp. 20, 21.
11. *Ibid.*
12. *Ibid.*, p. 12.
13. Elizabeth Cady Stanton, as quoted by Goldenberg, *Changing of the Gods*, p. 13,
14. Goldenberg, *ibid.*, p. 13.
15. *Ibid.*, p. 25.
16. Francis A. Schaeffer, *The Great Evangelical Disaster* (Westchester, IL: Crossway Books, 1984), pp. 43, 44.

CHAPTER TWENTY: *The Slippery Slope*

1. Michael Novak, *Will It Liberate? Questions About Liberation Theology* (Mahwah, NJ: Paulist Press, 1986), p. 27.
2. Mary Daly, *The Church and the Second Sex* (Boston: Beacon Press, 1968), Autobiographical Preface (1975), p. 14.
3. Mary Daly, *Beyond God the Father* (Boston: Beacon Press, 1973), p. xxxiii.
4. *Ibid.,* Original Reintroduction of 1985, p. xvii.
5. *Ibid.*
6. *Ibid.,* p. 40.
7. Mary Daly, *Gyn/Ecology: The Metaethics of Radical Feminism* (Boston: Beacon Press, 1978), p. xi.
8. *Ibid.,* pp. xi, xiii.
9. *Ibid.,* p. 9.
10. *Ibid.*
11. *Ibid.,* p. 10.
12. *Ibid.*
13. *Ibid.,* pp. 10-11.
14. *Ibid.,* p. 14.
15. *Ibid.,* p. 6.
16. *Ibid.,* p. 424.
17. Mary Daly, *Pure Lust: Elemental Feminist Philosophy* (Boston: Beacon Press, 1984), p. 1.
18. *Ibid.,* p. 1.
19. *Ibid.,* pp. 2, 3.
20. *Ibid.,* p. 3.
21. *Ibid.*
22. Mary Daly, *Webster's First New Intergalactic Wickedary of the English Language* (Boston: Beacon Press, 1987), p. 75.
23. *Ibid.,* p. 78.
24. *Ibid.,* p. 87.
25. *Ibid.,* p. 203.
26. Rosemary Radford Ruether, *Disputed Questions: On Being a Christian* (Maryknoll, NY: Orbis Books, 1989), p. 109.
27. *Ibid.,* p. 18.
28. *Ibid.,* p. 110.
29. *Ibid.,* p. 112.
30. *Ibid.*
31. *Ibid.,* p. 28.
32. *Ibid.,* p. 115.
33. *Ibid.*
34. *Ibid.,* p. 116.
35. *Ibid.,* p. 117.
36. *Ibid.,* p. 118.
37. *Ibid.,* p. 76.
38. *Ibid.,* p. 82.
39. *Ibid.,* p. 54.
40. *Ibid.,* p. 127.
41. *Ibid.,* pp. 138, 139.
42. *Ibid.,* p. 134.
43. Virginia R. Mollenkott, "Church Women, Theologians, and the Burden of Proof," *The Reformed Journal* (July/August, 1975), pp. 18-20.
44. Virginia R. Mollenkott, *Women, Men & the Bible* (Nashville: Abingdon, 1977), p. 121.

45. Virginia Ramey Mollenkott, "The Bible & Linguistic Change," *The Other Side* (June 1981), p. 19.
46. Virginia Ramey Mollenkott, *The Divine Feminine: The Biblical Imagery of God as Female* (New York: Crossroad Publishing Co., 1988).
47. Virginia Ramey Mollenkott, *Godding: Human Responsibility and the Bible* (New York: Crossroad Publishing Co., 1988), pp. 64, 65.
48. *Ibid.*, p. 6.
49. *Ibid.*, pp. 46-48.
50. *Ibid.*, p. 106.

CHAPTER TWENTY-ONE: *Fighting on Two Fronts*

1. Francis Schaeffer, *The Great Evangelical Disaster* (Wheaton, IL: Crossway Books, 1984), pp. 98-99.
2. *Ibid.*
3. Dr. Lawrence J. Crabb, *Men & Women: Enjoying the Difference* (Grand Rapids, MI: Zondervan, 1991), p. 33.
4. Donald Bloesch, *The Battle for the Trinity: The Debate over Inclusive God-Language* (Ann Arbor, MI: Servant Books, 1985), p. 25.
5. *Ibid.*
6. *Ibid.*, pp. 25, 26.
7. Job 38:4, 5, 25, 31-33.
8. For further reading on this point, I would suggest Donald G. Bloesch, *The Battle for the Trinity: The Debate over Inclusive God-Language*, Dr. Larry Crabb, *Men & Women: Enjoying the Difference, Recovering Biblical Manhood & Womanhood*, eds. John Piper and Wayne Grudem (Wheaton, IL: Crossway Books, 1991), and Leanne Payne, *Crisis in Masculinity* (Wheaton, IL: Crossway Books, 1985).
9. Leanne Payne, *The Healing Presence* (Wheaton, IL: Crossway Books, 1989), pp. 125, 129.
10. Schaeffer, *The Great Evangelical Disaster*, p. 134.
11. *Ibid.*
12. *Ibid.*, p. 135
13. *Ibid.*

CHAPTER TWENTY-TWO: *The Future of Feminism*

1. Danielle Crittenden, "Let's Junk the Feminist Slogans: The War's Over," *Chatelaine* (August, 1990), p. 38.
2. Patricia Davies, "Mysticism Goes Mainstream," *Chatelaine* (March, 1990), pp. 86-88.
3. Crittenden, "Let's Junk the Feminist Slogans: The War's Over," *Chatelaine*, p. 37.
4. *Ibid.*, p. 38.
5. *Ibid.*
6. *Ibid.*, pp. 38, 39.

INDEX